THE EXTENT OF MARKETIZATION
OF ECONOMIC SYSTEMS IN CHINA

China in the 21st Century: Economy, Society and Politics
Xiaowen Tian (Editor)

The Extent of Marketization of Economic Systems in China
Chen Zongsheng, Wu Zhe, Xie Siquan, et al.
ISBN 1-56072-778-0

Business Communication in China
Dr. Zhu Yunxia
ISBN 1-56072-655-5

China's Relations with Japan
in an Era of Economic Liberalisation
Dong Dong Zhang
ISBN 1-56072-625-3

Dynamics of Development in an Opening Economy:
China since 1978
Xiaowen Tian
ISBN 1-56072-551-6

THE EXTENT OF MARKETIZATION OF ECONOMIC SYSTEMS IN CHINA

CHEN ZONGSHENG, WU ZHE, XIE SIQUAN, ET AL.

Nova Science Publishers, Inc.
Huntington, New York

Editorial Production:	Susan Boriotti
Office Manager:	Annette Hellinger
Graphics:	Frank Grucci and Jennifer Lucas
Information Editor:	Tatiana Shohov
Book Production:	Patrick Davin, Cathy DeGregory, Donna Dennis, Jennifer Kuenzig, and Lynette Van Helden
Circulation:	John Bakewell, Lisa DeGangi and Michael Pazy Mino

Library of Congress Cataloging-in-Publication Data
Chen, Zongsheng.
     The extent of marketization of economic systems in China / Chen Zongsheng, Wu Zhe, Xie Siquan, et al.
         p.   cm.
     Includes bibliographical references and index.
     ISBN 1-56072-778-0
         1. China—Economic conditions—1976- 2. China—Economic policy—1976- I. Wu, Ch'e. II. Xie, Siquan.
HC427.92.C35857   2000   CIP
338.951—dc21   00-025987

Copyright 2000 by Nova Science Publishers, Inc.
     227 Main Street, Suite 100
     Huntington, New York 11743
     Tele. 631-424-6682 Fax 631-424-4666
     e-mail: Novascience@earthlink.net
     e-mail: Novascil@aol.com
     Web Site: http://www.nexusworld.com/nova

Printed in the United States of America

CONTENTS

TABLES

FIGURES

ACKNOWLEDGEMENTS

We thank the advisors of this research project: Professors Gu Shutang, Ji Renjun, Liu Fuding, and Pang Jinju, who offered many revision suggestions and comments during the research. Professor, Zhou Liqun, Liu Xin, who were visiting scholars abroad at that time, sent us as references a lot of measuring indexes which the foreign scholars used in their researches. Professors Zhu Guanghua, Wei Xun, Xiong Xingmei, Cai Xiaozhen, and Zhang Rende gave the research group a lot of encourages. Some parts of the project were introduced at the "Academic Seminar Fortnightly" at Nankai Institute of Economics and helpfully commented on by scholars on and out of the campus. The overall report and several sub-reports were addressed at the "Academic Conference for Celebrating the 70th Anniversary of Nankai Institute of Economics", and on them valuable comments were made by Professors Dong Furen, Justin Y.F. Lin, Hai Wen, Zang Xuheng, Zhang Shuguang, Chang Xiuze, Cao Yuanzheng, Li Luoli, Zhao Renwei and so on. Finally, We are also grateful to Dr. Chen Chunjiang, Wang Jianmin, Shi Guangqing for their careful proof of this English version, Dr. Tian Xiaowen for his helping with publishing affairs, and to Mr. Fan Zhenyi, Zhu Fengxiang, Cao Xiaohui, secretaries of the Institute, for their typing all the manuscripts.

Chen Zongsheng
Professor and Director
Nankai Institute of Economics,
Nankai University, China

PREFACE

After mankind entered the last 20 years of 20th century, several great events which influence to the progress of history have taken place. Among them the economic system reform in China is a very important one. Since the 3rd Plenary Session of the 11th Central Committee of Communist Party of China started the economic system reform, the reform has been carried out for 20 years, during which China has changed earth-shockingly and become the focus of world attentions. In the 20 years the national economic power of China has grown significantly, the living standards of Chinese people improved obviously, and the position of China in the world has risen steadily. Especially, after 1997's Asian financial crisis, economies in many Asian countries have been struck seriously. Chinese economy, however, not only remained steady but also offered a lot of support for other countries to counter the crisis and earned respect from the world. All of the important changes, without doubt, owed much to the social and economic reforms pushed firmly by Chinese government and people. Therefore, it is necessary and important for us to summarize the experiences of the 20 years, to check the progress of 20 years' reforms, to measure the paths and extents of Chinese economic reforms, to judge how far from the target systems and so on.

In fact, if possible, or, if the analysis techniques are ripe and the measurement methods are sophisticated, the measurements for economic system reforms should be done frequently. In 1991, before my visit to Yale University, I had suggested that, while focusing on the study of course changes of economic development, Nankai Institute of Economics should pay more attention to quantitative research into the reform progress of economic system, designing measuring indexes, and tracking the paths and trends of reform scale. But at that time, the research force and funds were not adequate to deal with such a task. In 1996, Chinese reform has been carried on for 18 years, which is long enough for us to do the research, and more people have recognized the requirement of quantity aspects for summarizing the reforms; as a matter of fact, several small-scale researches have been done already. Moreover, the research force and funds were further improved through some efforts and could bear to do this job. Therefore, in 1996 we started the project and spent two years to finish it. In 1998 publication of this research result is just taken as the best memory of the opening of the 3rd Plenary Session of 11th Conference of Communist Party of China.

A research on the extent of marketization of China's economic system includes plentiful contents and covers a wider research scope. Literatures show us that there are some very important views put forward in the existing researches (see the references), but most of the researches are scattered and only involved in certain one or a few aspects. The most important characteristic of this book is that it has a wide research range -- dealing with almost all main aspects or fields. Its contents are relatively rich and all of the important issues, such as the progress of system reforms, measuring indexes, extents of promotion, effects, problems and policies, are analyzed. This book is composed of four parts and 12 chapters. There is only one chapter in the 1st part, which focuses on the total marketization and abstracts the main views and contents of the other chapters, so it is the outline of the whole book. There are seven chapters (from the 2nd to 8th chapter) in the 2nd part, which focuses on the marketization of enterprises, governments and markets from the angle of the compositions of economic systems. The 3rd part includes 3 chapters (from the 9th to 11th chapter), which refer to the study of marketization of agriculture, industry and foreign trade from the angle of industrial sectors. The 4th part only includes one chapter, the 12th chapter, in which comparative studies are made about the marketization extents of several large areas from the angle of regional differences.

The basic framework of this book is consistent with the composition of target model of economic system reform in our country. The basic views of the authors are that the purpose to research the progress of system reforms is to understand how far we have stepped forward to the target model since the start of reform. Therefore, it is reasonable for us to arrange the logical system of this book according to the composition of market economic systems to be carried out in the future. Based on our understanding, the target model of Chinese market economy may be defined as: governments adjust markets and markets guide enterprises. Specifically, governments adjust markets through various economic parameters and economic means, and markets guide enterprises with the information including various macro preferences and economic variables and enterprises autonomously operate in economic environments adjusted by various macro measurements. This target model comprises three layers or links: government---market---enterprise. In order to emphasize the key points and for the convenience of discussions the analyses in this book follow the sequence of enterprise---government---market. The systems of enterprises are the core of market economic system, so to study them first is advantageous to catch the key. The contents of market systems are quite varied, including consumer goods, production materials as well as the main factors of markets such as labor, capital, funds, real estate, housing, technology, and foreign exchange markets and so on. So it is convenient to discuss them lastly. Doubtlessly, the marketizaton of economic systems may also be researched according to main industrial sectors. Therefore, the research of marketization according to main composition of systems is followed by the studies on agriculture, industry and foreign trade. Finally, the differences of marketization of several large areas such as the east, middle and west or the south, middle and north parts of China are explored. I think this arrangement of the logical system of this book is unique, and it is quite comprehensive to research the extent of marketization of our economic systems both primarily and secondarily from three angles of system composition, industry sectors and area disparity.

There are three general issues discussed intensively many times by the research group. One is the criterion judging marketization of economic system. The target model of China's economic reform is the socialist market economy, hence, the course of system reform equals to that of marketization. But how to judge or evaluate whether or not the reforms reach to its target? Obviously the marketization extent of the target model must be defined. However, there are two standards: one is the 100% of marketization in theory; the other is the actual marketization extent of some market economy. Which criterion to be adopted? If the latter, the marketization extents in different countries and their different fields are much different. Then, which country's extent should be adopted as the criterion? Or maybe the average of several countries? Obviously, this is a complex issue. Yet, without a united standard it is impossible to reach the general conclusions. This book handles the range of marketization in the way: the complete marketization is defined as 100% and the complete planned economy defined as 0%, which is mainly for standard to be united and convenience to sum up. In fact we know well that even in an autocratic and planned economy, it is impossible to completely avoid any market activity; on the other hand, even the most advanced market economy marketization cannot reach 100% because there is no economy that can reject any government intervention. But the extents of government interventions in various market economies and in different fields or periods are much different. So if we do not define the complete marketization as 100%, but define the actual extent of marketization of certain advanced market country as 100%, then it is difficult for us to compare among different fields or periods in the same country or different countries.

The second one is the implication of marketization and the design of measurement indexes of marketization. Does there exist a set of united indexes that are completely suitable to all aspects of the economic system? The answer is definitely no. It is impossible because the features in various fields are different. For example, indexes in measuring enterprises' marketization can not be the same as those in measuring technology markets. However, different indexes in various fields must be consistent with the united or the same definition of marketization. Then what is marketization? The common knowledge of the authors is that marketization means a process in which the resources allocation role of market mechanism in the economy continually intensifies, and the dependency of economy upon market mechanism increases. Market mechanism includes supply and demand, competition, pricing, risk and interest mechanisms and so on, and it further annotates the theoretical implications of economy marketization. During the transformation from planned system to market system, the behaviors of governments or enterprises and other aspects of markets will be changed to some extent, and then the characteristics of marketization will be exposed. There are many features such as decentralization, multiplicity, self-interest, autonomousness, less-intervention, normalization, legalization, which embody respectively from different aspects the theoretical implication of marketization and hold the designing and choosing of indexes to measure marketization.

The third one is the considerations and methodology measuring overall marketization. The measurement of overall marketization is undoubtedly more important and complex than that of each individual component. The general conclusion of marketization of economic system is based upon the former. Besides, overall marketization covers more layers and aspects than the individual marketization. The analysis involves several complicated issues, such as from what point, what methodology to adopt, whether and what weight to be applied in the analysis. Generally speaking, there are different considerations in measuring the overall marketization of economic system and each one has its own strength and drawback. To avoid one-sidedness, and for the sake of comparison, especially to be more accurate, we have adopted simultaneously five considerations in our analysis, which is also an important characteristics of our research. Their five considerations are:

- "composition weighting of society gross product" marketization, i.e., measuring overall marketization extent of economic system by weighting the composition of society gross product;
- "algebra weighting of the price of input elements" marketization, i.e., the indexes of all input elements in production function as the weight in measuring marketization;
- "three industrial composition weighting" marketization;
- "general weighting of GNP composition" marketization
- "simple averaging of market parameters" marketization, defining marketization extent by averaging price parameters of all markets.

The first four considerations involve weighting, but in appearance, they are economic development parameter rather than economic system parameter. However, as economic development is represented in the change of system reform, they are the same in essence. We have measured the marketization of the economic system with the five considerations. There is difference among the five considerations, for instance, the overall marketization extent for 1997 are 62.5%, 62.8%, 64.9%, 61.4% and 55%. Despite the difference, the extent is around 60%, which proves the scientific quality of the research consideration.

The basic conclusions of this book are: China's economic system reform has evolved to institutional renovation period, i.e., setting up new framework of market economy. The development of marketization of economic system is significant and substantial. Overall marketization degree of Chinese economy has reached about 60%, which is a remarkable achievement. But the development of different layers of the economy is unbalanced. Judging by fields, the marketization of commodity market is highest of all, about 85% while other fields are relatively low. Judging by sectors, agriculture sector has reached to about 65%, while other sectors are relatively lower. Judging by regions, the East and South of China are 70%, whereas the West and North are lower. Despite the fluctuation of the marketization, its general trend is upward. The performance of China's marketization reform is striking to the world, and China's development pattern is ascending from low-income group to middle-income group. Therefore, the only correct policy is to strengthen the weak parts of economic system reforms, to keep the harmony of the reforms among all main fields, sectors and regions, and to continue the reform towards our anticipated targets.

As one key topic of Nankai Institute of Economics, this program was headed by the Director, Professor Chen Zongsheng and assisted by deputy directors, Professors Wu Zhe and Xie Siqun. The research group held more than 10 meetings to agree on the research framework, main contents, definition of marketization and measuring indexes. This book is the result of collective researches and most authors are the young scholars from Nankai Institute of Economics and Nankai College of Economics as well as some of universities of Beijing and research institutes of State department. The authors of each chapter are as follows respectively: preface: Chen Zongsheng; the first chapter, the overall marketization of Chinese economic system: Chen Zongsheng, Zhou Bing, zhong Maochu, Gu Jie, Ning Yong; the second chapter, the marketization of Chinese enterprises: Gao Minghua, Zhen Rongjun, Li Ya; the third chapter, the marketization of China government behaviors: Zhou Bing, Wen Guang; the fourth chapter, the marketization of commodity pricing system: Gao Xiaohui, Zhou Jianyun, Guo Yongfeng, Zhang Shufen; the fifth chapter, marketization of labour market: Zhang Can, Xie Siquan, Dong Li; the sixth chapter, the marketization of finance market: Ci Hongfei; the seventh chapter, the marketization of real estate: Cao Zhenliang, Fu Shihe; the eighth chapter, the marketization of technology market: Xie Siquan, Zhang Can, He Jingtong; the ninth chapter, the marketization of agriculture: Chen Zongsheng, Chen Sheng; the tenth chapter, the marketization of industry: Zhong Maochu, Wang Xiaochun; the eleventh chapter, the marketization of foreign trade: Wang Yuru, Cheng Zhang, Ma Zhiguang; the twelfth chapter, the marketization differences of various large areas: Wu Zhe.

Chen Zongsheng
Professor and Director
Nankai Institute of Economics,
Nankai University, China

PART I: MARKETIZATION OF CHINA'S ECONOMIC SYSTEM: IMPLICATIONS, PROCESS AND OVERALL MARKETIZATION DEGREE

Chapter 1

MARKETIZATION DEGREE OF CHINA'S ECONOMIC SYSTEM

THE STAGES AND FEATURES OF CHINA'S ECONOMIC REFORM

China's economy is undertaking double transformations or transitions: the system pattern is transforming from the central-planned economy into market economy, and development frame is ascending from low-income type to middle-income type. That the double transitions take place simultaneously in a developing and socialist country, China, is quite significant for the whole world. They have attracted and will continuously attract the world-wide attentions. What people are interested in and try to understand is in what way and in what degree the current development is different from traditional China; in what degree and in which aspect it is associated with the roads that developed countries have passed. This is the essential parts of the new exploration for human social development roads. (Chen Zongsheng, 1995)

The double transitions are related to each other. However, this book centers on the transformation of economic system pattern. It endeavors to define the transformation extents of China's economic system pattern up to now and to measure the paces of marketization progress. Before specific measuring, we must first describe the stages and features of China's economic system reform as well as the features of the target pattern. Then we will elucidate the implications and features of marketization because they are the basis for the design of measurement indicators.

Since 1978, China has adopted a gradualist reform approach in accordance with the old Chinese adage: "Crossing a river by feeling the stones". China has adhered to its reform principles by absorbing the helpful experiences from developed market economies but not copying them and followed the order of economic system reforms before political system reforms. After 20 years' market-orientated reforms, China's economic system has changed greatly.

With the symbol of public ownership, the ownership pattern of "mixed economy" has been established, which consists of many kinds of ownership such as state, collective, individual, private, foreign and joint venture. The operation mechanism of state-owned enterprises has been adjusted initially through empowering autonomy and profit retention as well as other experimental reforms including responsibility system, joint-stock system, and shareholding system. The range and degree regulated by market mechanisms are increasingly enhanced. Prices of production materials, consumer materials and services are almost determined by the supply and demand in markets. Government's management on economy has converted from direct control with administrative orders into indirect regulation mainly through economic and legal measures, and from direct intervention with firm's operation into macro regulation. Household responsibility system in rural economy has been consolidated, improved and perfected, and town and village enterprises have developed drastically, which shows positive roles in absorbing surplus labor force and integrating urban and rural economies. Since open-door policy was introduced in 1978, foreign economic and technological cooperation has been implemented widespread, and the new open-door pattern in all levels and aspects has been formed basically.

In 1993 the 3rd Plenary of the 14th Central Committee of the Communist Party of China characterized the framework of the new socialist market economic system. The Party officially sanctioned the target pattern of system reform. In our understanding, the target model of Chinese socialist market economy can be described as follows: *Government regulates markets while market guides enterprises. That is, the government regulates the markets through economic parameters and means; the market guides enterprises with the information of macro preferences and economic variables, and the enterprises operate autonomously in the market environments that are regulated by macro economic regulations.* Towards this target pattern, China's economic reform has been carried out in three levels in recent years.

First, it has defined property rights and developed modern enterprise system. The reform of state owned enterprises is converted from the favorable reform that empowers autonomy and profit retention into the institutional innovation reform that focuses on clear relations of property rights. That is, large firms are transformed into shareholding or modern legal-person system while middle and small firms change their operation mechanisms by contracting, renting, selling and trusting.

Secondly, it has cultivated, developed and perfected the market system. The reform has begun to pay more attention to factor markets, such as capital, labor, land, technology, than to commodity markets.

Thirdly, it has set up and improved effective macro regulation system. It has converted from direct administrative and economic coordination into indirect economic coordination, including monetary policy, fiscal policy and planned regulation. Additionally, it has carried out some supplementary reforms, for instance, social protection systems and legal systems. In one word, economic system as a whole is approaching to the target pattern. It is predicted that the framework of new system would be completed in 2005 or so and perfected in 20 more years, i.e., 2025.

There are obvious stages in the reform process, some major and some minor. In 1992 the Party's 14th Central Committee established the market economy as the target pattern, which signaled the beginning of a new long stage. The year of 1992 is a turning point. The reform before it can be named as "the perceptual development stage" or "the stage of destroying traditional system". Its features are trial, dispersion, interest-orientated and breaking traditional systems. People did not reach consensus on some important issues such as the necessity, ways and directions of reform. Furthermore, the major stage can be divided into two short stages: the stage prior to 1984 focused on rural reform while the stage post 1985 focused on urban reform. Accordingly, the reform after 1992 can be called as "the rational advancement stage" or "the stage of building new system" which has well-defined goals and objectives. Its major features are systematization, initiative, institutional innovation and building up the framework of market economy. Most people have been unanimously in support of the reform. This long stage also has two short sub-stages. The first one is to build up the framework of market economic system before 2005. The second one is to perfect the new market economic system before after 2005. China's current system reform is in the early stage of the rational advancement stage, that is, building the framework of new system. The above analysis is shown in Table 1.1.

Table 1.1 Stages of China's Economic System Reform

	Period	1978-1992		1992-2020	
Long stages	Features	the perceptual development stage: trial, tentativeness, destroying traditional system		the rational advancement stage: systematization, self-consciousness, institutional innovation	
Short sub-stages	Period	1978-1984	1984-1992	1992-2005	2005-2020
	Features	emphasis on rural reform	emphasis on urban reform	building up the framework of the new system	Perfecting the new system

Source: Chen Zongsheng, *Walking out the Predicament of Stagflation*, Chinese Economics Press, 1995.

THE IMPLICATIONS AND FEATURES OF ECONOMIC SYSTEM MARKETIZATION

The outline of reform stages shows that since 1978 China's economic system reform has been advancing towards marketization. It has already made great strides towards its goals. The basic framework of socialist market economy has been set up and the degree of marketization is steadily increased, which prompts economic growth and development faster. At present, the reform lies in the stage of deepening and many key problems need to be solved. Therefore, it is necessary for us to draw some lessons in time, to make researches on the degree of marketization and to determine studies on the direction and ways for further reform. The study of the marketization progress needs to design some indicators that must be in concordance with the implications of marketization. Hence, above all, we should understand the implications of market economy and marketization and grasp the features of modern market economy.

What is Market Economy and What is Marketization?

Market economy is economy where resources are allocated by market mechanism. Judging by the difference of economic adjusting mechanisms, economic systems may be divided into several types, such as market economy, central-planned economy and primitive economy. Marketization means a process where the market mechanism in an economy plays an increasingly important role in resource allocation, the economy relies on market mechanisms, and the market system evolves from generation, growth to mature. Historically, there were two types of marketization for human society. The first one refers to a transformation from primitive economy to market economy, in which the shares of production for self-sufficiency are gradually reduced whereas the shares for exchange through market are steadily increased. The second one refers to a transformation from central-planned economy to market economy, in which the direct intervention with economic activities by government authorities is continuously decreased and planning mechanism plays weaker roles while spontaneous market adjusting is more and more important. The economy prior to the reform in China was socialist central-planned economy, so what Chinese economic system reform pushes forward is the second marketization. That is, planned system and mechanism are gradually weakened and finally replaced by market system and market mechanism. However, as a less developed country, China's economy may retain primitive economy to some extent in rural areas before the reform. Thus, the first marketization, the transformation from primitive economy to market economy, is also involved in China's reform. Nevertheless, this book emphasizes on the second one even when discussing the administrative system of rural reform because it is the main body of China's reform. We will seldom discuss the first one except in some necessary cases.

Because the nature of marketization is the process of enhancement of market mechanism's role, thus, understanding market mechanism will be helpful to add up the knowledge of marketization. Market mechanism is an economic mechanism or means that adjusts and allocates resources. Theoretically, it is just equal to "the Law of Value" advocated by Karl Marx or "invisible hand" described by Adam Smith. Specifically, it should include five mechanisms: supply and demand, competition, price, risk and interest mechanisms.

1. The supply and demand mechanism balances economic development. The mechanism will act to adjust the economy whenever supply or demand is not equal. However, their balance is occasional while the unbalance is frequent. Consequently, the market economy is economy that often needs to be adjusted. Of course, the adjustment relies on the mini-adjustment of economic agents rather than government planning.
2. The competition mechanism, different from the contest promoted in central-planned economy, determines the economic efficiency. The contest occurs under the premise that all firms survive. However, competition is a process of "natural selection", in which more efficient firms can be the incumbents whereas inefficient firms have to

go bankrupt and be eliminated. Therefore, market economy generally is high efficiency economy.

3. The price mechanism is a lever. It is affected by supply and demand, in turn, it adjusts supply and demand. Included in price are commodity prices, as well as factor prices, such as interest rates, wage rates, land rents and so on.

4. The risk mechanism is an economic constraint one, that is, self-responsibility for profits and losses. Under such mechanism, economic subjects have to be responsible for their behaviors and benefits so that they are driven by an incentive motive to improve their performance.

5. The most important and fundamental mechanism is the interest mechanism, which is also the cornerstone of market mechanism. The interest mechanism supposes that economic agents have their own benefits. It recognizes that each person or firm may have egotistical behaviors and pursue its own interest. However, egotism is not equal to selfishness that cares only for one's own advantage in the light of others. Egotism shows the rational motives towards the economic subjects' own benefits. That is to say, here egotism means self-benefit. Based on the egotism of economic agents, market economy guides people to satisfy other's and social benefits in the process of obtaining their own benefits. This is completely different from that of the central planned economy that denies the egotism of economic agents. In planned economy government tries to make enterprises produce directly for social demand but not for profits, and finally enterprises can not obtain their own benefits and so have no motives to achieve social benefits, thus economic stagnation.

Egotism gives an impetus to economy. It admits and satisfies self-interest. So long as self-interest is recognized and satisfied, economic subjects will have incentives, vigor and efficiency. For example, enterprises' benefits are profits and entrepreneurs' subjective attempts to set up enterprises are to get profits rather than producing some products directly for society. Nevertheless, getting profits implies that they have to do something for the society, either products or service. Furthermore, the more they provide and the better the quality is, the more they get profits. It can be seen that market economy is the mechanism that when the enterprises pursue their own benefits, the needs of society are satisfied simultaneously. In short, it brings the objective needs and subjective purposes into uniformity.

In general, the function of these mechanisms is gradually enhancing, i.e., they are playing a more and more important role in economic activities, or, the degree of marketization will be increased greatly. Further analysis must expound the detailed features of marketization because they are theoretical essence of marketization implications and observable indicators in the marketization progress. Moreover, the features have laid the foundation of designing the indicators for the measurement of marketization degree, which makes it easy for us to transform the theoretical implications of marketization into countable statistical indicators.

What are the Basic Features of Marketization?

In the transition from central-planned mechanism to market mechanism, significant changes will take place in the government behaviors and enterprises government behaviors as well as other aspects of the market. Marketization is embodied in the changes. Therefore, with the exposition of distinguishing features in the changes, the marketization features are exposed.

1. Increasing of the independence and autonomy of economic subjects. The economic subjects are comprised of enterprises and farmers as well as individuals. As labor or consumer, if the dependence of these subjects falls with increases of the independence and autonomy as well as the expansion of their choices (such as the choices of behavior manner, living style, profit-seeking manner and institution), then the marketization will tend to deepen.
2. Decentralizing of decision-making rights. The governments make their effects only on macro-decisions and other required fields but withdraw from micro decision-making fields. Transformation from authoritarian control by plans to autonomous adjustment by market must drive governments to withdraw from some micro-fields. The transferring, transformation and dispersion of decision-making rights all represent marketization.
3. Multiplicity of ownership structures and ownership realization modes. Historically, market economy evolved from private economy. It is observed that non-state or non-public-owned sectors have inherent close relation to market economy. In contrast, public ownership is associated with centralization. Therefore, ownership structure and ownership realization modes are required to respond to the market-orientation reform and change accordingly. A new structure that public ownership is accompanied by multi-ownership forms needs to be established to adapt to the requirement of market economy.
4. Marketization of product price. Prices of consumer goods and production materials are determined by the supply and demand. In other words, the producers determine them according to the conditions of supply and demand as well as the cost rather than the government authorities' plans.
5. Marketization of factor price. Prices of labor, capital, funds, technology, real estate and foreign exchange are respectively wage, stock price, interest, transferring charges of patents, land price and exchange rate. To what extent the prices are determined by the conditions of supply and demand, or to what extent the authorities do not control directly, may be a vital symbol of market economy's maturity extent.   ·
6. Normalizing (or contractualization), legalization, orderliness and creditability of economic subjects' behaviors. Mature market economy is not disorder or entirely laissez faire, but is restricted and regulated by law, rules and norms (e.g., commercial morality). Hence, legalization of bankruptcy and ratio of contract fulfillment are also important symbols of marketization.

There may be many other features of marketization that are not involved, but the ones shown above must be most essential. These features imply the theoretical implications of marketization and circumscribe the bounds of the selection of statistical measurement indicators for marketization.

THE MARKETIZATION DEGREE OF MAIN FIELDS IN CHINA'S ECONOMY

Considering the explanation of the implications and marketization features, we design some indicators to measure marketization degrees in the 11 selected fields of Chinese economy (see Table 1.2). The indicators are basically consistent with the above marketization features. What we need to explain is that, first of all, it is impossible for us to use exactly the same indicators in different fields because of different conditions. For example, the indicators of agricultural marketization are different from that of industry, and the indicators for technological marketization are also distinct from those in labor market. However, all of the selected indicators are appropriate to show marketization degree in various fields. Secondly, we define complete marketization as 100% and complete planned economy as 0%, which will be taken as the bounds of marketization degree, because this definition is convenient for us to uniformity standards and thereby adds up related data. In reality, as we know, on one hand, there does not exist a planned economy that is exclusive of any market activity; on the other hand, marketization can not reach 100% even in the most developed market economies because there is more or less government intervention in any economy. Of course, the extents of government intervention in various market economies are different, and so is that of different times in the same country. In other words, they are different in various fields, different countries or different times. Therefore, if we take the actual marketization degree of some developed market economy rather than that of complete market economy as 100%, it would lose the uniform standards for comparison among nations or different fields in the same country. Thirdly, the measurement results only have relative meanings. People may use other different methods and indicators to measure the marketization and get different results. Thus, what is important are the trends implied in data queues.

According to the structure of target pattern of China's economic systems, first, we will analyze the marketization progress by the order of enterprise—government--market. Here market refers to the products markets (including consumer goods and service market as well as production goods market) and factors markets (including labor, capital, funds, real estate, technology and foreign exchange). Second, by sectors we illustrate the marketization degree of agriculture, industry and tertiary. Third, we discuss the differences of marketization degree among several large regions. In this chapter, we merely analyze the indicators and list measurement results, which in fact sorts out and takes a comprehensive elaboration for the contents of following chapters in the rest of the book, where the marketization degree of various fields will be expounded in detail, but the total marketization degree of China's economy will be examined in the next section of this chapter.

Table 1.2 Major Selected Indicators for 11 Fields

Major fields	1. Industrial and commercial enterprises	2. Government behavior	3. Commodity market	4. Labor market
Indicators	✧Freedom to choose enterprise's ownership ✧Ratio of executives appointed through competition ✧Ratio of observance of operation autonomy (14 Stipulations) ✧Ratio of the enterprise taking maximizing profits as the predominant goal. ✧Extent of legalization of bankruptcy ✧Ratio of contract fulfillment ✧Share of non-public enterprises ✧Share of non-public sector's assets ✧Share of output value of non-public sector	✧Indicators for transformation of government role: drops of the share of tax over revenue ✧Indicators for government's withdrawing micro economy activities: drop of the share of construction expenditures in total fiscal revenues drop of the share of state appropriation over total investment in fixed assets ✧Indicators for transformation of government's regulation manner: share of price subsidies over government expenditures share of price subsidies over GNP ✧Share of officials and functionaries in total employment[1] ✧Share of group consumption over total consumption[1] ✧Share of government institution number over total institution number[1]	✧Consumer goods: share of controlled, directive and market prices ✧Farm and sideline products: share of controlled, directive and market prices ✧Producer material: share of controlled, directive and market prices ✧Service: share of controlled, directive and market prices	✧Freedom to choose jobs: duty transference, re-employing, newly added labor in urban and rural areas ✧Freedom to hire or fire employees: some typical units such as state and non-state enterprises, services and social organizations ✧Mobility of labor: ratio of contractual employment mobility of rural labor. ✧Marketization of wages: relation with profits, contracts, farmer income and inflation

Table 1.2 Major Selected Indicators for 11 Fields (continued)

Major fields	5. Financial market	6. Real estate market	7. Technology market	8. Agriculture
Indicators	✞Ratio of financial assets over GNP ✞Independence of central and business banks ✞Regulating manner and operation of financial policy package by central bank ✞ commercialization of business banks operating as enterprises ✞Share of security value over total financial assets ✞Marketization of interest	✞Rate of private housing ✞Share of housing consumption in total expenditures ✞Ratio of housing price over income ✞Ratio of real estate finance to total financial assets ✞ Marketization of land exchange ✞ Marketization of housing price	✞Growth rate of transaction value in technology market ✞Growth rate of examined patent applications ✞Growth of examined paten applied by jobless and foreigners in China ✞Growth rate of technological funds raised by themselves	✞Share of farmer's input from market ✞Share of farmer's product transacted directly in market over total transacted product ✞Ratio of labor flowing into urban areas and labor in non-agriculture of rural over total rural labor force ✞Shares of rural fixed assets invested by collective, private and foreign enterprises to total rural fixed assets ✞Share of farm product prices determined by market

Table 1.2 Major Selected Indicators for 11 Fields (continued)

Major fields	9. Industry	10. Foreign trade	11. Regional differences
Indicators	✛Real employment rate in industry ✛Relative ratio of capital sets over output value ✛Rate of products sales over output value ✛Share of assets of non-state industrial enterprises ✛Opposite indicator of the direct intervention of government the rate of the surplus output value without planning controlled part[2] ✛Extent of enterprise services socialization	✛Rate of enterprises empowered to engage autonomously in foreign trade ✛Share of the value of foreign enterprises' import and export ✛Marketization degree of foreign exchange rate ✛Rate of fall of customs tariff ✛Rate of decrease of non-tariff trade barriers ✛Rate of rise of trade dependence	✛Prerequisites of marketization: Ratio of added value of tertiary over GNP, ratio of labor of tertiary over total labor, ratio of added value of non-state industrial sectors over gross output value, rate of non-agriculture output value over gross output value in rural areas ✛Establishment of market systems: number of outlets in wholesale and retail sale trade, personnel, free market in urban and rural areas, financial institutions averaged by per 10000 persons by regions ✛Marketization degree of commodites ratio of industrial product purchases in the sector of wholesale and retail trade over gross output value of industry, ratio of farm and sideline product purchases in the sector of wholesale and retail trade over gross output value of agriculture, ratio of import over purchase of goods in the sector of wholesale and retail sales, ratio of export over gross output value of industry and agriculture ✛Factor market: Share of contractual workers in total workers, ratio of registered persons of labor force flow over the urban unemployed, ratio of advertisement business volume over social gross output, ratio of transaction value in technological market over gross output of industry and agriculture, ratio of flooring size of the sold houses over the flooring size of total finished houses ✛Extent of social security in market economy: share of insurance and welfare funds in employee wages, share of the towns and villages having social security systems in total

Source: Eleven sub-reports of the 1996's project entitled by "The degree of marketization progress of China's economic system" supported by Gushutang Funds of Nankai Institute of Economics

Note· (1) The relation between the later three indicators and others in government behavior are: if their growth rates are positive then subtract them, if they are negative then add up them These numbers represent the marketization of government behavior (2) Method for calculating the indicators of intervention of government in industry field is as follows: the disparity between 1 and the ratio of the controlled part over total output value is the ratio of the market regulation Because the data of planning controlled are available, we use subtraction for it. (3) Because of liimted data some indicators are omitted or displaced by other available indicators See the detailed interpretation below and the analysis in the related chapters

Marketization of Industrial and Commercial Enterprises

By ownership, there are two types of industrial and commercial enterprises in China, that is, the state-owned and non-state-owned enterprises. System reform for state-owned enterprises is the key of economic system reform. In comparison with it, the non-state-owned-enterprises may be regarded as already being in the market (in fact, not all of them). In view of this, we will discuss the marketization of the public-owned enterprises, especially, of the state-owned enterprises. Then we add up the weighted marketization degrees of state-owned enterprises and non-state-owned enterprises. So far the reform of state-owned enterprises has carried out the approach of "empowering autonomy and retaining profits". Consequently, the marketization here actually refers to that the governments hand back enterprises the rights associated with enterprise's resources allocation. Thus, the selected indicators must reflect the degrees of empowering autonomy and retaining profits. In fact, we choose the next indicators;

1. The freedom for enterprise to choose ownership. It refers to the right that enterprises are able to choose their ownership for themselves, for example, shareholding, partnership, individual and private ownership. Enterprises in modern market economy have enough right to freely choose their ownership. It is noted that enterprises' choices are not arbitrary. In contrast, their choices have to be based on the market and laws. Therefore, the ownership forms of enterprises are just the results of market competition, which further proves that the indicator of the freedom for enterprise to choose ownership is a reasonable indicator to measure marketization process.
2. Ratio of executives or entrepreneurs appointed through market competition. The indicator reflects the transition situation under which enterprise chiefs are appointed gradually through market competition rather than by the governments. It is well known that in central-planned economy, the chiefs of state-owned enterprises are selected mainly by the governments. However, in modern market economy they are selected mainly through executive or entrepreneur markets or elected democratically in the enterprises (also belong to market behavior).
3. Ratio of operation autonomy rights of enterprises. The ratio of operation autonomy rights suggests the enhancement of enterprise independence and the establishment of autonomy operation agents. At present, the observable and recognizable operation autonomy rights are 14 items stipulated by the Regulations of Transforming Operation Mechanisms for State Owned Industrial Enterprise issued by the State Council in July 1992. The extent of implements of these stipulations may reflect the progress of enterprise marketization.
4. Ratio of the enterprises taking profit maximum as the predominant goal. Maximizing profits is a survival condition in market economy and indicates that enterprises have taken part in competition. Nevertheless, enterprises in centrally planned economy take output or maximum employment as their major goals that are entirely different from the goal of maximum profit.

5. Degree of bankruptcy legalization. So far, it has been believed that Chinese enterprise's bankruptcy is the result of administrative interference. After the Bankruptcy Law was taken into effect in 1988, there were merely 3010 cases against bankruptcy up to 1994, and enterprise bankruptcy rate was less than 0.01%. However, the process from no bankruptcy to having it and further to bankruptcy by law describes the marketization progress appropriately.

6. Ratio of contract fulfillment. Market economy is the one that is both legal and contractual. Creditability is one of essential attributions of modern economy. For instance, how many transactions of enterprises do sign contracts (the ratio of signing contracts), and how many contracts be fulfilled (the ratio of fulfilling contracts), which reflect the marketization degree, in particular in modern market economy and are totally different from the behavior of enterprises in central planned economy.

7. Ratios of non-public enterprises. It refers to ratios of the number of non-public enterprises, employees and output value. Usually, non-public enterprises may be assumed to be complete marketization.

Averaging the above indicators, we obtain the total marketization degree of Chinese industrial and commercial enterprises. The figures in Table 1.3 show that the marketization degrees of Chinese industrial and commercial enterprises are relative low, less than 50%, but the data before 1988 are estimated by author.

Table 1.3 Marketization of Industrial and Commercial Enterprises

Year	1978	1984	1988	1990	1992	1993	1994	1995	1997
M.D.(%)	0	10	23	15	25	34.7	40	46.4	48

Source: See Chapter 2 of this book.
Note: M.D. refers to marketization degree.

Marketization Degree of Government Behaviors

As the general representative of economy, the government is the decision-maker of economy. In socialist countries, government is also the representative of state enterprises' property and the owner of state-owned property. Therefore, the transformation of government behaviors includes the changes of government functions, management ranges and adjustment means. The core of the transformation is that government only acts as the manager of macro economic activities but withdraws from some fields of direct operation and production. Even in some fields needing intervention, the adjustment means must respond to the changes. Compared with the government functions in central-planned economy, the gradual decrease in management ranges and decisions of governments implies the increase of marketization degree of government behaviors (though the change of regulation means should be involved in, too). These decreases are just consistent with the increases of the enterprise decision-making rights and the independence.

Quantitatively, the power of government behavior is mainly reflected in fiscal revenue and expenditure. Moreover, its transformation is surely reflected in the changes of items and quantity of fiscal revenue and expenditure. Hence, we can examine the changes of fiscal items and balance status for measuring the changes of government behaviors from central planned economy to market economy.

1. Indicator of the transformation of government function identity. It can be measured by the composition of fiscal revenue. In general, as a social economic manager, government receives its income from tax. As a proprietor, it does from rents and interests. As a producer, it does from profit. (If producer operates with its own capital, its revenue should include both profit and interests.) In central planned economy, government is proprietor, manager and direct producer. Instead, in market economy government is mainly a macro manager. Fiscal revenue of China's government consists of tax, enterprise income (profits) and enterprise loss subsidies (negative profits). Tax reflects the function of social manager while enterprise income and loss subsidies do the function of proprietor. Thus, the transformation of government function may be shown in the two aspects. We can examine the marketization degree of government function by the indicator of fiscal revenue composition.

2. Indicator of government withdrawing from micro economic activities. In central planned economy, the government intervenes directly in economic activities and assigns mandatory planning quota. Market economy requires government to withdraw from these activities. To enable quantitative analysis, we choose two indicators: the share of economic construction expenditures in total fiscal expenditure and the share of state budget investment in social fixed asset investment. To some extent, the indicators may measure the extent of government participating in micro-economic activities. The bigger the figure, the more the participation into micro-activities of governments. Vice versa.

3. Indicator of the transformation of regulation means by government. In central planned economy, government uses direct controlling means, for example, giving instruction and issuing documents. Instead, in market economy indirect economic means such as monetary policy, fiscal policy and legal means are adopted. However, it is difficult to design indicators and obtain related data. To measure the changes from central planned economy to market economy, we try to take two indicators: the share of price subsidies over government expenditure and the share of price subsidies in GNP. In market economy, government is not assumed to give so many price subsidies to enterprises in order to guarantee the market parameters (including price) not to be distorted. Therefore, the smaller the above two indicators, the more close to market economy.

4. In summary, these indicators may measure the marketization degree of government behavior from three aspects: from proprietor of state property to social economic manager, from direct participant in micro economic activities to macro management, from direct administratively mandatory regulation to indirect economic regulation.

The simple average of these indicators is just the marketization degree of total government behaviors. See Table 1.4.

Table 1.4 Marketization Degree of Government Behavior

Year	1979	1980	1981	1982	1983	1984	1985	1986	1987
M.D.(%)	4	13	5.4	36	43	51	--	64.2	62.8

Year	1988	1989	1990	1991	1992	1993	1994	1995	1997
M.D.(%)	63.3	63.7	62.2	64.6	66.6	71.7	72	73	72

Source: See Chapter 3 of this book.

Marketization of Commodity (Service) Price

Price marketization of commodity and service is a major part in marketization-orientated economic reform. In fact, price reform took the lead in China's system reform. Usually, the marketization of commodity price refers to the process which producers autonomously determine the prices subjecting to market principles and the condition of supply and demand. It is comprised of three parts: relatively complete pricing rights for producers, relatively perfect competition in the pricing process and adjusting function to allocate resource and to balance the supply and demand by price. There are three kinds of pricing in China: the authority's price, the authority's guide price and the market price. Provided that market price is complete marketization (1), let the authority's guide price be half marketization (0.5) and the authority's price be complete non-marketization (0). Thus, the marketization degree of one commodity can be calculated by weighted shares of commodity value by using three forms of pricing.

The commodities in China's market can be divided into four types: retail commodity, agriculture and sideline product, producer material and service. With absence of service price in statistical yearbook, we only examine the former three types. Using the above method we can measure the marketization degree of commodity price of every type. Then taking sale values of various commodities as weights we may obtain the marketization degree of total commodity market. See Table 1.5. In 1995, 85% of prices of consumer and producer materials are determined by the conditions of supply and demand in market, which is an important symbol of initial establishment of market economic system.

Table 1.5 Marketization of Commodity Prices

Year	1979	1984	1988	1990	1991	1992	1993	1994	1995
M.D.(%)	2.25	15	60	54.5	64.1	84.7	88.5	85.9	84.5

Source: See Chapter 4 of this book.

Marketization of Labor Force

Labor is one of the most important production factors and labor market is one of the most important factors markets. The marketization of labor market has remarkable influence on the marketization of overall economy. Since reform and open-door the labor market has changed greatly. Qualitatively, the traditional concept that labor is not one of commodity has been denied in reality. Quantitatively, more and more labor force has entered labor markets, salary and wage have become a better sign of labor prices. To measure the maturity extent of labor market, we have set up the following indicators: the freedom to choose jobs, the freedom to hire or fire employees, labor force mobility and wage marketization.

1. The extent of freedom to choose jobs. One of the important parts of the labor marketization is to eradicate the mandatory arrangement for employment in planning system and to make laborers to choose jobs by their favors. The freedom of laborers to choose jobs covers three parts: the freedom of the first employment of new-added to labor force, job transference of employees and re-employment of the unemployed. Because of the lack of available data and the complexity for the latter two parts, we only examine the first employment of new-added labor force. As concerned with administrative system of labor force, the added labor force in urban areas is significantly different from that in rural areas. The new-added laborers in urban areas include the graduates from university, colleges and professional schools and peasants who immigrate into cities. The new-added labor force in rural areas includes farmers, flowing labor force who try to find jobs in cities, and laborers in town and village enterprises as well as individuals and laborers in private enterprises in rural areas. The freedom extents of every kind of laborers to choose jobs are weighted by the numbers of various laborers, then we may get the freedom extents of national labor force.

2. The extent of freedom of employment of the employers. This indicator reflects the demand in labor market while the preceding indicator does the supply. The supply and demand constitutes the integrate labor market. We may examine the extent of freedom of employment of the employers from three parts: employment freedom of the state owned and collective ownership enterprises, that of government and social organizations, and non-state enterprises and organizations.

3. Extent of mobility of labor force. We take the ratio of contractual employment as the indicator. It illustrates the results of two-way selection that refers to autonomy of choosing jobs by laborers and independence of recruitment by the employers. The mobility of labor force in urban areas is calculated by multiplying the ratios of contractual employees in state owned and collective ownership enterprises and other basic units by their labor weights. The laborers in rural areas are different from those in urban areas because the contractual ratios of laborers flowing to cities and agriculture labor are unattainable or simply absent. Therefore, we substitute the extent of freedom to choose jobs in rural areas for the mobility extent.

4. Marketization degree of wage. As labor price, wage that is determined by the supply and demand of labor characterizes a mature labor market. Labor income in conventional central planned economy is egalitarian and fixed while wages in market economy are associated with the economic efficiency of the enterprises, average levels in the same industries and the supply and demand condition. Specifically speaking, the wages in collective ownership enterprises in urban areas, foreign enterprises and non-state economy as well as new-added employees in all enterprises have been marketization. Although the wages of functionary are set by the authorities but in the same way as other market economies, they may be regarded as marketization. About 80% of wages in state-owned enterprises and 50% of wages in self-balanced organizations rely on benefits and market conditions. The marketization degrees of rural labor income in various industries are different from each other. The mean income of primary sector, 90% or so depends on the market prices of agriculture product prices. However, the income of labors in secondary and tertiary sectors in rural areas has been complete marketization.

In summary, averaging the above four indicators can attain the numerical results of the total marketization of labor market, shown in Table 1.6.

Table 1.6 Marketization of Labor Markets

Year	1979	1985	1990	1995
M.D.(%)	3.24	24.2	34.7	60.0

Source: See Chapter 5 of this book

Marketization of Finance

Financial Market, especially capital market, is an important factor market. Finance marketization is the necessary part and essential premise of total marketization of the economy. It is equal to "Finance Deepening" analyzed by modern economic theories. In a "finance deepening" economy, forms and duration types of financial assets increase significantly and so does the ratio of their value to national income or physical wealth; financial system is enlarged, organizations tend to be specialized, and interest as capital price can reflect exactly the supply and demand condition. China's financial system is gradually relaxed after long time's regulation. In recent years, the reform of finance marketization has speeded up in spite of low marketization degree. We use following indicators to examine the degree of finance marketization.

1. Ratio of financial assets to GNP. Rise of the ratio shows that China is running towards monetary economy which is an important symbol of marketization and that financial capital has many forms and various structures. For example, besides

conventional deposits and bank loans, various securities are also added, which is a kind of evidence for the deepening of finance marketization.

2. Independence of central bank. Central banks have high independence in developed market economies. Take an example, the United Reserve Bank of USA is independent of President and the fiscal Ministry as well as other state ministries. It can take action independently. In 1984 the China People Bank had the functions of central bank, but it was one of state department rather than the real central bank. In 1985, the People Bank of China was granted two functions by Law of Central Bank: First, to design and carry out monetary policies under the lead of the State Council; Second, to supervise and manage financial apparatus and not to give excess credits to the government. These two functions have taken great progress to make the China People Bank be a real central bank.

3. Marketization of central bank's operation tools and business bank. The China People Bank controls the overall financial system mainly through mandatory loan quota, which is one of administrative control. In developed market economies central bank use three financial tools to regulate the economies: open market operation, reserve rate and re-discount rate, which have been tentatively used in China before long. The effectiveness of these three policy tools relies on marketization degrees of various business banks. If business banks and non-bank financial organizations are government's cashiers or have no profitability goals, and if there are no private ownership (standing for efficiency) in financial system, then even a real central bank would not implement effective and sensitive regulations. Actually, here we examine the mature degree of financial system.

4. Ratio of securities to total financial assets. Negotiable securities consist of treasury bill, firm bonds, financial bonds and stocks, and so on. The ratio of securities to total financial assets is a major indicator for finance marketization because it stands for the share of direct capital, i.e., the share of funds directly raised from market. However, it cannot cover all fields since a part of loan in total financial assets comes from market. See next indicator.

5. Marketization of interest rate. It is another important indicator for finance marketization. The essence of marketization of interest rate is to let interest be determined by capital's supply and demand. In market economies central banks issue only re-discount rates for business banks, while interests of short-term capital market that are mainly comprised of business banks are fully free market interests with regard to supply and demand. In China the interests prior to reform were fixed, but the ones post reform are adjusted frequently by administrative forms and the adjustments are market orientation, that is, being close to market interests. When calculating, we use the share of the loans by floating interests in total loans, which obviously treat floating interests as market interests and fixed interests as non-market interests. Averaging these indicators we attain the overall finance marketization.

Table 1.7 Marketization of Finance

Year	1978	1985	1990	1995
M.D.(%)	1.0	3.6	6.3	9.1

Source: See Chapter 6 of this book.

Marketization of Real Estate

Real estate includes housing and land. The real estate marketization refers to the allocation of housing and landing through market mechanisms, that is, viewing real estate as commodity. Real estate market is one of important factor market. Its marketization degree is equal to the mature degree of real estate market, that is, the degree of allocated real estate resource through market. This book only examines urban real-estate markets. We have chosen following indicators for measurement.

1. Share of private ownership housing. In other countries the share of private housing refers to the ratio of urban household ownership (private ownership) housing to total housing. Owing to low share of apartments (about 50%) in our country, we use floor space to calculate the rate of private ownership, i.e., the ratio of the floor spaces of private housings to those of total housings. In the view of urban areas, we argue that this indicator show the housing marketization.
2. Share of housing expenditure. It means the ratio of housing expenditure of urban household over total consumption expenditure. The indicator in market economies mainly reflects the development level and the improvement of living standard but has no relation to the marketization of real estate. Nevertheless, due to low rents for a long time, the housing expenditure in China has accounted for a very small share of living expenditure. With the growth and development of housing market, money-distribution-oriented reforms of housing welfare increase rents, and housing investment marketization requires rents to match housing investment price. Hence, the level of housing expenditure has been approaching to the level of market rents, so we choose the share of housing expenditure in consumption expenditure as the indicator for housing marketization.
3. Ratio of house price over income. It refers to the ratio of average market price of common house over household income per year. Like the preceding indicator, it seems to show only the income level, but because of welfare housing the ratio of house prices over income can reflect housing marketization to some extent.
4. Marketization degree of land transferring. This refers to the share of land transferring through market in total transferred land. There are two kinds of land transferring: planning distribution and negotiable transferring. All three forms of negotiable transferring, contract, tender and auction, belong to market transaction in spite of different degrees.

5. Marketization degree of house price. This refers to the ratio of floor spaces transacted in market price over total space for transaction. There may be three types of house prices: real market price of commodity houses, cost price of houses for Housing Project (Anju Gongcheng) and favor or standard price of state owned houses for selling. Their weighted shares can reflect the marketization of house price.

According to the above indicators, we have calculated marketization degree of real estate. See the Table 1.8.

Table 1.8 Marketization of Real Estate of China and Tianjin (%)

Year	1978	1986	1987	1988	1989	1990	1991	1992	1993	1994	1995
China	0.0	21.1	24.0	27.8	28.8	22.8	24.0	21.9	28.9	38.2	39.3
Tianjin	0.0	-	-	-	-	-	-	-	-	-	30.2	37.4

Source: See Chapter 7 of this book.

Marketization of Technology

Technology is another important production factor and technology market is another important factor market. In particular, technology plays an increasingly important role in modern economy. Technology commodities are what people exchange in technology market. (Some technologies are ambiguous to define their bounds and thereby can not be commodity.) Technology market is the overall exchange relationship in which technology commodities are exchanged or transacted and become actual production forces. It has many forms, such as agency for transferring technologies, consultative and development organizations for technology, technology shops and technology markets. Some irregular and invisible technology transactions belong to technology markets, too. However, China's technology markets are less developed. In central planned economy there were no markets and transaction for technology. Thereby, the building of China's technology market does not need to reform conventional system but to cultivate new system for technology market. The mature degree of technology market is characterized by the indicators of technology commodity's transaction volume and value.

First, the growth rate of transaction value in technology market directly stands for the marketization degree of technology market because the rate represents the technology commodities transacted already. Second, the growth rate of examined patent applications. Patents include innovation, new practical forms and outward appearance design. The volumes of application and examination of three kinds of patents stand for technology's scale and openness. Third, the growth rate of examined patent applications by the jobless and foreigners as well as the openness of technology market. Prior to open of technology market, Chinese jobless persons and foreigners cannot apply for patents for their scientific achievements because only organizations can do. Therefore, these indicators can characterize the growth and development of China's technology market. Fourth, the growth rate of technology funds raised by one self. To raise funds is a full market-style action. The more funds are raised, the more developed the technology market is. Because of shortage of data, some other indicators such as the justice of technology market and the growth of technology transaction organizations are ignored. By averaging these explained indicators, it can be seen that the development of China's technology market has been fast.

Table 1.9 Marketization of Technology Markets

Year	1979	1985	1990	1995
M.D.(%)	0.0	46.3	54.1	70.8

Source: See Chapter 8 of this book.

Marketization of Agriculture

In the following text we will have an insight into the overall marketization of China's economy by sectors. Agriculture is both the starting point of China's economic system reform and the foundation of national economy. First of all, we describe the marketization degree of agriculture. With the weighted indicators of agriculture labor force, capitals for agriculture, transaction for agriculture products and agriculture product's price, we will calculate the overall marketization of agriculture.

1. Labor force, as an important production factor in agriculture production, has remarkable impact on agriculture marketization. In central planned economy, labor force in rural areas is fixed with land and can not be free to flow into market. With the advancement of agriculture reform in the form of household responsibility system (HRS), it is possible for farmers to extricate themselves from land farming. They have the freedom to flow and choose jobs, which is shown in the increase of the number of employment in non-agriculture industries and farmers into cities. Supposing that for labor force in town and village enterprises and farmers into cities come from labor market is reasonable. Hence, we can select the ratio of the number of employment in non-agriculture industries to total labor force in rural areas as the indicator of agriculture labor's marketization.

2. Agriculture capital consists of flowing capital and fixed asset investment that was controlled by authorities in central planned economy. Under HRS, flowing capital is raised by farmers themselves while fixed asset investment by state, collectives and individuals. Due to unattainable and small amount of flowing capital, we use the shares of collective, individual and foreign investments in total agriculture fixed assets to illustrate the marketization of agriculture capital approximately.

3. Agriculture product transaction refers to the transaction relationship of agriculture products in markets. An appropriate indicator may be the share of the direct transaction in total transaction in the markets. Obviously, marketization degree increases with growth of the share. In addition, it is argued that the ratio of

agriculture product's prices determined by the market force be better indicator. However, the key is to select and allocate the weights when adding up the indicators to attain the result of overall agriculture marketization. Given that the weights of production and transaction are 50% respectively. Production function is used to estimate the weights of labor and capital in production process. We suppose that price marketization and transaction marketization of agriculture products contribute to overall marketization equally. According to the results in table 1.10, agriculture marketization degrees after reform arise from 20% of 1981 to more than 60% of 1995.

Table 1.10 Marketization of Agriculture

Year	1978	1979	1980	1981	1982	1983	1984	1985	1986	1987	1988	1989	1990	1991	1992	1993	1994	1995
M.D	7.67	12.8	17.9	22.3	25.0	31.1	38.3	49.7	48.3	51.5	53.9	49.5	51.6	52.6	50.5	58.8	64.7	65.0

Source: See Chapter 9 of this book.

Marketization of Industry

Industry occupies an incomparable position in national economy. After reform, the state changed the strategy of putting strong emphasis on the development of heavy industries. With the decrease of intervention into industry field by administrative power, the marketization degree of industry has increased steadily. We will use some indicators to characterize this progress.

1. Rate of effective employment in industry. The number of effective employment in industry means the employment number in coordinate with capital under the market principles. In market economy firms have the goals of maximum profits and operate without redundancy labor. Thereby, the ratio of the effective employment to total labor force is suitable to describe industrial marketization. Dividing gross industrial product by labor productivity of foreign enterprises is the effective employment.

2. Ratio of industrial capital-output in comparison. Suppose that capital can be effectively allocated for maximum profits in market economy. The relative ratio of industrial capital output in comparison can be attained by the ratio of industrial output per 100 yuan China industry capital over that of per 100 yuan joined-venture industry capital.

3. Ratio of sold industrial products over gross products. In market economy production is market orientation, so only a very small share of products can be reserved in warehouses. High ratio indicates high degree of marketization. It is different from the situation in central planned economy where what types and how many products are produced mainly rely on firm's capacity with high stocks.

4. Share of the assets of non-state-owned industrial enterprise. The assets of non-state owned industrial enterprises are not invested by the governments but allocated by

market. Therefore, the share of the assets of non-state industrial enterprises in total industrial assets can measure industrial marketization progress.

5. Inverse rate of direct interference with industry by the authorities. The indicator is calculated by subtracting the part controlled by plans from gross products. We suppose that firms in market economy make decisions of production, purchase, pricing and selling according to the market conditions, and the authorities are allowed to guide but not to interfere with firms. Subtracting the summed products controlled by plans from gross products will be the indicator.

6. Extent of service socialization for enterprise. Divided the welfare provided by firms by total welfare. In market economy, firms are production organizations and only pay off the wage and concerned premium for personnel, but they do not assume any other social functions. That is, the governments or other organizations should provide welfare for workers' lives. Society should serve firms, not vice versa.

Averaging these indicators, we may get the marketization level of overall industry.

Table 1.11 Industrial Marketization

Year	1983	1985	1988	1991	1993	1994	1995
M.D.	7.96	23.5	32.1	37.3	46.5	48.4	49.9

Source: See Chapter 10 of this book.

Marketization of Foreign Trade

As far as logical and comprehensive analysis is concerned, it would be better to examine the marketization of tertiary sector after that of agriculture and industry. However, some fields of the tertiary sector such as real estate, finance and technology have been examined above. And some service prices in tertiary sector have already partially reflected in the commodity (and service) markets. Moreover, the tertiary sector is too complex to examine as a sole sector, so we will leave it for deep analysis. Here we begin to analysis the marketization of foreign trade. Above all, we examine the freedom extent of national trade system.

1. Increase of foreign trade subjects. If all the foreign trade subjects are designated by the state authorities, the marketization degree must be very low. This was the case at the beginning of economic reform. At present, there are over ten thousands of foreign trade enterprises; the subjects of foreign trade is now greatly diversified, such as national foreign trade corporations, national industry and trade corporations, local corporations of foreign trade, industry and trade, agriculture and trade, and technology and trade, industrial enterprises, research institutes, universities and colleges, commercial and material enterprises as well as more than twenty thousands foreign enterprises. The number of autonomous agents increases greatly.

2. Ratio of import and export of foreign enterprises. Foreign enterprises refer to joint ventures, cooperative enterprises and ventures exclusively with foreign investment and so forth. The marketization degree of foreign trade would surely increase if their shares in total of import and export grow. In 1993, the ratio increased to 34%.
3. Trade dependence ratio. The degree of trade dependence measures the openness and marketization degree of an economy. It has the positive correlation with economic openness and thereby overseas markets as well as marketization degree. This book argues that the current trade dependence degree reaches 20% or so despite some other figures by other methods.
4. Regulation system of foreign exchange. Foreign exchange rates had been regulated by authorities for a long time and been far away from the market rate. After some reforms, the exchange rates of Renminbi via Dollar have closed to the level of market rate.
5. Decrease of customs tariff. Low level of customs tariff is one of important indicators for the freedom of foreign trade system. It stands for the degree of openness. In the span of 1991-1997, China's customs tariff level decreased from over 43% to 17%. If we consider customs tariff of 45% as non-marketization of 100%, then the decrease of twenty-eight percentages (45%-17%) means that the marketization degree of customs tariff has reached 62%.
6. Decrease of non-tariff barriers. The non-tariff barriers include import or export quota, license system and mandatory control of import and export. However, all of the non-tariff barriers are the obstruction in the road towards foreign trade marketization. Although they are reduced in recent years, its fall is much slower than that of customs tariff.

Based on these indicators, we may show the result of foreign trade marketization in the following table.

Table 1.12 Marketization of Foreign Trade

Year	1978	1980	1985	1988	1991	1995	1997
M.D.	1.5	3.0	9.0	19.0	22.3	41.4	54.4

Source: See Chapter 11 of this book.

Difference of Regional Marketization

Finally, we discuss the difference of marketization among regions. China has wide territory and its development is not balanced and so is economic system reform. The differences of implement force of system reform, the favor reform policies entitled by central government and the economic development levels lead to the disparity of system marketization among regions. They have the positive correlation with marketization. We use several indicators to measure the regional marketization.

1. Prerequisites of marketization. Share of added value of tertiary in GNP, share of labor force of tertiary, share of industrial added value of non-state owned sectors in gross industrial products, and share of non-agriculture products in gross social product of rural areas, may suggest the economic base of marketization from the whole society, industry and rural areas.

2. Building of market system. It may be shown in the number of outlets in wholesale and retail sector, personnel, free markets in urban and rural areas, and financial institutions per 10 thousand.

3. Marketization degree of commodities. It may be shown in the share of industrial product purchases in wholesale and retail sector in gross industrial products, the share of farm and sideline product purchases in the whole sale and retail sector in gross agriculture products, the share of the import in commodity purchases of the whole sale and retail sector, and the share of export trade value in gross industrial and agriculture products. Commodity marketization among regions may be examined respectively in the markets of industrial and agriculture products as well as the import and export.

4. Factors markets. (1)The share of contractual employees in total workers. (2)The share of registered persons in urban unemployed persons. (3)The ratio of advertisement business volumes over gross social products. (4) The ratio of technology transaction volumes over gross industrial products. (5) The share of floor space of the sold houses in that of total completed houses.

5. Extent of social security. It can be shown in the share of insurance and welfare expenditures in wages and the share of the towns and villages with social security system in total towns and villages.

6. The weights of these indicators are given by experts. Then we can get the marketization degrees of the East, Middle, West, South and North of China. We select two groups of figures: the highest and lowest, shown in Table 1.13. According to highest group, there are marketization differences of 5 percentage points between the East and the West and 1.5 percentage points between the South and the North. Although smaller difference exits in the lowest group, the disparity is still evident.

Table 1.13 Marketization Differences in Regions

Region	East	Middle	West	North	South
M.D.	70.3	64.4	64.9	66.4	67.9
	(56.8)	(52.1)	(52.5)	(53.7)	(54.9)

Source: See Chapter 12 of this book.

Note: The figures with parentheses are lower group, and the figures without parentheses are higher one. According to the findings (see Table 1.14), we may draw some conclusions.

Table 1.14 Marketization Trends in Main Fields

Year	1979	1980	1981	1984	1985	1986	1987	1988	1989	1990	1991	1992	1993	1994	1995	1997
1. Industrial and commercial enterprises	0	-	-	10	-	-	-	23	-	15	-	25	34.7	39.6	46.4	48.0*
2. Government behavior	4	13	5.4	50.8	-	64.2	62.8	63.3	63.7	62.2	64.6	66.6	71.7	72*	73*	72*
3. Commodity market	2.25	-	-	15	-	-	-	60	-	54.5	64.1	84.7	88.5	85.9	84.5	85.0*
4. Labor market	3.2	-	-	-	24.2	-	-	-	-	34.7	-	-	-	-	60.0	65.0*
5. Finance market	1.0	-	-	-	-	3.6	-	-	-	6.3	-	-	-	-	9.1	10.0
6. Real estate market	0.0	-	-	-	-	21.1	24.0	27.8	28.8	22.8	24.0	21.9	28.9	38.2	39.3	40.0*
7. Technology market	7.67	17.9	22.3	38.3	49.7	48.3	51.5	53.9	49.5	51.6	52.6	50.5	58.8	54.7	65.0	66.0*
8. Agriculture	0.0	-	-	-	46.3	-	-	-	-	54.1	-	-	-	-	70.8	71.0
9. Industry	0.0	-	-	7.96	23.5	-	-	32.1	-	-	37.3	-	46.5	48.4	49.9	50.0*
10. Foreign trade	1.5	3.0	-	-	9.0	-	-	19.0	-	-	22.3	-	-	-	41.4	54.4
11. Regional	East				Middle			West			North				South	
Difference in 1996	70.3 (56.8)				64.4 (52.1)			64.9 (52.5)			54.9 (53.7)				67.9 (66.4)	

Source: The 11 sub-reports of the 1996's project entitled by "The degree of marketization progress of China's economic system" supported by Gushutang Funds of Nankai Institute of Economics.

Note: (1) "-" represents that it can not be calculated due to no available material. (2) "*" represents estimated values. (3) We obtain different value of regional difference using different weights. In the table, we choose two groups: the highest and lowest values. The latter are enclosed in parentheses.

1. The independence of economic subjects in China's economy is obviously increasing but still far away from the requirements of market economy. The marketization degree of industrial and commercial enterprises is about 47% which is much less than that of farmers in rural areas, 60%. As a consumer he or she has larger autonomy to choose commodities while as a laborer he or she is still confronted with many obstacles to choose or change jobs. State owned enterprises are still interfered by the authorities from some important aspects and have left a great deal of problems needed to be solved. With regard to market conditions, the restrictions are still significant in factors markets though they are moderated in producer raw market. Enterprises can not have real autonomy without development of factors markets. Another reason why industrial and commercial enterprises have low marketization is the small share of non-public sectors. In spite of enough independence for private enterprises, they only account for insignificant shares in China's economy. Slow privatizing of public sectors postpones the overall marketization progress of industrial and commercial enterprises. Independence of farmers in rural community is much bigger but its further development will be restricted mainly by the markets of social service (for example, seeds and pesticide) and factors (for example, land). The deregulation of the markets of consumer goods and service makes consumers have more choices but income level is the only determinant for consumption choices. Nevertheless, as production factor, laborers are still restricted by both traditional ideas and current system (for example, social security systems of medical aid and endowment)

2. Central and local governments have greatly loosened the control of whole economy (especially in commodity market), but they need to improve it further. Marketization degree of government behavior is 70% or so. The problems of over staffed organizations, redundancy, overlapping department and rights centralization, are not thoroughly solved. Although the intervention by direct quota is decreased evidently, "directly economic intervention" [1] and chief-responsibility system is still main and effective tools of regulation in transitional period. In fact, the administrative interventions among sectors and regions have been mainly made by local governments who have intercepted most powers transferred from central government and left little rights to enterprises, such as "loans based on fixed amount" and "turning over profit based on fixed ratio", while indirect economic regulations are yet rare and fruitless.

3. Markets systems have been generally set up but developed out of balance. Comprising consumer market, service market and producer raw market, the commodity market has developed fastest and best, over 85%. In these markets, commodity prices are almost determined by supply-demand and cost conditions. The

---

[1] "direct economic intervention" defined initially by us summarize the features of macro regulation in current transitional period. It differs from "direct administrative intervention" that passes mandatory planning from top to bottom and from "indirect economic control" through price parameters mechanisms. It regulates through size instructions, such as controlling loan base, total wages, turned-over tax base, funds for writing off uncollectable account or bankruptcy, and so on. That is, local governments or enterprises have a limited autonomy within a specified number or size prescribed directly by higher authorities.

second highest position is occupied by labor market. Although the freedom for labor to choose or change jobs and the freedom for firms to fire and hire workers are limited, the extent of labor wage marketization is relatively high, which lead overall labor market to 60% of marketization. Other markets like capital, funds, monetary (stock, bonds and future market), business bank system, housing, real estate, technology, and so forth, are initially established or are developing, more or less.

4. Marketization disparities among sectors are significant, too. Chinese economic reform originated from agriculture sector, then the reform spread to urban areas and the whole nation. Hence, marketization degree of rural economic system is much higher, about 70%. Slow reform of state-owned industrial enterprises hindered the marketization degree of the whole industrial system, only about 50%. In an effort to meet the requirement of World Trade Organization (WTO), the reform of foreign trade has been accelerated in recent years. In 1990s, China speeded up the process of further tariff reduction. China's weighted average tariff rate in 1997 stood at 17%. However, non-tariff trade barriers are still so high that overall marketization degree of foreign trade is less than 50%.

5. Finally, the marketization disparities among regions are evident. The marketization of the East part of China is 5% higher than those of the Middle and West. The South is 8% higher than that of North. The other group data has shown the same trends despite small disparities by figures.

6. The detailed analysis and suggestion from the above conclusion will be shown in final section. Next we will study the overall marketization degree of China's economy as a whole.

THE OVERALL MARKETIZATION DEGREE OF CHINA'S ECONOMY

After analyzing, measuring and judging the marketization degree of China's economic fields deeply and comprehensively, we will synthesize the overall marketization of China's economy and expect to draw a comprehensive and quantitative judgment on marketization progress since system reform.

We put forward some measurement approaches that reflect marketization degree of total economic systems. As concerns with the measurement methods and indicators of overall marketization, on one hand, they have to reflect and be logically in line with the theoretical implication and features of "marketization", such as decentralization, multiplicity, self-benefit, autonomy, less-interference, normalization, and so on. On the other hand, they have to be able to describe objectively the actual changes of all fields towards marketization. Subject to the principles, we make full use of existing research results of marketization in main fields for overall measurement. However, because of variation of measurement angles and non-consistency of expression, small changes have taken place on some concepts. For instance, price marketization degrees of consumer goods and producer raw goods are still equal to those above. Nevertheless, in this section wage marketization stands for the marketization degree of labor markets, monetary marketization for the marketization degree of financial markets, and stock capitalization of enterprise assets for capital marketization. Furthermore, those of primary and secondary sectors refer to agriculture and industry marketization degrees while the real-estate, banking and foreign trade marketization stand for that of tertiary sector. Finally, policy-allowed losses and price subsidy represent negative marketization of government interference, i.e., complete non-marketization. Obviously, the overall marketization is not only equal to the aggregation of marketization degree in all fields but the organic synthesis of marketization of various independent parts.

In the actual measurement process of organic synthesis, we deal appropriately with some thorny problems. (1) From which points of view do we divide the overall economic system into a few subsystems that do not overlap and are not omitted but can be added? This is to make it clear that which basic and independent subsystems comprise the structure of overall economic marketization. (2) What are the weights? Theoretically, we should choose the indicators that can best reflect the marketization sizes of all system levels. Unfortunately, the directly quantitative indicators are seldom or impossible. Consequently, we select shares of output value that indirectly reflect marketization size as weights because the recent years' development and growth in Chinese economy should be mainly regard as the function of system marketization. (3) How should weights be distributed to these parts? The position and roles of independent fields' marketization in the overall markets are embodied in the weights, which should be based on the actual shares and trends of parts in economy and avoid subjective opinions. (4) What are the summing methods? Because the methods of the addition, multiplication and mixed summing have significant difference, the summing methods should be based on the logical relations among parts.

The summing methods that satisfy the above requirements and conditions are not sole. Moreover, the theories of marketization are not fully ripe, and actual economic statistics are not completely accurate. Hence, it is rather difficult to find a perfectly reliable and accurate summing method and corresponding indicators. Therefore, when we measure the overall marketization degree of China's economy, we should go by the basic rules and choose relatively comprehensive, reasonable and less-error indicators by comparison among possible and existing methods and indicators. The following approaches for measuring overall marketization of China's economy come from different views on total economic structures and from different logical summing methods. By comparison and analysis, we believe that they are suitable for the features of China's economic system reform and the features of current economic conditions. Due to different measurement approaches, some calculating methods and data are complicated but some are not, so it is impossible for us to get the complete same measuring results. Every method has its own distinctive quality and errors. Generally, it is not easy to judge which method is better. As a result, choosing methods mainly depends on users' preference as well as availability and accurateness of the data. We here use five approaches and methods to measure the overall marketization of China's economy so that it is convenient for people to do comparison, supplementing and references.

Marketization "Weighted by Composition of Gross Social Products"

The flow of gross social products refers to the total economic value within one fiscal year in an economy, consisting of intermediate inputs and final outputs. The intermediate inputs include producer raw inputs and depreciation of fixed assets, or they may be also divided into the intermediate inputs of primary, secondary and tertiary industries. The final outputs comprise labor income and profits. The former includes wages and welfare income, and the later includes net profit, tax, losses and subsidy. Due to statistical classification, the economic flow commonly includes an item of "Others" that can not be defined accurately. Thus, eight parts constitute the flow of gross social products value: the intermediate inputs of primary, secondary and tertiary industries, depreciation of fixed assets, profits and taxes, losses and subsidiary, labor wages and welfare, and "others". Each part stands for one field of national economy.

Marketization "weighted by composition of gross social products" only means that shares of the components of the total economic value represent the roles and position, i.e., the weights, of marketization degrees of every field or levels in overall marketization. When measuring, we have to make some adjustment. First, in terms of intermediate inputs, we should consider both their production processes' marketization and their selling-prices' marketization. Hence, the marketization of intermediate inputs should be as: (ΣMarketization of each intermediate input sector $\times$ Each sector's share) $\times$ Marketization of producer raw materials' prices. Second, "policy-allowed losses and subsidies" are considered as non-marketization elements in opposition to marketization, i.e., and government interference, whose degree of marketization is -100%. Equations and results are as follows.

Overall marketization FF=[ΣMarketization of each intermediate input sector$\times$Each sector's share]$\times$ Marketization of producer raw materials' prices + [ΣMarketization of each final output sector $\times$ Each sector's share]=[Marketization of primary industry $A_1\times$Its share of intermediate input a_1+Marketization of secondary industry $A_2\times$Its share of intermediate input a_2+Marketization of tertiary industry A_3 $\times$Its share of intermediate input a_3]$\times$ Marketization of producer raw material' prices P +[marketization of enterprise assets $A_4\times$(share of depreciation a_4+share of profits and taxes a_7) + marketization of labor $A_7\times$share of labor income and welfare a_5 + marketization of tertiary industry $A_3\times$share of "others" a_6 + share of losses and subsidy $a_8 \times$ (-1)]

That is,

$$FF=[a_1A_1 +a_2A_2 +a_3A_3]P + (a_4+a_7)A_4 + a_5A_5 + a_6A_3-a_8$$

In addition, the compositions of gross social products as weights merely stand for independent influence of each field on economy, but not for actually complete influences of the fields because the interactive influences among some related fields have to be belonged to one of them. For instance, the influence of agriculture on total economy includes both the direct influences as the intermediate input and some indirect influences. Hence, it will make a mistake if we regard the share of agriculture as the sole role of agriculture marketization in overall economic marketization, because the other indirect influences have been calculated in the share of other fields. (This is also suitable for the other methods given blow, and not to repeat.)

The results for overall marketization measured by the method of marketization "weighted by composition of gross social products" are given out in Table 1.15, in which the weights of marketization are the shares of parts various parts of gross social products in the input-output table of 1990. The marketization indicators come from the chapters of this book whereas others do from *Statistical Yearbook of China* concerned. The following text has the same source. The indicators of tertiary marketization are attained from the related chapters involving tertiary marketization, and those of enterprise asset marketization are calculated with the share of non-state owned assets and shareholding state owned assets in total assets.

Marketization of "Geometric Weights of Input Factors Prices"

Production functions imply that national economic volume (Y) is comprised of input factors-capital, labor and so on-and their contributions to economy.

$$Y = AX_1^{a_1} X_2^{a_2} \cdots X_n^{a_n}$$

Where A is constant; X_i is the input factor; a_i is the contribution to economy. Thereby, the whole economy can be divided into parts by input factors. The exponents of input factors in production function represent their roles in the economy, i.e., the weights of marketization of various fields in overall marketization. This is the origin of the method of marketization of "geometric weights of input factors prices". The marketization of factor prices is the cornerstone of the marketization, so the synthesis of the marketization can completely and comprehensively reflect the marketization degree of overall economy, which has been embodied in the method of "geometric weights of input factors" marketization. The summing method is subject to the logical relationship of the input factors.

Price marketization of input factors (the basic physic input factors are capital and labor, and technology is embodied in them.) contains some kinds of marketization. Assets prices marketization, i.e., fixed assets (including land) marketization of enterprises, refers to the share of market-style enterprise assets in total assets, for example, the ratio of the sum of non-state-owned enterprises' assets and shareholding state-owned enterprises' assets over total social assets. Capital prices marketization refers to interest marketization or the share of the market-style loans in total loans. Labor marketization refers to wage marketization or the share of market-style wages in total wages. Producer raw material price marketization refers to the share of the producer raw material whose prices are adjusted by the supply and demand of market in total value of total production materials.

Table 1.15 The Results Measured by the Method of Marketization " Weighted by Compositions of Gross Social Products"

Year	A_1	a_1	A_2	a_2	A_3	a_3	P	A_4	a_4	A_5	a_5	a_6	a_7	a_8	FF
79*	0.10		0.005		0.10		0.03	0.20		0.03		0.052		-0.035	0.014
85	0.497		0.235		0.45		0.30	0.58		0.243		0.052		-0.035	0.208
88	0.539		0.321		0.60		0.60	0.63		0.350		0.057		-0.030	0.334
90	0.516	0.098	0.336	0.402	0.60	0.085	.055	0.65	0.046	0.350	0.205	0.055	0.141	-0.032	0.324
92	0.552		0.455		0.70		0.85	0.75		0.650		0.059		-0.028	0.539
94	0.647		0.484		0.75		0.88	0.78		0.680		0.062		-0.025	0.590
97**	0.680		0.530		0.80		0.88	0.80		0.700		0.063		-0.024	0.625

Source: Authors' own calculation according to involved data in *Statistical Yearbook of China*.

Note: "*" stands for estimated figures. "**" stands for predictive figures.

The weights of input factors are equal to their shares in the economic flow. That is, the share (b) of wages and welfare is the weight of labor price marketization (D). The share (a) of depreciation, profits and taxes in the total economic value is the weights of capital price marketization (A). The share (c) of intermediate input is the weight of producer raw material's price marketization (C). However, considering the interactive fact that the intermediate input have to rely on flowing capital and the flowing capital also have to depend on intermediate input, so the share of intermediate input may regard as an united weight of the price marketization of producer raw material and flowing capital (B), i.e., half and half respectively. The equation is

$$FF = A^a B^{c/2} C^{c/2} D^b$$

According to the input-output table of 1990, the shares are as follows: wage 20.5%(b), depreciation, profits and taxes (containing other and losses) 21.0% (a), intermediate input 58.5%(c) that is divided into the two equal parts for the price marketization of producer raw material and capital. With these weights overall marketization degree of 1979-1994 are calculated. (See Table 1.16)

Table 1.16 The Results Measured by the Method of Marketization of "Geometric Weights of Input Factors Prices"

Year	Capital Price (A)	Funds Price (B)	Producer Raw Material Price (C)	Labor Price (D)	Overall Marketization (%) $FF=A^{0.21}B^{0.293}C^{0.293}D^{0.205}$
1979[*]	0.20	0.02	0.03	0.03	4.4
1985	0.58	0.10	0.30	0.243	23.9
1988	0.63	0.15	0.60	0.35	36.1
1990	0.65	0.12	0.55	0.35	33.3
1992	0.75	0.25	0.85	0.65	54.7
1994	0.78	0.30	0.88	0.68	59.4
1997**	0.80	0.35	0.88	0.70	62.8

Source: Authors' own calculation according to involved data in *Statistical Yearbook of China*.
Note: "*" stands for estimated figures. "**" stands for predictive figures.

Marketization "Weighted by Shares of Three Sectors"

The common classification of economic sectors is that of three sectors. That is, the whole national economy consists of the primary, secondary and tertiary sectors. For instance, the added values of these sectors comprise the GNP. The method of measuring marketization weighted by shares of three sectors stems from this approach. We may get summing marketization degree with the weights of three sectors which are the shares of added values of three sectors in GNP.

That is, overall marketization degree FF= Marketization of primary industry A_1 × Its share a_1 +Marketization of secondary industry A_2 × Its share a_2 + Marketization of tertiary industry × Its share a_3. The equation is

$$FF = a_1A_1 + a_2A_2 + a_3A_3$$

Where the tertiary marketization degree is replaced with the marketization degrees of the real estate, finance and foreign trade. The others are the same as above. Table 1.17 shows the results by this method.

**Table 1.17 The Results Measured by the Method of
Marketization " Weighted by Shares of Three Sectors"**

year	a_1	A_1	a_2	A_2	a_3	A_3	FF=$\sum a_iA_i$
1979*	0.30	0.10	0.56	0.005	0.14	0.10	0.047
1985	0.30	0.497	0.53	0.235	0.17	0.45	0.354
1988	0.28	0.53	0.5	0.321	0.22	0.60	0.445
1990	0.27	0.516	0.48	0.336	0.25	0.60	0.451
1992	0.20	0.552	0.49	0.455	0.31	0.70	0.550
1994	0.21	0.647	0.48	0.484	0.31	0.75	0.600
1997**	0.20	0.68	0.47	0.530	0.33	0.80	0.649

Source: Authors' own calculation according to involved data in *Statistical Yearbook of China*.
Note: "*" stands for estimated figures. "**" stands for predictive figures.

Marketization of "GNP Compositions Synthetic Weighting"

The preceding method of "the marketization weighted by composition of gross social products" marketization covers very wide ranges of fields and thereby has quite comprehensive results. However, intermediate inputs merely have the function of transferring values and accounts for relative large share in national economy, so you may have the impression that marketization weight of intermediate input sector is not correspondent with the actual position in economy. Therefore, the method of "mixed share of GNP compositions" marketization is highlighted to solve this problem.

Gross national product (GNP) refers to the sum of added values within a fiscal year in an economy, which has six parts of depreciation, flowing capital interest, wages, profits and taxes, losses and subsidy, and other added values. Their shares can be viewed as their positions in GNP or their roles in economy and thereby as the weights of marketization of related fields. This is the approach of "marketization weighted by GNP compositions mixedly". Furthermore, the flowing elements are considered too: First, the actual performance of enterprise marketization. The profit rates of marketized enterprises are much higher than those of non-marketized enterprise, so the share of profits and taxes of marketized enterprises in GNP is directly used for the marketization weight of the fields concerned which considers both the marketization level of enterprise's asset and the influence of the actual performance of enterprise assets' marketization on economic performance and overall marketization. Second, price marketization is one of important parts of overall economic marketization, so when examining marketization of every field, we have to pay attention to the mixed influence of price marketization, i.e., multiplying the sum of marketization degrees of various fields by the levels of price marketization. Third, losses and subsidies as well as "others". Their definitions are the same as before. The equation is

$$FF = (a_1A_1 + a_2A_2 + a_3A_3 + a_4A_4 + A_5 - B) \times P$$

Where a_1, a_2, a_3 and a_4 are the shares of depreciation, interest of flowing capital, labor wages, other added value in GNP, respectively; A_1, A_2, A_3 and A_4 are the marketization of enterprise assets, capital, labor force and tertiary industry; A_5 refers to the share in GNP of profits and taxes of marketized enterprises; P is the marketization degree of product prices; B is the share of policy-allowed losses and price subsidy in GNP.

Table 1.18 is the results by the method of "marketization weighted by GNP compositions mixedly".

Table 1.18 The Results Measured by the Method of Marketization "Weighted by GNP Compositions Mixedly"

year	a_1	A_1	A_2	A_2	a_3	A_3	a_4	A_4	A_5	P	B	$FF=[\sum a_iA_i +A_5-B]\times P$
1979*		0.20		0.03		0.030		0.10	0.110	0.03	0.100	0.002
1985		0.58		0.10		0.243		0.45	0.289	0.30	0.100	0.127
1988		0.63		0.15		0.350		0.60	0.306	0.60	0.075	0.275
1990	0.130	0.65	0.180	0.12	0.180	0.350	0.080	0.60	0.318	0.55	0.080	0.251
1992		0.75		0.25		0.650		0.70	0.350	0.85	0.065	0.510
1994		0.78		0.30		0.68		0.75	0.368	0.88	0.055	0.573
1997**		0.80		0.35		0.700		0.80	0.390	0.88	0.050	0.614

Source: Authors' own calculation according to involved data in *Statistical Yearbook of China*.
Note: "*" stands for estimated figures. "**" stands for predictive figures.

Marketization of "Averaging Market Parameters"

In the above section, we have introduced four measurement approaches for overall economic marketization and their methods and results. It is evident that the four methods have to use weights. Here we attempt to introduce a simple measurement method without weight named marketization of "averaging market parameters". At first, we should expound its theoretical implications. Market economy adjust the economy mainly through market parameters, such as commodity prices in commodity market (including consumer materials and producer raw materials), wage rate in labor market, security prices in security market, interest rate in capital market, and technology transferring fee in technology market. Hence, dividing the sum of the marketization degrees (A_i) of all product and factor markets by number of various markets, n, we may attain the overall marketization degree (FF). The equation is

$$FF = (A_1 + A_2 + ... + A_n)/n$$

With limits of data, we sum up the four marketization degrees of product market, labor market, finance market and real estate market (the indicators of technology market are unsuitable), and then average the sum by n. For comparison, we give two group results, one containing the finance market and the other not.

Table 1.19 The Results Measured by Marketization of the Method of "Averaging Market Parameters"

Year	Commodity (1)	Labor (2)	Real Estate (3)	Result I (4)	Finance (5)	Result II (6)
1978	2.25	5.1	2.0	3.12	1.0	2.09
1985	15.0	24.3	21.1	20.1	3.6	16.0
1990	54.5	34.8	22.8	37.4	6.3	29.6
1995	84.5	64.7	39.3	62.8	9.1	49.4

Source: Authors' own calculation according to involved data in *Statistical Yearbook of China..*
Note: (4)=(1+2+3)/3, (6)=(1+2+3+5)/4

Comparison of Five Approaches

The results of the five approaches are shown in Table 1.20 for comparison.

Table 1.20 Comparison of Overall Marketization Degree of Five Approaches

Year	1	2	3	4	5
1979*	1.4	4.4	4.7	0.2	3.12 (2.09)
1985	20.8	23.9	35.4	12.7	20.1 (16.0)
1988	33.4	36.1	44.5	27.5	-- --
1990	32.4	33.3	45.1	25.1	37.4 (29.6)
1992	53.9	54.7	55.0	51.0	-- --
1994	59.0	59.4	60.0	57.3	62.8 (49.4)
1997**	62.5	62.8	64.9	61.4	68.0 (55)

Source: Table 1.15--1.19
Note: * estimated values; ** predicted values.

These approaches and methods from different perspectives have different theoretical and practical significance, respectively. The first four all use weights to measure. Therefore, both marketization degree and development level (i.e., share of output) in various fields have a great impact on the value of indicators. Theoretically, either high marketization degree and output share or low marketization degree but higher output share can both lead to higher values of indicators. For the later case it is evident that there are some flaws in the weight-methods themselves. However, theoretically, the flaws may be revised to some extent because of regarding output as the function of marketization. In fact, it is difficult to sum up marketization degree of various fields without weights.

It is hard for us to judge which approach is more accurate among these results because their results are almost the same. The authors believe that "geometric-weighted marketization of input factor prices" is the method which is worth propagation among the approaches because the marketization reflected by the method fits in with its theoretical implication very well. Further, the consideration for selecting weights is relatively precise, the summing method matches the logical relations of economic indicators, and the final measurement results are concordant with our intuition on marketization degree. In addition, the data used in the method are less than that in any other approach and are available.

Surely, the fifth method without weight is the simplest and most easy one. It overcomes the flaws of using weights and are intuitive and simply calculation with small amount of data. In most cases, it is satisfied for us to use this method to measure and get the basic status of marketization. However, the method can not be used directly and simply to average all of different fields, so some fields have to be left out or intentionally omitted, which is the flaw of the approach. The result by the method has relatively large difference from those of other approaches. Clearly, it is the key that how and what should be selected as sub-markets for summing and averaging. Anyway, these measurements may be used for the reference for further study.

Achievement of Chinese Economic System Marketization

Moreover, we pay great attention to the trends of overall marketization of China's economy and its impact on economic performance. Since China started reform and open-door policies, the overall marketization degree of China's economy have developed quickly from a low level 5% to a high level 60%. Especially after China established the concept and target of "Socialist Market Economy" in 1992, marketization progress has been accelerated evidently. As a result, in the meantime overall thirty percentage points increased marketization degree. The following figure show the trends of China's economic marketization of 1979-1997, where solid lines stand for the actual development process measured by above 5 approaches and dotted line stands for the long-term trends.

Figure 1.1 The Trends of China's Economic Marketization in 1979-1997

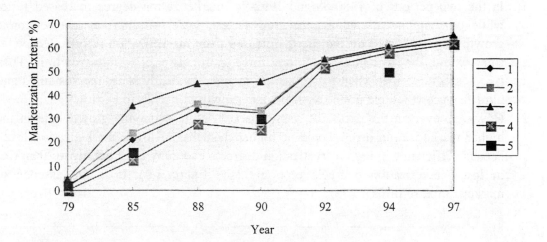

The main purpose why China started the marketization reform of economic system is to improve economic performance. Then has the 20-year's marketization of Chinese economic system reached its goal? To answer the question, we should analyze the relation between overall marketization degree in various periods and the corresponding indicators of economic performance. Table 1.20 presents the relationships between marketization degree and annuls growth rates of per capital national income from 1975 to 1997. "Annul growth rates of per capital income" as the indicator of economic performance filters out the influence of population and inflation and has positive relationship with other performance indicators. Thus, it is a better representative indicator.

Table 1.21 Overall Marketization and Economic Performance

Period	Average marketization degree (%)	Changes of marketization degree (percentage points)	Annul growth rate of per capital national income (%)
1975-79	4.4	0	4.5
1980-84	14.2	16.5	7.2
1985-88	30.0	15.2	9.3
1989-91	35.7	2.00	5.4
1992-94	52.9	20.9	13.1
1995-97	61.1	3.4	7.1

Source: Authors' own calculation according to involved data in *Statistical Yearbook of China*.

Two conclusions from Table 1.20 can be reached as follows.

1. In the two periods of 1980-88 and 1992-94, marketization degree increased faster while per capital national income grew fastest, which means that fast economic growth may be fueled by the energy released from marketization reform. Hence, to some extent, the more powerful reform force is, the faster economic growth is. Then it is conjectured that when marketization inclines to steady state, the sustained and ultra-fast growth might not be repeated, and growth rate tends to be slow.
2. However, even in the period of stable marketization, economic growth rate in the higher marketization level should be higher than that of lower marketization level, because efficiency in high marketization degree's economy is all but higher than that in low marketization degree's economy (see figure 1.2). It is the essence of marketization reforms.

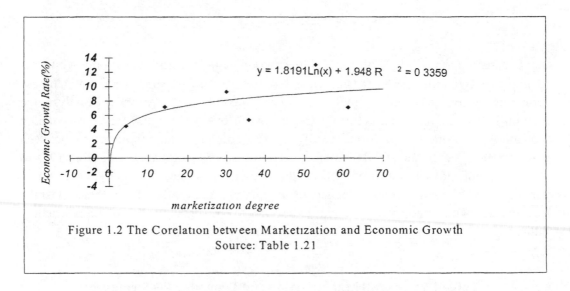

Figure 1.2 The Corelation between Marketization and Economic Growth

Source: Table 1.21

Moreover, how marketization of economic systems pushes economic growth? It is commonly agreed that economic system reform drives people to input more physical resources and more labor, but economic growth in this way does not lead long. In fact, economic system marketization expedites economic growth generally through two channels. The first is to raise the usage efficiency of resources in production. Because of inefficiency caused by lack of stimulation in centrally planned economy, the actual output in economy is much lower than maximum potential output. There is a long distance from production possibility frontier. However, marketization reform may make actual production close to the production possibility frontier. The second is to accelerate technology progress. The stimulus to technology progress is rather poor in central-planned economy. Slow technology progress leads to inefficiency and fixed production possibility frontier. In contrast, economic system marketization can propel technology progress, and thus push production possibility frontier outward (Wu, 1997).

In short, economic system marketization expedites economic growth essentially by means of the increase of total factor productivity. A scholar constructs a model of "dual pure added values" and proves the market efficiency in marketization reform. The basic model is $\Delta Y = F(\Delta L, \Delta P, \Delta H, \Delta D, \Delta I)$, where the symbols stand for the added values of gross national product, labor force, physical capital and human resource, domestic market efficiency and foreign market efficiency, respectively. The results of its estimation show that since the reform and the open-door policy are initiated in 1978, 25% of economic growth may have owed to added physical capitals, 33% to added input of human resource (e.g., education investment), and 42% to increase in market efficiency (Tian, 1997).[2]

This study proves that economic system marketization has a remarkable impact on economic growth or economic performance, which is the fundamental grounds to continue the reform.

CONCLUSIONS AND SUGGESTIONS FOR FURTHER MARKETIZATION

According to the above analysis, we may reach following basic conclusions:

1. As a result of market-oriented economic reform, the Chinese economy has already made great strides towards marketization of economic system. As a whole, marketization of China's economy has been enhanced continuously, from 5% in early time to 60% or so now. It is a wonderful accomplishment in 20 years' reform progress. In China the dual-tracks gradualist strategy has worked successfully. Seriously speaking, it should be observed that it will be a long way to arrive at the target pattern (that is not the 100% marketization, but according to the above interpretation, the marketization close to an ideal pattern with reference to the marketization degree of some advanced market economies in reality). More efforts are needed to continue the reform and more difficulties will be confronted in current stage (i.e., the rational advancement stage with the basic features of institutional innovation) than that in last stages.

2. Marketization degrees among different fields are significantly different Marketization progresses in some fields advance fast. For instance, the marketization degree of commodity markets is almost close to the anticipated level. As far as the extent of price is concerned, it is approaching to the level of market economies, over 85%. However, marketization reform of other fields (particularly production factors markets) maybe only takes their first steps, merely 15% or so, such as financial and technology markets.

3. Each field has fluctuated over time, which is dominated mainly by national situations and policies. For example, there was a big undulation around 1989. Before 1989, the

---

[2] This estimation entirely contradicts the prevailing argument, in which China's economic growth had been achieved by pouring in more capital and more labor with little or no growth in total factor productivity (Krugman, 1994). The estimation seems to be higher than that of the expected, which may owe to model constructing and used material. In addition, its market efficiency seems to have different implications in contrast with the efficiency of marketization reform in the paper

progress is almost stable with steadily increasing marketization, then because of the political turmoil it decreased at the beginning of 1990's. It has not increased until the establishment of target system of "Market economy" in 1993. Indeed, political situation has an essential impact on the fluctuation of marketization.

4. Marketization degrees among regions develop unbalancedely, too. Generally, marketization in the East is higher than that in the West and Middle, and that in the South is higher than in the North. For instance, the marketization of the East China is 70.3%, the West 65%, the South 68%, and the North only 55%. These disparities are quite significant.

5. Marketization reform is the most reliable institution safeguard and the most effective policy measures for fast economic development of China. Due to marketization reform, the Chinese economy grows remarkably, per capital national income enhances uninterruptedly, poverty rate decreases a great deal, living standard is raised significantly, national power is strengthened evidently, and China can enact more and more important role in the world. The reality convincingly proves that both the reform directions towards marketization and socialist market economic system objectives are quite correct without question. It is the fundamental road for China to get sustainable, fast and harmonica development through pushing marketization reform forward firmly.

Consequently, we propose following basic countermeasures and suggestions to accelerate marketization.

1. As a whole, property rights system reform is the critical issues of the acceleration of Chinese economic marketization progress because it is the institutional base for decision-making decentralization, economic agent independence and the establishment of market economy. In the past reforms of various aspects, ownership reform is the biggest constrains. When China's economy sticks to the absolute main body of state-owned or public-owned economy, the economy can not be set up on a solid market foundation, markets can not have enough room for regulation, and the economy can not reach the same marketization degree as modern market economies. We argue that Chinese economy advance the reform of ownership structure steadily in the aid of ideology liberation after the Party's 15th National Congress. With regard to the ownership, it is necessary to adopt a mixed economy with a relative preponderance of public ownership. That is, whatever the indicators, such as assets, output or labor force, are used, public economy as a whole should not be compared with the whole non-public economy, but with every kind of non-public ownership such as private, individual, joint venture and foreign, respectively. As long as public economy occupies relative preponderance in these comparisons, economic development can be guaranteed to be stable. Under the prerequisites that the shares of public economy are reduced appropriately, we should pay great attention to improving the quality of pubic economy, i.e., to enhancing efficiency of state-owned economy. Governments should control the major fields, i.e., control the commanding elevations, and consolidate the foundation of public economy. The next step is to

liberate ideology and regard ownership only as means of allocating property and resource, and give up the tight relation between public ownership and socialist. By this approach, reforms will make a great leap towards marketization.

2. As concerns the marketization of enterprises, under the prerequisites of proper shrinkage state-owned enterprises, state enterprises reform should focus on the principles of "grasping large enterprises but enlivening small ones", adopting joint-stock system for large-scale-enterprises, restructuring enterprise assets, canceling administrative ranks of enterprises and entitling enterprise autonomy over decisions of leadership and management, personnel, finance and assets. The authorities should evaluate the enterprises' performance only through profits and taxes.

3. Government, being the agent of the macro economy management, its reform concentrates most energies on transformation of government functions and reduces its intervention into economic activities in accordance with the principle of "small government but big society". However, the most important step of the reform is to simplify government apparatus because "Buddhist monks really have to leave only after their temples are dismantled". Of course, it should be in tune with political system reform. Therefore, once the opportunity is ripe, the political system reform or at least administrative system reform should be speeded up.

4. Building of the market systems is also an important step. Price reform in commodity market has been basically accomplished, leaving further improvement. The key task is to reform factors markets. At present, all kinds of factors markets are far away from right tracks. Except that labor market has a little higher extent, the markets of real estate, stocks, capital and technology are not set up entirely. However, if these markets do not work, enterprises can not get necessary factors from the markets and can not have really independent autonomy. The key measures are to reform current housing system in real estate market, to encourage legal-person-shares and state-shares to exchange in the security market, to reform banking system in capital market to establish really central bank and business bank, and to improve patent system in technology market. To sum up, macro-regulations of governments would be lack of carriers without perfect factor markets.

5. By sectors, agriculture marketization has reached the national average level, over 60%. Its next step is mainly to reform land system, to introduce competition into responsibility contract system and to establish social service system. Industry marketization exceeds 50%. Its reform approaches have been addressed in preceding sections. The tertiary industry, taking finance as example, lies on initial level. Despite reducing tariffs for many times, governments has still controlled a large amount of non-tariff fields. On principle, it should liberalize foreign trade gradually and disengage the state monopoly in the open-door process, which will connect domestic markets tightly with international markets.

6. By regions, unbalanced marketization degree among regions owe to difference in ideology liberation, and are also related with favored policy towards some regions that are carried out by the central government. Difference in ideology liberation is associated with the cadres' quality that is related to education levels. Therefore, we should restructure the education structures of cadre force on a large scale and

promote intellectual officials. The difference regarding favored policy may be eliminated once after removing the preference that means to discriminate against other regions. Impartial national treatment on all regions is needed for unified national market and improvement of the overall marketization.

With regard to ironing overall marketization fluctuations over time, we should mainly reduce political intervention and drastic turbulence and gradually push political system reform such as, acceleration of political democratization, punishing corruption and establishing stronger legal framework. Furthermore, we should always guard against transforming some serious economic problems such as inflation, unemployment, illegal parvenus and so forth, into political crises. We should solve the social ambivalence in time and prevent them from sharpening the problems and then may prevent economic system reform from drastic changes and vacillation. Like economic system reform, it is better for us to adopt gradualist strategy for political system reform. Keeping up stability to some extent will create necessary prerequisites for reform and development. However, political system reform can not be postponed or canceled, otherwise the accumulation of contradictories may result in drastic upheavals.

7. By fields, sectors and regions, we should reinforce the marketization reforms of some weak aspects, or there will be seriously unbalanced marketization that leads to mismatching and disharmony and can constrain marketization, in turn.

In summary, we hold that under the push of the Party's 15th National Congress, as long as we liberate ideology and follow the above major approaches, Chinese marketization of economic system will be continuously enhanced towards anticipated target systems. Socialist Market Economic system with Chinese features which are full of vigor and moderate will propel China's economy to grow quickly from low-income style to middle-income style.

REFERENCES

Chen Wentong, *"On the Compatibility of Socialist System and Market Economic Means"*, Academic Communication, No. 3. 1996

Chen Zongsheng, *"Macro Economic Analysis in the Institutional Transformation"*, Economic Research Journal, No. 7. 1987

Chen Zongsheng, *"Income Distribution in the Economic Development"*, Shanghai Sanlian Press, 1991

Chen Zongsheng, *"On the Major Background of the Operation of China's Economy"*, Tianjin Social Science, No. 6, 1995

Chen Zongsheng, *"A Research on the Road of Chinese Ownership Reform from the Natures of Sectors and Products"* (Chinese), Discussion Paper at Nankai Institute of Economics, 1997

Fan Gang and Zhang Shuguang, *"The Outline of Macro Economic Theory of Public Ownership"* , Shanghai Sanlian Press, 1990

Gu Shutang (1994), *"The Growth of China's Market Economy and the System Transformation"*, Tianjin People's Press.

Journal of Xinhua, 1990-1997.

Krugman, P., *"The Myth of Asia's Miracle"*, *Foreign Affairs*, December 9, 1994

Li Jingwen, *"China's Economy towards the 21st Century"*, Economics and Management Press, 1992

Lin Yifu, et al., *"China's Miracle"*, Shanghai Sanlian Press, 1994

Lu, Zhongyuan and Hu Angang, *"An Impact of Marketization Reform on China's Economic Operation"* (Chinese), *Economic Research Journal*, No. 5. 1993

Pan Jinju, *"Economic Fluctuation and Economic Adjustment"*, Nankai University Press. 1993

Sheng Hong, *"Labor Division and Transaction"*, Shanghai Sanlian Press, 1994

State Statistical Bureau (1985-1996), *"Statistical Yearbook of China"*, Chinese Statistics Press.

Stiglier, G. J., *"Industry Organizations and Government Regulation"*, Shanghai Sanlian Press. 1989

Tian Xiaowen, *"A Model of Dual Pure Added Value"*, *Economic Research* Journal, No. 11. (1997)

Wu Yanrui, *"Is China's Economic Growth Sustainable?"* Discussion Paper at Department of Economics, University of Western Australia, Australia. 1997

Zhang Shuguang et al., *"Empirical Analysis on Tradeoff of China Trade Protect"*, *Economic Research* Journal, No. 2. 1997

Zhang Zhuoyuan, *"Review and Prospect on China's Economic Theories Since Reform and Opening"*, *Economic Research* Journal, No. 6. 1997

Zhong Maochu, *"A Quantitative Analysis on Transformation of China's Economic System"*, *Tianjin Statistics*, No. 6. 1996

Zhou Bing, *"Unreachable Goals"*, Changchun Press, 1996

Zhou Bing and Xie Hui, *"A Research on Government and Industrial Authority"*, Discussion Paper at Nankai Institute of Economics. 1997

Zhou Liqun, *"On State -Owned Asset Organizations"*, Shanxi People's Press, 1994

PART II
MARKETIZATION OF MAIN FIELDS IN CHINA'S ECONOMY: MEASUREMENTS OF MARKETIZATION OF ENTERPRISE, GOVERNMENT AND VARIOUS MARKETS

CHINESE ENTERPRISE MARKETIZATION: CONTENTS, EVALUATION AND INTERNATIONAL COMPARISON

Actively expediting the course of enterprise marketization and establishing modern enterprise system are the main content and core of Chinese economic system reform. It is nearly 20 years since the reform and opening up of China. What is the degree of Chinese enterprise marketization? It is a focal problem that every Chinese person of insight cares. Obviously, correctly evaluating the course of Chinese enterprise marketization is of great importance to deepen the enterprise reform. Studying the enterprise marketization may start from many respects or angles, hereby we begin our research from the point of rights allocation between the government and enterprises.

CONTENTS AND THEORETICAL BOUNDARIES OF ENTERPRISE MARKETIZATION

Marketization, a dynamic concept, indicates that the means of resource allocation is changed from the government to the market pattern. The government pattern means that resource allocation is accomplished by the government according to the state plans and administrative directions, in which the main role is the government and its departments, i.e., the government owns all the rights of resources allocation. The market pattern indicates that the resource allocation is accomplished according to the supply and demand of market and the price change resulting from the change of supply and demand, in which the important roles are enterprises, families and individuals as the producers and managers of commodity, i.e., enterprises, families and individuals own all the market rights of resource allocation according to the efficient principle.

Enterprise marketization means that resource allocation behaviors of all kinds of enterprises change from the government dominance to the equal and voluntary transactions through market. It also means that the set of enterprises' transactions of products and factors change from the government control (for example: price, output, profit and the freedom of entrance and exit) to the market harmonization (Sheng Hong, 1992). The enterprise marketization can result in the maximum increase of enterprise efficiency, which has been proved by the reform of Chinese enterprise marketization since 1978. During the last 20 years, the scope of enterprise marketization, especially the non-state–owned enterprises, has gradually expanded. The achievement is remarkable. Statistical data indicate that the profits and taxes of state-owned industrial enterprises with independent accounting increased at average rate of 8.2% during the period of 1978- - 1997, while the increase rate of profits and taxes of the non-state-owned industrial enterprises with independent accounting even amounts to about 20.5%. Even in the U.S.A. where the market system is much developed, some people still advocate to push on the marketization reform because they think that the marketization degree is not high enough. For example, J.M. Buchanan (1986) thinks that the government plays a role far beyond the appropriate scope in the American economy, thus in many economic areas market instead of the government can bring the increase of social wealth. R.H.Coase (1959) who holds the same point of view, pointed out that actually it is much better that many functions that ought to be implemented by government according to the traditional economics and ideas are accomplished by market. Though what Buchanan and Coase said does not only refer to enterprise, it is obvious that the non-marketized or less marketized enterprises should deepen their marketization.

However, the enterprise marketization is not pure or absolute. The resource allocation behaviors of enterprises are not sole market transaction ones, and at any time the non-market transaction behaviors between the enterprises and the government objectively exist. Moreover, if the market is perfect competition and highly efficient, enterprises can take place of the market, i.e., the transactions inside the enterprises are also non-market transactions, but we will not discuss this topic in this chapter.

The market transaction behaviors of enterprises are on the basis of equality and voluntaries. The realization of transactions depends on the consensus of the two parts. The consensus indicates that the transaction can bring the increase of welfare or efficiency to the two parts. If the transaction cannot result in the increase of welfare or efficiency to the two parts or can only do good to one part, then the consensus contract cannot be made and the transaction cannot be realized, the parts have to search for other transaction partners. Whereas the consensus contract and the ensuing transaction behaviors may produce "the third part effect" or external effect, which may do good or harm to the third party. When the enterprises' market transaction behaviors bring out externality, they cannot assure to result in the maximum efficiency to the enterprises. If the external effect is positive, the third part can freely get some benefits from the enterprises' market transactions; vice versa, if the external effect is negative, the enterprises that make transactions can freely get some benefits from the third part, i.e., the third part bears some cost of the former transactions. It should be emphasized that the third part may be singular or plural, which refers to the enterprises or other economic agents influenced by the specific two parts of market transaction, in brief, the other parts involved in specific transaction. Under the condition of external effect, the market transactions among enterprises will lose their incentives because part of the benefits are occupied by the third part without pay, or will be resisted by the third part because the enterprises occupy part of the benefits without pay. These are two kinds of tort behaviors. The market transactions between enterprises will certainly have low efficiency if the tort cannot be compensated or relieved.

The possible "third part effect" resulting from enterprises' market transactions afford a basis for the government to participate in the enterprises' transactions. But the government's involvement is not universal, it only occurs on occasion of external effect. In modern market system, the government's participation is regulated by the law. Because only in event of externality does the government participate in the transactions. The involved actors are not two but three or more than three, i.e., the government and other two or more than two economic agents. All the agents involved in the transactions including the government are equal. The final transaction contracts are made on the basis of agreement of equal agents. The difference is that the agreement is not always consensus, more often, it is expressed as the agreement of majority, and the contracts are made according to the principle of "the minority are subject to the majority". The rights of the contract parts are acknowledged and protected by the law. In fact, due to the nature of "economic man", the market transactions of economic agents (such as enterprises) will probably result in external effect without restrictions. Therefore relative laws and regulations will be made to defend the market equality and to protect the equal rights of transaction agents, so as to restrict the externality resulting from the enterprises' market transactions. In addition, the establishment and the perfect of laws can reduce the transaction cost of government's frequently participating in enterprises' market transactions to a minimum.

As to the economic activities with strong or stronger externality, such as the produce and supply of public goods and public services, however, the cost to put them into market transactions made by common enterprises will be very high, because the laws applicable to the common enterprises cannot bring into play the full functions due to the lack of definite usage boundaries of such economic activities. Thus the government has to frequently participate in the transaction activities of these areas, that is to say, the transaction of these areas become the special economic behavior of the government. This kind of transaction, a non-market transaction, has the characteristic of natural monopoly. No matter the relative parts agree or do not agree, get benefits or do not get benefits, the government will monopolize the produce and supply of these products or services, by levying tax on the users, and protect the right of imposing tax by law at the same time.

In general, in modern market system with perfect legislation, the transaction in which the government participate (or governmental transaction) occurs in the produce and management areas of public goods and public services with strong externality. A great number of transactions of common enterprises are market transactions, which are normalized and directed by the government through making laws and policies. Only under some special conditions does the government enter these areas. Some scholars summarize the link and difference between market transactions and government transactions as follows:" Market transaction and government transaction are based on the agreement of equal agents. The difference is that market transaction between two agents is more efficient without direct externality; while government transaction between two agents is more efficient with direct externality. Therefore the boundary between market and government exist between transactions of two agents and transactions of more than two agents"(Sheng Hong, 1992). Obviously, these summaries are more theoretical

THE EVALUATION OF ENTERPRISE MARKETIZATION: INDEXES DESIGN

According to the above analysis about the contents and boundary of enterprise marketization, we can see that the essence of enterprise marketization is to transfer the rights of resource allocation controlled by the government to enterprises. Thus the selected indexes should firstly reflect the situation of rights transfer; meanwhile, we should fully consider the exactness and comprehensiveness of the indices. In addition, because in China the rights are transferred gradually, not at once, the selected indexes can only roughly reflect the rights transfer course that happened. Along with the deepening and expediting of the rights transfer, we will list some new indices. Hereby we select eight indices elaborately explained in the following sections.

The Autonomous Extent of Selecting Enterprise System

The autonomous extent of selecting enterprise system refers to the extent that the enterprises decide their system existence formality on their own, for example, to what extent enterprises can autonomously select share-holding system, partnership system or other systems. In modern market system, enterprises are independent market agents, who have full rights to select their system existence formalities to adapt to the keen market competition. Because the different choice of enterprise system is relative to the change of property relationship, the transformation of inside management mechanism, the expansion of funds channels and enterprise scale, if an enterprise can select its system, that indicate the enterprise has strong market adaptability. If the selected enterprise system is not appropriate, it will not increase but reduce the enterprise efficiency, even bring great disaster, because specific enterprise system needs specific conditions, especially the listed companies need more strict restrictions. For example, in the developed market economy country, U.S.A., the rate of limited-liability companies to the total enterprises is only 14.5%, the majority are proprietorship enterprises which amount to 78% of the total, the other 7.5% are partnership enterprises (Gregory, 1988). These indicate that the selection of enterprise system is not arbitrary, it depends on the market conditions and developing situations of enterprise systems, i.e., enterprise systems are the results of market choice. When the government interfere in the selection of enterprise system or directly select the enterprise system, it means that enterprises as complete market agents are not mature. Thus this index, the autonomous extent of selecting enterprise system, can reflect the maturity extent of enterprises as market agents and how many rights the government has transferred to the enterprises.

The Market Choice Rate of Enterprise Managers

The market choice rate of enterprise managers reflects the transitional situations of selecting enterprise leaders from the government appointment to market choice through competition. In the classical planned system, the enterprise leaders were completely appointed by the government, so the enterprise leaders were not true managers but governmental officials who directed production by administrative powers. Correspondingly, the operation of enterprise through administrative powers did not meet the demand of economic laws and objective facts. In modern market system, the enterprise leaders, except the sole-investor enterprises (including state-owned and individual-owned enterprises), are almost chosen through the competition of manager market, or through the democratic election inside the enterprise (the essence is also market choice through competition). Therefore it can assure the high qualities of enterprise leaders which can make the enterprise leaders grasp the market operational laws in the fast changing market situations and maintain the sustainable efficiency of enterprise. Actually the market choice rate of enterprise managers is an important index to reflect the autonomy and scientific of enterprise decisions.

The Implement Extent of Autonomous Management Rights of Enterprise

Enterprises as independent market agents should have complete right to independently make decisions. But it is difficult to definitely specify which management right the enterprise should own to get the optimum efficiency. As to the individual proprietorship enterprises, obviously they own the entire market rights of independent management, so it is unnecessary to distinguish these rights. But to the state-owned enterprises or share-holding companies, the rights of autonomous management are not the entire market rights, because the property owners outside the enterprise (including the government) also own some rights. The key of assuring the high enterprise efficiency does not rest on that the property owners outside the enterprise have no rights to the enterprise, but rest on whether the rights the enterprise owning are autonomous and the outside rights can make effective incentives or constraints to the enterprise. To the Chinese enterprises during the marketization proceedings, clearly specifying the autonomous management rights the enterprise should own is a gradual process. Presently the known autonomous management rights of enterprise are the 14 items specified in the Regulation On The Management Mechanism Transformation Of State-owned Industrial Enterprises promulgated by the State Counsel in July, 1992. Certainly these 14 items of rights are applicable not only to industrial enterprises, but also to other kinds of enterprises. Studying the implement extent of the 14 items of rights can reflect the course of rights transfer and enterprise marketization from another angle.

The Proportion of Enterprises with the First Aim of Maximizing Profit

The property owners of modern enterprises are outside enterprises. Though property owners do not directly participate in the enterprise management, they have the right to determine the important decisions and the appointment and removal of managers. Thus as long as the management aims of enterprise are the same with the property owners', can the managers get the owners' acknowledgement and encouragement. To the owners, their aim is to maximize the dividend and bonus which originate from the enterprise' profit. That determines the first important aim of enterprise management is to maximize profit. Even in the case of multifarious aims, the other aims are subject to the aim of maximizing profit. In fact the other aims cannot be realized unless the enterprise can get maximum profit. Furthermore, the aim of maximizing profit is the outcome of market choice. The existence competition of enterprises depends on their profit. The profit rate is the main symbol of enterprise efficiency.

The Assumption Extent of Enterprise Property Rights Subjects

The assumption extent of Chinese enterprise property rights subjects mainly refers to the state-owned enterprises because the reform of Chinese enterprise marketization is mainly the reform of state-owned enterprise marketization, i.e., pushing the state-owned enterprises to the market and let them compete with other market agents under the same conditions. The basic prerequisite of the state-owned enterprise marketization is to cultivate independent subjects of state-owned property rights. In the case that the subjects of state property rights are not present or assume the office unindependently, the reform of state enterprise marketization will not be completed. Due to the decisive position of state enterprises in Chinese economy, the assumption extent of subjects of state enterprise property rights directly influences the whole assumption extent of enterprise property rights subjects, so the assumption extent of enterprise property rights subjects is an important manifestation of enterprise marketization.

The Legalization Extent of Enterprise Bankruptcy

Enterprise bankruptcy is the main symbol of market competition according to the principle of "selecting the superior and eliminating the inferior". If the unsuccessful enterprise management brings about great loss and the enterprise cannot repay the due debts, it should declare its bankruptcy according to the law. During the course of Chinese enterprise reform, from non-bankruptcy to bankruptcy, and to legalized bankruptcy, the enterprise marketization has gradually progressed. From November 1, 1988, the *Bankruptcy Law of the People's Republic of China* came into force. What is the implement extent of the bankruptcy law? We can get answers from the index of the legalization extent of enterprise bankruptcy.

The Proportion of Contracts Fulfilled

Enterprise will sign contracts when making market transactions. In market economy which is legalized economy, the contracts are acknowledged and protected by the law. In addition, honesty and credit, which rest on the law, is the main characteristic of enterprise behavior in market economy. Without perfect law, honesty and credit will be substituted by the speculative behaviors of "economic man". Therefore we adopt this index of the proportion of contracts fulfilled to measure the enterprise marketization degree from point of legislation.

The Synthetic Proportion of Non-publicly-owned Enterprises

The synthetic proportion of non-publicly-owned enterprises refers to the proportions of the number, the employees and the output of non-publicly-owned enterprises. Because the non-publicly-owned enterprises are scarcely interfered by the government, their operation is near to complete marketization. All the indices of the non-publicly-owned enterprises can comprehensively reflect the influence of the development of non-publicly-owned enterprises to Chinese enterprise marketization course.

EVALUATING THE CHINESE ENTERPRISE MARKETIZATION

According to the former indices, by using relative data, we can get the results of evaluating the Chinese enterprise marketization.

The Autonomous Extent of Selecting Enterprise Systems

The autonomous extent of selecting enterprise systems of Chinese enterprises is the weighted average, which consists of this index value of state-owned and non-state-owned enterprises, the weights are the proportions of the output of the two kinds of enterprises to GNP. At present time, these two kinds of enterprises own different rights to select enterprise system. The system selection (for example, transforming to limited companies) of state-owned enterprises is almost completely ratified by the relative government departments, which is compatible with the economic system reform background of "government pushing pattern". Therefore the state-owned enterprises' autonomous extent of selecting enterprise system can be taken as zero. The non-state enterprises are scarcely interfered by the government when selecting enterprise systems, so we can infer that they are completely independent, and their autonomous extent is 100%. According to the typical industrial enterprises, we can compute the weights. Relative data indicate that the proportion of output of the state industrial enterprises to the total industrial output were 47%, 37.3%,34%,28.5%,26.5% of 1993,1994,1995,1996,1997 respectively. Therefore we can get the value of autonomous extent of Chinese enterprises to select enterprise systems (See Table 2.1). It is clear that the tendency of this index is gradually increasing.

Table 2.1 The Autonomous Extent of Chinese Enterprises to Select Enterprise Systems

1993	1994	1995	1996	1997
47%*0+	37.3%*0+	34%*0+	28.5%*0+	26.5%*0+
(1-47%)	(1-37.3%)	(1-34%)	(1-28.5%)	(1-26.5%)
*100%=53%	*100%=62.7%	*100%=66%	*100%=71.5%	*100%=73.5%

Source: *A Statistical Survey of China, 1998.*

The Market Choice Rate of Enterprise Managers

The market choice rate of enterprise managers can be calculated according to the data afforded by the Chinese Entrepreneur Survey System(See Tables 2.2, 2.3).

Table 2.2 The Produce Methods of Enterprise Managers (%)

	In general		State-owned enterprise		Collective enterprise		Foreign-funded and other Enterprise	
	93	94	93	94	93	94	93	94
Appointed by the upper departments in charge	85.5	75.3	92.2	86.0	75.3	58.4	48.6	33.2
Elected by the employees' representative meeting	6.3	9.0	4.4	7.4	16.8	21.4	2.2	5.0
Public tender	3.3	2.4	2.7	2.2	5.2	3.1	2.2	1.5
Appointed by board of directors	3.8	11.1	0.1	2.5	1.0	14.0	44.9	58.3
Others	0.8	2.2	0.6	1.9	1.7	3.1	2.1	2.0

Source: Chinese Entrepreneur Survey System, The Special Survey Report on the Growth and Development of Chinese Entrepreneurs, 1995.

Table 2.3 The Produce Method of Enterprise Managers (%), 1995

	In general	State-owned enterprise	Collective enterprise	Foreign-funded and other enterprise
Appointed by the personnel department, they themselves feel reluctantly	26.3	29.9	15.9	18.5
Appointed by the personnel department, they are voluntary	39.9	41.4	33.6	42.7
Getting the position by their own striving	8.4	5.7	17.1	12.9
Getting the position by their competence	25.4	23.0	33.4	25.9

Source: Chinese Entrepreneur Survey System, *The Special Survey Report on the Growth and Development of Chinese Entrepreneurs, 1996.*

Approximately, we can take the first two rows Tables 2.2 and 2.3 as the government appointment, the later three rows as market choice, then the produce method of enterprise managers can be expressed as Table 2.4.

Table 2.4 The Produce Method of Enterprise Managers(%)

	In general			State-owned enterprise			Collective enterprise			Foreign-funded and other enterprise		
	93	94	95	93	94	95	93	94	95	93	94	95
Appointed by the government	92.1	84.3	66.2	96.6	93.4	71.3	92.1	79.8	49.5	50.8	38.2	61.2
Market choice through competition	7.9	15.7	33.8	3.4	6.6	28.7	7.9	20.2	50.5	49.2	61.8	38.8

Source: Tables 2.2 and 2.3.

From Table 2.4 we can see that in general, among the produce method of enterprise managers, the proportion of market choice is gradually increasing, while the rate of government appointment are reducing. So do the state-owned enterprise and collective enterprise and foreign-funded and other enterprises, except the foreign-funded and other enterprises in 1995.

The Implementation Extent of the Enterprise Rights of Autonomous Management

As to the implement extent of the enterprise rights of autonomous management, the Chinese entrepreneur survey system has made three-year successive following survey from 1993 to 1995. The data they got are more authoritative and we can directly quote them to compute this index (See Table 2.5). The survey results indicate that the implement of the 14 items autonomous rights of management all tends to increase at a remarkable rate, which reflects that the government has achieve great success on transferring rights to enterprises, for example, the implement rate of the enterprise's labor employment right in 1997 increasing by 9.5% and 23.3% and 40.8% compared with 1995 and 1994 and 1993 respectively, and the increase right is higher among all these rights. The items of right whose implement rate are more than 80% increase from 3 and 5 and 8 of 1993 and 1994 and 1995 to 10 of 1997. The average implement rate increase from 54.9% and 65.8% and 76.4% in 1993 and 1994 and 1995 to 82.4% in 1997. From this index we can see that the enterprise marketization advances rapidly.

Table 2.5 The Implement Rate of the 14 Items Rights of Autonomous Management (%)

Year	1993	1994	1995	1997
Right of produce and management decision	88.7	94.0	97.3	98.3
Right of setting price on product and service	75.9	73.6	85.4	92.0
Right of marketing product	88.5	90.5	95.9	96.8
Right of purchasing material	90.9	95.0	97.8	98.8
Right of import and export	15.3	25.8	41.3	54.0
Right of investment decision	38.9	61.2	72.8	82.5
Right of allocating the profit after tax	63.7	73.8	88.3	90.6
Right of disposing assets	29.4	46.6	68.2	76.5
Right of allying and merging	23.3	39.7	59.7	61.4
Right of labor employment	43.5	61.0	74.8	84.3
Right of personnel management	53.7	73.3	83.5	90.3
Right of distributing wage and bonus	70.2	86.0	93.1	96.0
Right of establishing internal organizations	79.3	90.5	94.4	97.3
Right of refusing arbitrary apportion	7.0	10.3	17.4	35.1
Average implement rate	54.9	65.8	76.4	82.4

Source: The Chinese Entrepreneur Survey System, *The Report of the Chinese Enterprise Managers Questionnaire Survey, 1997*."Management World", Vol. 1, 1998, Beijing.

The Proportion of the Enterprises with the First Goal of Maximizing Profit

According to the reports afforded by the Chinese entrepreneur survey system (See Table 2.6,2.7,2.8), the management aims of the enterprises have changed from 1993 to 1995.

Table 2.6 The Selection of Enterprises' Management Aims (Accumulated Frequency, %), 1993

Increasing the employees' income	Fulfilling the contract task	Increasing the sales profit
77.4	51.8	39.0

Source: The Chinese Entrepreneur Survey System, The Special Report of Share-holding Enterprises (Dec. 31, 1993--May 6, 1994).

Table 2.7 The Order of the Three Management Goals Enterprises Care Most (%), 1994

	In general	State-owned enterprise	Collective enterprise	Foreign-funded and other enterprise
Increasing the employees' income	43.8	47.7	39.4	30.2
Pursuing the maximum profit	40.7	40.7	32.6	42.4
Increasing the market shares	38.4	37.2	40.0	52.3
Establishing fine enterprise image	33.2	31.0	41.4	44.0
Expanding enterprise scale	27.5	26.3	36.5	21.2
Fulfilling contracting task	14.8	17.1	10.0	9.9

Source: The Chinese Entrepreneur Survey System, The Special Survey Report on the Growth and Development of Chinese Entrepreneurs, 1995.

If enterprises' pursuing maximum profit is unitary with the aim of accomplishing profit and tax indices and increasing sales profit (actually the profit and tax indices may exaggerate the aim of pursuing maximum profit), then from Table 2.6, 2.7, 2.8, we can see that on the whole, the rank of the goal of pursuing maximum profit has changed from the third, second of 1993, 1994 respectively to the first of 1995; and the fairly diverse goals became relatively concentrating. But the proportion of the enterprises whose first aim is to maximizing profit is not high, only about 59.5%; and there exist no notable difference among state-owned enterprises, collective, foreign-funded, and other enterprises. This indicates that as to the management aims, the pursuit of enterprises is not clear. There still exist many abnormal factors. There is a long way to the formation of marketization aims.

Table 2.8 The Management Goals That Enterprises Care Most (%), 1995

	In general	State-owned enterprise	Collective enterprise	Foreign-funded and other enterprise
Profit and tax indices	59.5	59.6	61.1	54.8
Sales scale and market shares	38.6	38.2	37.8	44.6
Employees' wage and welfare	1.1	1.2	0.9	--
Social contribution	0.1	0.1	--	--
The increase of enterprise' tangible and intangible assets	0.5	0.6	0.2	0.6
The increment of the market value of enterprise	0.1	0.2	--	--
Others	0.1	0.1	--	--

Source: The Chinese Entrepreneur Survey System, The Special Survey Report on the Growth and Development of Chinese Entrepreneurs, 1996.

The Assumption Extent of Enterprise Property Rights Subjects

Up to now it is no doubt that the assumption extent of state-owned enterprise property rights subjects is zero, i.e., the subjects of state-owned property rights are absent or nominal. The absence of the state-owned property rights subjects result in the serious "insider control" in the state-owned enterprises and the great loss of state assets. It means that Chinese state-owned enterprises, as actual market agents, are not mature. Because the behaviors of market agents are not absolute freedom, but freedom with restrictions. One of the indispensable restrictions is property rights constraint, which is protected by law. The absence of state property rights subjects has great influence on the course of enterprise marketization, which can be evaluated according to the proportion of the output of state-owned industrial enterprises to the national industrial output. If we assume the assumption extent of non-state-owned enterprises' property rights subjects is approximately 100%(in fact, lower than 100%), then the assumption extent of the whole enterprises' property rights subjects is the same with the autonomous extent of selecting enterprise systems, i.e., 53% in 1993, 62.7% in 1994, 66% in 1995, 71.5% in 1996,73.5% in 1997,which are obviously more optimistic estimation.

The Legalization Extent of Enterprise Bankruptcy

The bankruptcy process of Chinese enterprises is almost completely non-marketized or completely administrated. Since the Law of Enterprise Bankruptcy of People's Republic of Chins took effect on November 1, 1988, there were 3010 items of registrations of bankruptcy application by the end of 1994. The proportion of bankrupt enterprises is one in ten thousand, while in western developed countries, it is about 1%. Moreover, there exists serious administrative interference in the process of enterprise bankruptcy. Chinese enterprises cannot go bankruptcy without the ratification of the government department in charge and the well settlement of employees. The operation and implementation of Chinese enterprise bankruptcy are far from being able to meet the demand of developing market economy and it is difficult to make enterprise go bankruptcy according to the law. The legalization extent of enterprise bankruptcy is next to zero before 1995, and rises slightly in 1996 and 1997, which is 1.2% and 2.3%.

The Proportion of Contracts Fulfilled

Owing to imperfect law system, there comes administrative interference from the government now and then. So it is common that Chinese enterprises do not keep promise and break the law. According to the statistical data, there were 3000 million contracts signed in 1992 in China, among which only 30% were fulfilled. From 1993 to 1995 this situation had not changed to be better, the proportion of contracts fulfilled is still about 30% (Lu Xianxiang, 1996). The proportion is only 31.2% and 33.5% in 1996 and 1997. The low proportion of contracts fulfilled indicates that there is a long way full of difficulties to the enterprise marketization.

The Synthetically Proportion of Non-publicly-owned Enterprises

We can compute out this index according to the relative data (See Table 2.9).

Table 2.9 The Synthetic Proportions of Non-publicly-owned Enterprises (%)

Year	1993	1994	1995	1996	1997
Proportion of units	62.8	61.0	60.7	61.4	65.6
Proportion of employees	31.0	26.5	27.8	28.2	34.5
Proportion of output	25.2	28.2	30.1	31.3	32.9
Synthetic proportion	39.7	38.6	39.5	40.3	44.3

Source: *China Statistical Yearbook, 1996; A Statistical Survey of China, 1998.*

Integral Estimation

We can approximately estimate out the course of Chinese enterprise marketization from 1993 to 1997 by simply averaging the above eight indices value (See Table 2.10). The result is that the Chinese enterprises marketization degree are 34.7%, 39.5%, 46.4%, 48.8%, 52.6% in the years of 1993,1994, 1995,1996,1997 respectively. It is more optimistic evaluation. Obviously, though the market transactions among Chinese enterprises are gradually expanding in these years, they do not dominate the enterprises' operation. Therefore it is necessary to expedite the enterprise marketization.

Table 2.10 The Integral Estimation of Chinese Enterprise Marketization (%)

Index Year	(1)	(2)	(3)	(4)	(5)	(6)	(7)	(8)	Average
1993	53	7.9	54.9	39.0	53	0	30	39.7	34.7
1994	62.7	15.7	65.8	40.7	62.7	0	30	38.6	39.5
1995	66	33.8	76.4	59.5	66	0	30	39.5	46.4
1996	71.5	37.5*	77.6*	59.8*	71.5	1.2	31.2	40.3	48.8
1977	73.5	47.4*	82.4	63.7*	73.5	2.3	33.5	44.3	52.6

Note * Predicted Data.
Source: The Former Tables.

THE BRIEF RETROSPECTION OF THE COURSE
OF CHINESE ENTERPRISE MARKETIZATION

The Chinese enterprise marketization began in 1978. The original motive is to improve the management mechanism of state-owned enterprises without autonomy, and increase the efficiency of state-owned enterprises. Up to now, the reform of enterprise marketization can be divided into three stages.

The First Stage (1978--1984): Transferring Rights and Benefits

Before the reform of 1978, the Chinese enterprise marketization degree was nearly zero. Corresponding to the highly centralized planned system, the universal enterprise system was the enterprise owned by the whole people, i.e., the state-owned enterprise; collective enterprise is similar to the state-owned enterprise. There existed no enterprises with other kinds of ownership. Under the highly centralized planned economy, enterprises had few rights, whose operation completely depended on the administrative direction from the government, and there were no other competitors. The lack of internal benefit incentive and external pressure of market competition resulted in the inertia of produce and management and the lasting low efficiency. These maladies brought forth the reform guideline of "transferring rights and benefits to the enterprises" in the end of 1970s.

"Transferring rights and benefits" means to arouse the enterprises' enthusiasm of production and management through transferring autonomous rights and material incentives to the enterprises. However, it is a kind of completely government behavior, when "transferring rights and benefits" was beyond the government's original intention or against the government's will, the government would retake the rights and reduce the benefits by administrative power. During the reform course, it is inevitable to form a vicious circle--"when the government transfers rights, the enterprises will be active; when the enterprises are active, they will be in disorder; when they are in the disorder, the government will retake the right; when the government retake the right, the enterprises will die". It indicates that "transferring rights and benefits" did not create the market space for the growth of the state-owned enterprises. At the beginning, the national reform focused on the countryside, while the reform of urban enterprises were not put on the agenda, and "transferring rights and benefits was only the "by-product" of countryside reform. But "transferring rights and benefits" has loosed the rigid planned system of resources allocation, and induced the government to exert less control on the non-state-owned enterprises. Especially, the appearance and rapid growth of township enterprises was out of the government's expectation (Lin Yifu, 1995). In addition, the reform of countryside, as a key point of reform, has had great incentive to the growth and development of the non-state-owned enterprises (mainly are township enterprises). The entrance of non-state-owned enterprises indicated that the market mechanism which have been dormant for many years in China now reappeared and began to develop. Because the non-state-owned enterprises were the outcome of market, they had to acquire production factors and market their products through the market competitions, so they had the hard budget constraint. As early as they grew, the non-state-owned enterprises showed higher vigor and efficiency than that of the traditional state-owned enterprises, and had pressure on the state-owned enterprises. According to the data from the World Bank (1992), from 1980 to 1984, the average increase rate of output and the total factor productivity were 6.77% and 1.8% in state-owned section, and 14.03%,3.45% in the collective section(mainly are township enterprises) respectively. The later is far higher than the former.

If we say that the enterprise marketization in the first stage has made some progress, it is the non-state-owned enterprises that almost made the entire contribution. However we should notice that in this stage, the non-state-owned enterprises were fairly weak compared with the traditional state-owned enterprises, and the Chinese enterprise marketization backed by them (especially township enterprises) has only started, not getting the essential progress. In 1984, the proportion of the total output of non-state-owned enterprises to the total industrial output were only 30.9%; the proportion of industrial output of township industrial enterprises was 16.3%. Because all the rights of the state-owned enterprises, which were all over the economy area and whose output occupied the absolute proportion, were grasped by the government, and the urban collective enterprises did not open to the outside, the Chinese enterprise marketization (averaging the values of eight indices), even though we do not consider that the township enterprises and other non-publicly-owned enterprises interfered by the government frequently, are not more than 10%. Obviously, in the first stage of reform, the Chinese enterprise marketization advanced very slowly.

The Second Stage(1985--1992): The Experiment of Strengthening the Management Rights

From 1984, the focus of economic system reform switched from countryside to cities. The reform of state-owned enterprise was clarified as the core of reform, the main content of which was to make experiment of strengthening the enterprise' management rights. This experiment originated from the abnormalism of "transferring rights and benefits". Because "transferring rights and benefits" was completely government behavior, the arbitrariness of the government's interference resulted in the unstable expectation and short term actions of enterprise managers, which had influence on the optimization of enterprise structure and the increase of efficiency, and caused the inflation of investment and consumption in 1994. Under the former conditions, people changed their sights to the managers, and expected to initiate "manager revolution" inside the state ownership to make managers responsible for the efficiency of state-owned assets, by rebuilding the micro benefit mechanism and rights subjects. Thus the economic responsibility system that aimed to clarify the rights and duties of enterprise managers were implemented, among which the main kinds were rental system, contracted responsibility system and economic responsibility system of assets management. It was the system of contracted responsibility that was implemented in the widest scope and had great influence on the state-owned enterprises.

Compared with "transferring rights and benefits" at the first stage, economic responsibility system expanded the market space for the growth of state-owned enterprises. Enterprise behaviors were optimized and the efficiency increased slightly. But it was undisputed that economic responsibility system could not rescue the state-owned enterprises from the low-efficiency straits because it was still limited in the framework of transferring rights by administrative power. Let's take contracted system as an example. In order to assure the enterprise property revenues which was the basic right of the owners, the government had the power to determine the profit distribution(not through the market negotiation of equal agents) and to interfere the appointment and removal of enterprise managers(not through the market choice with competition). As to the nomination and dismiss of managers, 73% were nominated by the government, 13%by the election of employees' representatives meeting, 12.4% by public tender,1.6% by the recommendation of the contracting group, according to the questionnaire survey on 403 state-owned enterprises in 1988 (Dong Fureng, 1992). In fact, it is the public tender that is really market choice through competition, others, which proportion is 87.6%, are the outcomes of government appointment or involvement. From the angels of other indices, except that the aim of maximizing profit that aroused the care of few state-owned enterprises and those enterprises have acquired few unstable management autonomy, the government completely controlled the enterprises on system choice and bankruptcy. Enterprises were still not independent property rights subjects, the contracts were not stable, and the proportion of contracts fulfilled was less than 10%. Obviously, though the marketization of state-owned enterprises began, it progresses slowly.

Contrary to the slow progress of state-owned enterprises, the marketization of non-state-owned enterprises got essential breakthrough in the second stage. From 1985 to 1992, the yearly increase rate of output value of state-owned industrial enterprises was 8.3%, while that of non-state-owned industrial enterprises amounted to 28%. Also in 1992, the proportion of output value of non-state-owned industrial enterprises, which was 48.5%, was nearly 50%. Thus indicated that the efficiency of non-state-owned enterprises brought about by the marketization was far higher that of state-owned enterprises which were controlled by the government. Compared with the state-owned enterprises, the non-state-owned enterprises, on the whole, were independent property rights subjects, pursuing for the relatively independent economic benefits (maximizing the profit). In brief, the behaviors of non-state-owned enterprises had the typical features of market.

Whereas in the same existence space, these two kinds of enterprises with different behavior features will inevitably conflict. Because the state-owned enterprises under administrative control were in the dominant position during the second stage, this kind of administration will inevitably infiltrate to the non-state-owned enterprises. The prominent manifestations were as follows: the law and regulations were not perfect; the enterprises' market rights could not get effective protection, for example, breaking contracts could not be halted and compensated; the bankruptcy settlement did not reflect the reasonable rights and will of the relative parts. Due to these situations, the marketization degree of non-state-owned enterprises may be much discounted. During the period of improvement and rectification from 1989 to 1991, the marketization of both state-owned and non-state-owned enterprises went backward.

On the whole, the enterprise marketization from 1985 to 1988 progress more rapidly, amounting to about 23% in 1988; retrogressed from 1989 to 1990, reducing to about 15% or even less in 1990. In 1991, the enterprise marketization degree rebounded. In 1992, Mr. Deng Xiaoping's south-trip speech had great incentive to the enterprise marketization course, which amounted to about 25%.

The Third Stage (1993--): Transplanting The Modern Enterprise System

In 1992, the Fourteenth National Session of the Chinese Communist Party take the socialism market economy as the aim of Chinese economic reform, which was the turning point of expediting the Chinese enterprise marketization. The striking features of this stage was that the state-owned enterprises absorbed the modern enterprise system, which were in experiment but have had great incentive to the marketization of non-state-owned enterprises. We have computed out the Chinese enterprise marketization degree from 1993 to 1997 in the former section, hereby we do not repeat.

According to the estimated values, we can describe the approximate locus of Chinese enterprise marketization (See Figure 2.1).

Figure 2.1 The Approximate Locus of Chinese Enterprise Marketization Degree

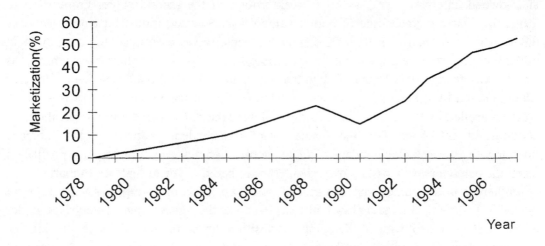

THE INTERNATIONAL COMPARISON OF ENTERPRISE MARKETIZATION

Comparing the Chinese enterprise marketization with foreign countries, we can set a reasonable standard for Chinese enterprise marketization. The enterprise marketization standard can be used to judge the enterprise marketization degree is rational or enough in accordance with modern market economy. However, it is difficult and unnecessary to set up a completely accurate standard. Hereby we analyze the enterprise marketization degree of several western countries with developed market economy to afford reference for the reform of Chinese enterprise marketization.

The enterprise system of western countries with developed market economy is free enterprise system, the government has influence on the market activities of free enterprises mainly by relative policies and state-owned enterprises, not by the direct administrative interference. Especially the state-owned enterprises, as a policy instrument and method of implementing economic plan of government, play an important role in influencing the behaviors of free enterprises. Therefore, by studying the scale of state-owned enterprises in the western developed countries and other relative factors, we can make appropriate evaluation on the enterprise marketization of these countries. We also analyze the indices one by one in the following paragraphs.

Table 2.11 The Proportion of State-owned Economy in the Western Countries with Developed Market Economy in 1977(%)

	Postal service	Broadcast and communication	Power station	Gas industry	Oil exploration	Coal industry	Railway transportation	Aviation transportation	Automobile industry	Iron and steel Industry	Shipbuilding industry
Britain	100	100	100	100	25	100	100	75	50	75	100
France	100	100	100	100		100	100	75	50	75	P
West German	100	100	75	50	25	50	100	100	25	P	25
Japan	100	100	P	100		p	72	25	p	P	P
U.S.A.	100	P	25	p	p	P	25	p	p	p	P

Note: "P" means "Private"

Source P.39 *"Economist"*(Britain), Dec. 30, 1978,. Cited from "History of World History" (second half). P86. Edited by Song Zexing, Chinese Social Science Press. 1989

The Autonomous Extent of Selecting Enterprise System

In developed western countries, the enterprise systems except the state-ownership which is determined by the government, are completely independently determined by enterprises. By studying the distribution of the state-owned enterprises in several developed countries, we can see that the majority of state-owned enterprises undertake public infrastructure and fundamental industry (See Table 2.11), and the proportion of state-owned enterprises to the total enterprises is very small, only 1%--10%. The proportion of output of the state-owned enterprises is less than 20%, for example, in Britain, 11%(1979); in France, 18%(1991); West German, 9%(1985); Japan, 10%(1980); the U.S.A., 2%(1982). Thus we can estimate out the autonomous extent of selecting enterprise system are 89%, 82%, 91%, 90%, 98% in Britain, France, West German, Japan and the U.S.A. respectively.

The Market Choice Rate of Enterprise Managers

There exists perfect manager market in developed western countries. Except that the managers of state-owned enterprises are appointed by the government, the other kinds of enterprises select managers according to their own benefits and market principle; and the individuals select enterprise managers on the basis of their characteristic and market principle. Thus in general, there are two ways for enterprises to select managers: one is from the inside of enterprise, the other is from the outside. Though the proportion of these two ways to select managers varies in different countries, they are belonging to the market choice pattern. If all the managers of the state-owned enterprises are assumed to be appointed by the government, we can estimate the market choice rate of enterprise managers of different countries according to the proportion of state-owned enterprises to the total enterprises units. The proportion of state-owned enterprises in Britain and the U.S.A. is less than 1%, in Federal German, less then 5%, in France and Japan, less than 10%; correspondingly, the market choice rate of enterprise managers in Britain and the U.S.A. is about 98%, in West German, about 95%; in France and Japan, about 90%.

The Implementation Extent of Enterprise Rights of Autonomous Management

Free management and free competition is the basic characteristic of enterprise operation in developed western countries. But the functions of government cannot be neglected, which are embodied in many respects. First, the government directly afford service for enterprises by setting up public services (or state-owned enterprises); second, the government adjust and control the private enterprises so as to make them serve the public welfare as possible as they can by many ways; thirdly, the government can directly support the enterprise, for example, imposing tariff to prevent some national product from foreign competition to protect the national enterprise and infant industry. Under these circumstances, the government has certain influence on the enterprise autonomous management rights. Recently, the rank of the government interference extent is as follows: Britain, U.S.A., West German, Japan, France, from the weakest to the strongest. In addition, to the share-holding company, the share-holders will impose some restrictions on the autonomy of enterprises. If we assume that the share-holders' restrictions to the enterprise autonomy is the same in different countries, then, the implement extent of enterprise rights of autonomous management are about 92%, 88%, 85%, 80%, 78% in Britain, U.S.A., West German, Japan and France respectively.

The Proportion of Enterprises with the First Aim of Maximizing Profit

Profit is the best criteria of enterprise behavior. In the western market economy countries where resources are scarce and competition are fierce, to enterprises, as "economic men" in the market, pursuing maximum profit is the prerequisite for them to survive and develop. But undoubtedly, the profit aim of some enterprises is subject to the realization of other aims. There are two probable cases: one is the interference from outside power, especially the government; the other is that when the enterprise situation become worse, whittling down cost, reorganization and contraction will spread among the enterprise circles (Thompson, 1990). The later often results from the worse macro situation created by the government. Therefore, approximately, the proportion of enterprises with the first aim of maximizing profit is the same with the implement extent of enterprise rights of autonomous management, i.e., the value of this index are 92%, 88%, 85%, 80%, 78% in Britain, U.S.A., West German, Japan, France respectively.

The Assumption Extent of Enterprise Property Rights Subjects

Theoretically speaking, the property rights subjects of enterprises including state-owned enterprises in western developed countries are present. The problem is that the property rights subjects of great companies, especially the listed great corporations, are vacated, which results in the lack of property rights constraint and the "insider control". "Insider control" is the manifestation of unperfected market economy. Modern market economy should take the enterprise property rights subjects assume their positions with sufficient power. At present time, due to the difference of development scale, market construction and law normalization in western countries, the property rights constraint and the assumption extent of enterprise property rights subjects are various. In the U.S.A., there are many giant enterprises, and the stock rights are dispersal, the "insider control" problem is remarkable, the assumption rate is about 90%. Britain has not so many great enterprises with dispersal stock rights as the U.S.A., and has implemented privatization continuously, so the assumption rate is slightly higher, about 95%. West German has very strict qualifications to the listed share-holding companies, so its assumption rate is near 95%. France adopts the market economy of "state-dominant pattern", the excessive interference from state will deprive the enterprise rights, so the assumption rate is 80%. The main characteristic of Japanese share rights structure is " corporation-holding shares" and the subjects of enterprise property rights are not nominal, so the assumption rate is about 98%.

The Legalization Extent of Enterprise Bankruptcy

In western developed countries, there are fairly perfect laws and regulations. Enterprises should act on the normalization and restriction of laws. As to the enterprise bankruptcy, the developed countries have many years of practice of legalized bankruptcy. The fundamental purposes of the bankruptcy law are as follows: to liquidate the debtors' property fair and reasonably according to the legal process to protect the debtors' interests when the debtors cannot repay the due debts, and to improve the debtors' assets structure; to remit partial debts of the debtors who are really insolvent to give them new chances of life. Presently in western countries, almost all the enterprises acknowledge and obey the legalization of enterprise bankruptcy. So we can estimate that the legalization extent of enterprise bankruptcy is no less than 95%.

The Proportion of Contracts Fulfilled

In developed western counties, market transactions universally depend on the contracts of agents with equal rights. All the contracts are acknowledged and strictly protected by the law. Since the enterprises should act on the normalization and restriction of laws, breaking the law will incur punishment, so the rate of contracts fulfilled in transactions in western countries is very high. But owing to the nature of "economic person" of enterprises, violating contracts is inevitable. We estimate that the proportions of contracts fulfilled in western developed countries are nearly the same, about 85%.

The Synthetic Proportion of Non-publicly-owned Enterprises

Western developed countries adopt private ownership or market economy system with private ownership, non-publicly-owned enterprises, whatever their units, employees or output, occupy absolute proportion. Correspondingly, the synthetic proportion of non-publicly-owned enterprises is very high. According to the former analysis of the first, second index in this section, we estimate that the synthetic proportion of the non-publicly-owned enterprises are 94% in Britain and the U.S.A.,91% in Federal German and Japan, 82% in France respectively.

Integral Measurement

According to the above estimation of he indices, we can compute out the enterprise marketization degree in each developed western country. They are 92.5%, 84.9%, 90.3%, 88.6%, 92% in Britain, France, West German, Japan, U.S.A. respectively(See Table 2.12).

Table 2.12 The Enterprise Marketization Degree in the Main Western Countries with Developed Market Economy (%)

Index Country	(1)	(2)	(3)	(4)	(5)	(6)	(7)	(8)	Average
Britain	89	98	92	92	95	95	85	94	92.5
France	82	90	78	78	89	95	85	82	84.9
West German	91	95	85	85	95	95	85	91	90.3
Japan	90	90	80	80	98	95	85	91	88.6
U.S.A.	98	98	88	88	90	95	85	94	92

Source: The Former Tables

The Chinese social system determines that on all accounts the enterprise marketization cannot reach the high level of western developed market countries. However, since we have taken setting up modern market economy as the direction of economic system reform, and we also have acknowledged that enterprise marketization has deterministic influence on increasing the enterprise efficiency, the enterprise marketization degree of China will not much less than that of western developed countries in the future. We think the reasonable extent of Chinese enterprise marketization extent is between 75% and 80%. The reasons are as follows: firstly, the state-owned enterprises that dominate Chinese economy will be interfered by the government more or less; secondly, the dominance of state-owned enterprises does not mean that they will occupy absolute proportion among all the enterprises, we estimate the proportion of state-owned enterprise is less than 15%; thirdly, China has a vast territory and various economic structure, it will helpful to motivate the economic vitality to let the enterprises freely participate in the market competition; fourthly, it is indispensable for the government to support enterprises, but the government should adjust enterprises through market as an intermediate, not through the direct administrative interference; fifthly, perfect law normalization is necessary for marketization. Only from these points, can we understand the contents of marketization completely. Obviously, it is a difficult task for Chinese enterprise marketization degree reach 75%--80%.

PROPOSALS ON EXPEDITING CHINESE ENTERPRISE MARKETIZATION

Devoting More Efforts to Developing Non-state-owned Enterprises

The non-state-owned enterprises are the main power to expedite Chinese enterprise marketization. Because the management mechanism of non-state-owned enterprises is more suitable for market economy, and they are less intervened by the government; their efficiency is higher, and their competitive capacity is stronger, which results in the gradual development and expansion of their economic strength. Now the proportion of output of non-state-owned enterprises to GNP is over 50%, and the proportion of output of non-state-owned industrial enterprises to the total industrial output amounts to 73.5%. However, the development of non-state-owned enterprises is still not enough. In the main western developed countries of market economy, the proportion of output of non-state-owned enterprises to GNP is about 93%, which is far higher that of China. Therefore, expediting Chinese enterprise marketization depends on the great development of non-state-owned enterprises.

First, we should create fair competition circumstances for the development of non-state-owned enterprises. Since the reform the main factors disturbing the development of non-state-owned enterprises areas are as follows: difficult to get bank loan; too many restrictions; unfavorable public opinions to them, especially to the private enterprises (including individual enterprises). In order to solve these problems, we should abolish the traditional method that making laws and policies according to the ownership, and implement the market principle that all kinds of ownership compete fairly. Except the state-owned enterprises on areas of national safeguard, national economic lifelines and public services, the other state-owned enterprises should fairly compete with the non-state-owned enterprises under the same market conditions, and face the principle of "survival of the fittest".

Secondly, we should actively support the intermediary organizations. Presently almost all the large Chinese enterprises are state-owned, the scale of non-state-owned enterprises are smaller and their grades are lower, inevitably they suffer the contradiction between small-scale production and wide market. In addition, the non-state-owned enterprises, especially the private enterprises are weak in their self-constraint ability and the consciousness of accepting the monitor and check, it is necessary to establish some non-governmental economic intermediary organizations, such as professional association, industrial and commercial association, entrepreneur society, etc. These are to afford services and directions for non-state-owned enterprises, including harmonizing relationship, communicating, publicizing laws and regulations, etc, to make the non-state-owned enterprises develop rapidly and healthily.

Strengthening the Reform of State-owned Enterprise Marketization

Sticking to the dominant status of state-owned economy is a prerequisite of Chinese enterprise marketization reform. But if we limit us in this prerequisite, the reform of Chinese enterprise marketization will be full of difficulty. "Dominance" is only a direction. The share-holding company can control other enterprises even it holds small proportion of shares, analogously, as long as the state-owned economy dominate some key areas, they will achieve the dominant position. Therefore it is wise to let most of state-owned enterprises participate in the market and manage freely. Thus we should accomplish the following tasks:

First, normalizing the external management system of the state-owned enterprises. A congenial external management system is the guarantee of the healthy development of state enterprises. Currently the relationships between state-owned enterprises and external management system are not smooth yet, especially the relationships between the enterprises, people's congress, party's organization, government and other departments should be clarified urgently to form the mechanism of legalized guarantee, administrative management, audit and monitor and department services. The direction of the reform is to establish a specialized non-political state assets management center, separated from the government. The center acts as the subject of state-owned property and implements the functions of state-owned property ownership. The administrative departments of the government recede from the operation and management of state property, and are responsible for the market construction, the improvement of macro economic situations and other necessary services.

Secondly, rebuilding the relationship between banks and enterprises. Presently the bad debts of enterprises and bad assets of banks are main obstacles to the marketization of state-owned enterprises, which is relative to the over-emphasis of enterprise marketization reform and the negligence of the marketization reform of banks. In fact, in modern market economy countries, banks are also enterprises pursuing for profit. Except that the central bank is governmental organization, the other banks are all commercial banks. To take banks as enterprises is to put banks to the position of rights subjects that manage independently according to the market change. If we take banks as enterprises, then the enterprise marketization reform should synchronize with the bank marketization reform, which is the fundamental countermeasure to improve the relationship between banks and enterprises. As to the bad debts and bad assets resulting from the wrong policies, they may be separated from the account and gradually disposed by the government. After that, the relationships between banks and enterprises are subject to market principles.

Thirdly, separating the social functions from enterprises. Another obstacle to the marketization of state-owned enterprises is that state enterprises bear a great number of social functions. The best way to solve this problem is to separate the social functions from the enterprises, and the government should establish good social security system to be responsible for these social functions. After the social functions are separated, there is no reason for the government to interfere in the enterprises, what remains is the property relationship between enterprises and state assets management center. This is very important to rebuild the corporate governance structure with property constraint and high efficiency, and is also an important step for the marketization of state-owned enterprises. As to the sources of funds which will be used to establish social security system by the government, there may be three channels in short term: the revenues from selling insolvent, low-profit or small state-owned enterprises; the income from selling partial state shares; the dividend and bonus from partial state shares (Gu Shutang, 1995).

Strengthening and Perfecting the Legislation Construction

Market economy is legalized economy. Marketization inevitably comes along with legalization. Marketization without the normalization of legislation is not real marketization. The weakest link of Chinese enterprise marketization is legislation construction. Due to the lack of effective legal normalization and constraint, administrative interference often gets a chance to step in, which makes the enterprise marketization become a mere formality. The most important legal problem in the course of enterprise marketization is to determine the rights and duties between the government and enterprises, i.e., putting the behaviors of the government and enterprises into the strict legal constraint. Meanwhile, we should set up the idea of "law is more important than power" in the whole society. Thus can the operational mechanism of enterprise marketization with both incentives and constraint produce, can the maximum enterprise efficiency be motivated from the internal system.

REFERENCES

Arthur. A. Thompson, *"Enterprise Economics"*, Shanghai People's Press. 1990

Chinese Entrepreneur Survey System, *"The Special Survey Report on the Growth and Development of Chinese Entrepreneurs"*. 1995

Chinese Entrepreneur Survey System, *"The Special Survey Report on the Growth and Development of Chinese Entrepreneurs"*. 1996,

Chinese Entrepreneur Survey System, *"The Report of Questionnaire Survey on Chinese Enterprise Managers"*. 1997,

Chinese Entrepreneur Survey System, *"The Special Survey Report on Share-holding Companies"* (Dec.31, 1993--May 6,1994).

Coase, Ronald H., *"The Federal Communications Commission,* Journal Law and Economics", Vol.2. 1959

Dong Fureng, Tang Zongkun, *"The Reform of Chinese State-owned Enterprises: Institutions and Efficiency"*, Chinese Plan Press. 1992,

Graygly, Paul R., *Comparative Economic Systematology,* Chinese edition, Shanghai Sanlian Bookstore. 1988

Gu Shutang, Gao Minghua, *"The Mechanism Transformation of State-owned Enterprises: Obstacles and Countermeasures"*, "Economic Survey", Vol.12. 1995,

He Zili, Zheng Zibing, *"French Market Economy System"*, Lanzhou University Press. 1994,

Lin Jue, *"American Market Economy System"*, Lanzhou University Press. 1994,

Lin Yifu, *"Chinese Economic Reform And Economics Development*, In "Economics And Chinese Economic Reform", Shanghai People's Press. 1995,

Lu Xianxiang, "Moral Risk Theory In Foreign Countries*", Economics Information*, Vol.8. 1996,

Sheng Hong, "The Condition, Limitation and Formality of Marketization*", Economic* Research Journal, Vol.11. 1992,

World Bank, *Reform and Role of Plan In the 1990s,* Washington, D.C.. 1992,

Xia Yongxiang, Dang Guoying, *"British Market Economy System"*, Lanzhou University Press. 1994,

Zhang Jinghua, *"Germany Market Economy System"*, Lanzhou University Press. 1994,

Zuo Zhonghai, *"Japanese Market Economy System"*, Lanzhou University Press. 1993,

Chapter 3

MEASUREMENT OF THE ADAPTATION OF CHINESE GOVERNMENT BEHAVIORS TO MARKETIZATION

PROBLEMS AND APPROACHES

This chapter is primarily concerned with the degree of relevant change of government behaviors during the course of Chinese economic reform of marketization, or, the degree of adaptation of Chinese government behaviors to marketization. It reflects, from an aspect, the degree of economic marketization degree in China.

The government behaviors reflect and, to a great extent, determine the system pattern of the social economy in any society since state emerged. The specialized function of government is to provide people with necessary order, justice and security, that is, to provide a system environment of social and economic activity. So in a market economic society, government is not the market behavior subject in normal sense, but is a supervisor administering and controlling the economy outside and above market. Government also has market activities such as consumption and investment, but its role under this circumstance is an ordinary microeconomic market subject rather than a special supervisor. Generally speaking, government always lies outside market. In this sense, there does not exist the problem of the marketization of government behaviors.

However, government behaviors greatly influence the course and features of marketization. Different government behaviors may promote or suppress the generation and development of markets, impel or retard market process, and even wither a developed market reverse the whole process. The reason is that government as the main institutional supplier can determine a country's economic direction and regulate market function and the room of market development through policy and rule. Government behaviors are especially important during the period of transformation. From another point of view, there exists significant discrepancy in government behaviors between different economic systems. During the process of economic system reform, to the government activity, there are also problems of adaptation to the market reform. For instance, should the economic activities of government, including the acquisition and the disbursement of the financial income, follow the rules of market economy or run counter to it? This has a significant impact upon the marketization progress.

The chapter is a positive study in order to measure the degree of marketization of Chinese government behaviors. The traditional planned economic system has two features: the close combination of government with enterprises in organizational structure and the high centralization of decision-making powers in economic functioning. For the marketization reform, the government is both the primary promoter and the target of the reform. The government behaviors will inevitably change along with the development of market economy and the deepening of reform, but the direction is not undoubted and determined. Theoretically, there are two opposite directions in the transformation of government behaviors and the possibility of oscillation between the two directions. Therefore, whether and to what extent the Chinese government behaviors will evolve towards market economy needs to be revealed by the positive study. This chapter objectively describes the historical tenor of marketization of Chinese government behaviors and elucidates the current development. It is a real historical record rather than a theoretical research, and so there is no the author's subjective evaluation in it.

As a record of significant historical events, its academic value will be increased if this work would continue. For this purpose, the data employed must have comparability and the same effect during a long historical period. Hence we must select data from the public statistic instead of individual investigation. The economic variables that reflect the conversion of government behaviors are the ones found in both market and planned economic systems, but both have quantitative discrepancy, rather than those variables only existing in a specific economic system or a specific period of a system. We find that only the financial statistics of income and expenses can meet this requirement.

Since the government behavior is embodied in financial income and expenses, the transformation of government behaviors surely can be reflected from the financial data. So it is probable to study this conversion through the change of financial income and expenses. Our discussion excludes the action of government as an institutional supplier. This is because such action is usually intangible and difficult to quantify and measure directly.

The government behaviors include central and local government behaviors. During the marketization of China, local government plays an important role. But as a subordinate, local government can not exceed the limitation which central government permit in the extent of behavioral conversion and the action of promoting market economy. It is the central government that determines the progress of conversion. To simplify discussion, we concentrate our research only on the measurement of degree in the change of central government behaviors.

THE RETROSPECT OF THE REFORM OF ECONOMIC MANAGEMENT SYSTEM OF CHINESE GOVERNMENT

The transformation of Chinese government behaviors to adaptation to marketization is achieved gradually through the progress of the reform of traditional government economic management system. By and large, the reform of Chinese government economic management system since 1979 is performed with three main clues:

1. Giving enterprises the independent rights to achieve the separation of government and enterprise. This policy includes two sides: one is that the central government transfers the economic decision-making power to professional government departments and local governments in order to form a macro-economic hierarchical-supervisory pattern. The other is that government directly gives the independent managing rights to enterprise, and changes its economic function, withdraws from microeconomic managing region.

2. Changing the methods that government administers economy from direct administrative command to indirect adjustment with economic levers. The change includes a series of reform, such as the reform of planned system, price administrative system, personnel managing system, wage distributive system, commercial system, foreign trade system, fiscal and financial system and investment system.

3. Reforming government institutions includes not only the reform of central and local governments, but also the institutional reform of grass-roots governments and enterprises. The latter one has started in late 1980's.

Reviewed from the reform progress, the reform of economic management system of Chinese government can be divided into three stages.

The first stage (1979 to 1986) was the beginning one of government reform, and also a step characterized by breaking down old system. Although the reform was elementary, it had spread in almost every aspects of economic managing system of government. The most representative measures included: a. increasing the probation units of enterprises independence rights; isolating central finance from local finance; transferring the approval power of investment projects to lower level of authority; conducting pilot run of comprehensive urban system reform; clarifying the adjustment means of economy by mandatory plan, instructive plan and market adjustment, decreasing mandatory plan; implementing "two track" system of prices of production materials; releasing control upon some industrial products and agricultural and sideline products; changing the original government purchasing system to contract purchasing; loosening state monopoly over the operation of commodities and materials; permitting the existence of competition of all kinds of economic components; implementing the reform of the two step "profit to tax"

The second stage (1986 to 1991). The government reform develops and deepens steadily. The most obvious characteristic in this stage is stressing the transformation of government function in theoretical cognition. The center of each reform of economic managing system all revolves around functional transformation. In this period, contract responsibility operation system have been widely adopted

The period after 1992 is the third stage when the macro adjustment and control system was set up according to the mode of socialist market economy. Among the measures of government economic management in this period, there are four outstanding aspects: (1) The implementation of modern enterprise institution and the appearance of managing agency of state-owned assets made a big pace toward the direction of government-enterprise separation. (2) The practice of labor contrast system in enterprises and civil servant system in government agency thoroughly changed the old labor and personnel system. (3) The reform of tax apportionment made the relationship between central and local government close with the norm of market economy. (4) The government accelerated the pace of reform of financial system and foreign trade system, set up the policy bank and commercial bank, opened the stock market and futures market, all of which made the factor market burgeon quickly. The reform of exchange rate made the domestic and foreign market concatenate together.

THE CONNOTATION OF ADAPTATION OF GOVERNMENT BEHAVIORS TO MARKETIZATION

Marketization is a trend through which the economic system of a society develops toward the orientation of market economy. The so-called market economy is a kind of economic form where social resources are regulated by market. Therefore, marketization is a dynamic concept reflecting the degree of market development. In fact, there are two different meanings about the concept of marketization: one is the development from natural economy to market economy in developing countries, and the other is the reform of traditional planned economy in socialist countries. These are two kinds of marketization with different features and contents. As a developing socialist country, China has both of the two kinds of marketization at present. The first kind is mainly a spontaneous and natural process, which can be affected but not replaced by the government behaviors. Meanwhile, it is in a subordinate position in the present marketization of China. However, marketization of the second kind, especially for socialist countries, is promoted by the government. To a great extent it is the transformation of the change of government behaviors. Therefore, our concern is on the marketization with the second meaning, that is, the transformation and its extent in the progress of transformation from traditional planned economy to market economy in China.

In socialist planned economy, the most important attribute of government is it is the owner of public-ownership economy. This is the most essential difference of it from other types of governments. Therefore, the government in planned economy is both the administrator of social economy and the owner of public-ownership economy. Since the traditional planned economy is a uniform economic organization which covers all the society, the government as the owner of public economy, does not conduct capital operation and profit like the owners in market economy, but like those in natural economy, is engaged in self-sufficient production. The government is both the owner and producer, carrying out the function of production operator.

In market economy, however, government carries out three economic functions:

1. To stipulate and maintain the market economic regulation. Government uses its special position to stipulate and maintain the market economic rules, fight against illegal behaviors, protect the legal rights of market participants and ensure the smooth running of market economy.

2. To regulate market economy. Government uses various economic leverages to regulate supply-demand relationship, to keep the stability of macro-economy, promote the development of economy and maintain a stable economic environment.
3. To participate in market as an ordinary subject. Government buys products as a customer and produces as an investor.

During the period of transformation from traditional planned economy to modern market economy, the transformation of government behaviors mainly embodies in three aspects:

1. The separation of dual roles. Government should mainly act as the administrator of social economy. The government should gradually clarify its identity and function as the owner and social administrator, and form a mutual control and mutual serving mechanism. The purpose of reform is to seek an effective combined point at which not only the state-owned asset could be protected and increased, but also the social managing function of government could be exerted effectively.
2. The change from directly participating in micro-economy activity to macro-regulation. In traditional planned economy, government directly takes part in the activities of microeconomic organizations, and became to "general manager" of every individual enterprise. This is closely related to the government system, enterprises system and market environment in planned economy system. However, in market economy the government system and the enterprise institution are essentially different from that in planned economy, the object of government regulation changes from enterprises to market, modulating economic activities by means of macro adjustment. It guides the goal of enterprise to be in conformity with that of the state by market adjustment.
3. The changes from direct control to indirect adjustment. In traditional planned economy, government controls the economy with direct administrative methods, adapting to the direct intervention with enterprise operation. In market economy, enterprise is independent economic subject rather that the subordinate of government. It has its own independent profit target and won't complete abide by the instructions of government. The behaviors of enterprise are adjusted by market information. An effective market system is the essential guarantee of economic development. To avoid the disturbance and distortion of market parameters, government should cut down the direct intervention of market parameters as much as possible, and adjust the economy mainly through fiscal policy and monetary policy.

THE EVALUATION INDEXES OF ADAPTATION OF GOVERNMENT BEHAVIORS TO MARKETIZATION

According to previous analysis, we devise a set of evaluation indexes measuring the adaptation of government behaviors to marketization, indicated by F. F consists of three parts: $F1$ is the index of financial income structure, or the index of government function changing. $F2$ denotes the index of government withdrawing from the microeconomic region and $F3$ the index of conversion of government modulatory method. This set of indexes only reflect the government behaviors, without including the scale of government activity, and also purely show the progress of economic reform, without including the index of economic development. The target of economic system reform is promote economic development, Either the transformation of planned economy, or the breakdown of natural economy, is definitely accompanied by economic development. However, they are not the same and usually non-synchronize. Generally speaking, system change (marketization) is the cause and precondition of economic development, and economic development is the result and representation of system change. But, the indexes of national economic statistics mainly reflect the economic development rather than the marketization of economic system. When measuring the degree of adaptation of government behaviors to market, to exclude the factors of economic development, we all use relative values, to reflect the degree of the changes of the system itself. For example, $F1$ reflects the change of government function by the variation of fiscal income proportion. Because we observe the composing of income rather than the amount of financial income, the influence of fluctuation factors induced by economic development, thus, is excluded. These indexes can suit different levels of economic development, or it will not be invalid with the change of time.. We now explain these indexes in details.

F1: the Index of Change of Financial Income Structure or the Government Function Identity

Generally, as the administrator of social economy, the benefit of the government is represented by tax revenue; as the owner, the realization of its economic benefit is by rent and interest, and as the producer, its benefit is achieved by profit. However, the government of planned economy is a combination of administrator, owner and producer, and so its benefit includes both revenue and profit of state-owned enterprises. The benefit of Chinese government is represented by fiscal incomes that mainly include revenue, enterprise income (profit) and subsidy to enterprise (negative profit). Revenue reflects the role of administrator of government, enterprise income and subsidy are the embodiment of owner's function. The change of government function will be reflected through the proportion of the, so we can measure the degree of the change of government function by the index of financial income structure:

$$F1 = \frac{revenue - (income - subsidy)}{total\ income}$$

The income and subsidy are both profit of owner with only one difference: the former positive, and the latter negative. The sum of their absolute value represents the activity scale of government as an owner, so we connect them with symbol "-"in the expression. The scope of F1 is [-1,1]. When the fiscal income wholly comes from revenue, (income-subsidy)=0, F1=1, government completely avoid intervening the microeconomic activity. This is the absolute market economy. When fiscal income =income-subsidy, revenue =0, F1=-1, government totally plays a role of owner. This is the pure planned economy. In the real world, F1 cannot be at extreme positions but lies between them.

F2: the Index of Government Withdrawal from the Microeconomic Region

Government's direct participation in micro economic activities in planned economy can be seen in the following areas: issuing mandatory instructions to enterprises, allocating production elements, directly appraising of all economic indexes of enterprises, appointing leaders of enterprises, deciding the investment and profit allocation of enterprises. The change of government behaviors adapting to marketization is withdrawing form the microeconomic region, loosening, even giving up the control over enterprises. But the reform of mandatory plan and reforms of allocation system of labor forces, capital and production materials are discrete and discontinuous, and so hard to analyze quantitatively. In order to analyze and compare quantitatively, we choose two indexes to measure the extent of government taking part in the microeconomic activity, they are proportion of economic construction in aggregate fiscal expenditure and proportion of investment in national budget in whole social investment on capital assets. The equations for them are:

$$F2_A = - \frac{the\ expenditure\ used\ in\ economic\ construction}{aggregate\ fiscal\ expenditure}$$

$$F2_B = - \frac{the\ investment\ in\ national\ budget}{the\ whole\ social\ investment\ on\ capital\ asserts}$$

Both $F2_A$ and $F2_B$ reflect the extent of government participation in the microeconomic activity, the larger the absolute value is, the more government participates in microeconomic activity; the smaller this absolute value is, the less participant extent is. Obviously, they are both negative indexes of government behavior's adaptation to market progress, so we add negative symbol "-"in front of them. Obviously the scope of $F2_A$ and $F2_B$ are both [-1,0].

$$F_2 = \frac{1}{2}\left(F_A + F_B\right)$$

These indexes overlap and mutually reflect the extent of government withdrawing from microeconomic region. Among them, $F2_A$ indicates the composing of government expenditure that reflects the change of government behavior. F_B indicates the extent of government withdrawing from the view of whole society. There are the same changing direction of $F2_A$ and $F2_B$, so we take their arithmetic average of the two.

F2 is the index of government withdrawing from the microeconomic region.

F3: the Index of Conversion of Government Regulatory Method

Government in planned economy directly controls the economy with administrational methods, including promulgating regulations, sending out redheaded writs, meetings and debriefing. The conversion towards indirect modulation is reflected on using economic and legal methods, which includes legislation, fiscal policy and monetary policy instead of administrational methods. Therefore, the conversion of government modulatory method should be reflected from the comparison between the number of laws and the number of regulations, and from the comparison between the law execution and the administrative meetings. However, it is difficult to design an index like that and collect information, so we select following two indexes as substitute: the proportion of price subsidy in fiscal income and the proportion of price subsidy in GNP. In fact, they are not the reflections of government intervening economy through administrative method, but we think that although the price subsidy is not the direct administrative intervention, it makes market parameters distorted, affects the function of market mechanism. Since price subsidy is analogous to government intervention, so it can be seen an index of government intervening market to some extent. Because the extent of distortion of market parameters by subsidy contorting is much less serious than that by administrative intervention, the precision of this index is accordingly lower than other indexes.

F3 consists of two sub-indexes: $F3_A$ is the proportion of price subsidy in fiscal income, $F3_B$ is the proportion of price subsidy in GNP:

$$F3_A = -\frac{\text{price subsidy}}{\text{fiscal income}}$$

$$F3_B = -\frac{\text{price subsidy}}{\text{GNP}}$$

Both $F3_A$ and $F3_B$ reflect the extent of government intervening market economy, the larger the absolute value, the more government intervenes the market; the smaller this absolute value, the less the intervention. Obviously, they are all negative indexes of government behaviors adapting to marketization, so we add negative symbol "-"in front of them. Consequently, the scope of F3 $_A$ and F3$_B$ are both [-1,0]. F3$_A$ stands for the decrease of government intervention from the view of fiscal expenditure and F3$_B$ from the view of whole society. The difference between F3 $_A$ and F3 $_B$ in their reflection is that F3 $_A$ is from the view of the government itself, while F3 $_B$ is for the whole society. There are the same changing direction of F3 $_A$ and F3$_B$, so we take the arithmetic average of them.

$$F3 = \frac{1}{2}\left(F3_A + F3_B\right)$$

F3 is the index of conversion of government modulatory method.

F: the Index of Adaptation of Government Behaviors to Marketization

F1, F2, F3 are three aspects of government behaviors adaptation to marketization, that is, the change from the owner to the administrator of social economy, the change from a producer directly taking part in the microeconomic activity to a macro-administrator and the change from direct modulation to indirect modulation. When we take their arithmetic average, we arrive at:

$$F4 = \frac{1}{3}\left(F1 + F2 + F3\right)$$

F4 is the index of government behaviors adapting to marketization. The scope of F4 is [-1,1/3].

Let

$$F = \frac{3}{4}(F4 + 1)$$

Then the scope of F becomes [0,1], the simple transformation above will not alter the changing trend but simplify the expression of F. So we use F to indicate the extent of government behaviors adapting to marketization. F=0 is the complete non-market economy, and F=1, the complete market economy.

THE MEASUREMENT OF ADAPTATION OF CHINESE GOVERNMENT BEHAVIORS TO MARKETIZATION SINCE REFORM

We have measured the extent of Chinese government behaviors adaptation to marketization since the reform in 1979. See the data in Table 3.1.

Table 3.1 The Indexes of Government Behaviors Adaptation to Marketization

Year	F	F1	F2	F2$_A$	F2$_B$	F3	F3$_A$	F3$_B$
1979		0.041		-0.598		-0.041	-0.062	-0.020
1980		0.126		-0.553		-0.062	-0.097	-0.026
1981	0.573	0.236	-0.384	-0.448	-0.279	-0.088	-0143	-0.033
1982	0.688	0.359	-0.349	-0.471	-0.227	-0.093	-0.149	-0.036
1983	0.728	0.428	-0.365	-0.492	-0.238	-0.093	-0.153	-0.034
1984	0.779	0.447	-0.369	-0.507	-0.230	-0.086	-0.141	-0.030
1985		-*	-0.322	-0.485	-0.160	-0.086	-0.142	-0.029
1986	0.839	0.763	-0.338	-0.530	-0.146	-0.068	-0.111	-0.025
1987	0.833	0.727	-0.323	-0.515	-0.131	-0.073	-0.120	-0.025
1988	0.837	0.720	-0.303	-0.516	-0.090	-0.069	-0.117	-0.021
1989	0.837	0.700	-0.277	-0.472	-0.083	-0.075	-0.128	-0.022
1990	0.830	0.654	-0.268	-0.448	-0.071	-0.065	-0.110	-0.021
1991	0.841	0.666	-0.245	-0.422	-0.068	-0.058	-0.098	-0.017
1992	0.850	0.672	-0.229	-0.415	-0.043	-0.043	-0.073	-0.012
1993	0.873	0.746	-0.221	-0.405	-0.038	-0.033	-0.057	-0.009
1994	0.911	0.912	-0.235	-0.437	-0.032	-0.031	-0.054	-0.009
1995	0.914	0.915	-0.222	-0.413	-0.031	-0.035	-0.063	-0.006
1996	0.908	0.887	-0.223	-0.419	-0.027	-0.032	-0.057	-0.007

Source: all data from "*Chinese Statistics Yearbook*".
* According to calculation, the F1 in this year is larger than 1, so it is omitted.

The result above has two problems. First, the value is too large. F reaches 80% in the middle 1980s and even 90% in the middle of 1990s, which does not correspond with people's usual consideration. Second, the diversity among years is too small, and the curve that draws according to table 1 is almost a straight line, which is hard to reflect the change of government administrative system.

The main reasons are that the temporal frame of reference we have chosen is too large. The scope of F changes from complete non-market economy to complete market economy, which reflects a time span from the generation of commodity and nation to the modern market economy, involving the whole history of evolution of social economy system. In addition, the traditional planned economy system in socialist country is not a complete non-market economy, which includes a certain extent of market economy. All of these factors make the scope of index F much narrower; it might change, say, from 0.5 to 1 rather than from 0 to 1. So it is necessary to change the temporal frame of reference of our measurement, in other words, to use a larger scale. We take the traditional planned system in commencement of reform as zero point, so the original expression of F can be transferred to:

$$F0 = \frac{1}{a}F - \left(\frac{1}{a} - 1\right)$$

In the equation, a stands for the extent of government behaviors adaptation to marketization in traditional system, which can be represented by the extent of government behaviors in 1960 when the extent of administrative control is highest in the history. F0 is the extent of Chinese government behaviors adaptation to marketization in contrast to the traditional system. The scope of F0 is [0,1]; 0 means a complete planned economy, and 1 a complete market economy. Before 1981, the financial statistical items are inadequate, and the only figures available are F1 and $F2_A$. These data tell us that the extent of government behaviors adaptation to market economy is lowest in 1960, which is about 44.9% according to the average of F1 and $F2_A$. Let a=0.449, calculate the relevant F0, the result is in table 3-2.

Table 3.2 The degree of Chinese Government Behaviors Adapting to Marketization

Year	F0	Year	F0	Year	F0
1981	5.4	1987	62.8	1992	66.6
1982	30.5	1988	63.7	1993	71.7
1983	39.4	1989	63.7	1994	80.2
1984	50.8	1990	62.2	1995	80.9
1986	64.2	1991	64.6	1996	79.5

We can use graph to represent the extent of Chinese government behaviors adapting to market economy clearly

Figure 3.1 The Curve of Chinese Government Behaviors Adapting to Marketization

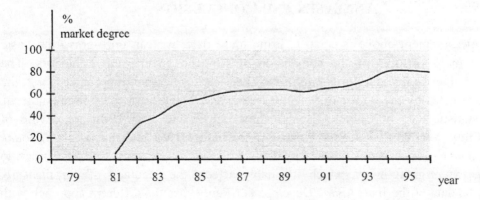

In the result above, the value of a is obtained according to the equation $\alpha = \frac{1}{2}(F1 + F2_A)$. In the three components of F, F3 is quite small and may be omitted without affecting the accuracy. Besides, $F2_A$ and $F2_B$ are complementary parts of F, so it is feasible to use $F2_A$ only when $F2_B$ absents. Therefore, equation $a = \frac{1}{2}(F1 + F2_A)$ becomes a succinct index of government behaviors adapting to marketization. We can compare the extent of Chinese government behaviors adapting to marketization with other countries using this succinct index.

In the annual statistic data of the *World Bank Development Report*, there are two indexes, which are the proportion of non-tax income in the fiscal income and the proportion of expenditure of economic activity in aggregate fiscal expenditure, respectively resemble our indexes of F1 and $F2_A$. So we can use our succinct index and the annual statistic data of the *World Bank Development Report* to measure the extent of government behaviors of mature market economy countries adapting to market, and compare them with that of Chinese government. Because we lack data of Japanese government, we only measure the other six main market economy countries. The result is in table 3.3.

Table 3.3 The Comparison of Government Behaviors Adapting to Marketization with China and Other Mature Market Economy Countries

Country	China	U.S	U.K	France	Germany	Italy	Canada	The Mean
F0(%)	79.5	95.7	95.1	96.7	96.8	96.7	93.5	95.8
Year	1996	Average of 1972 and 1980-1992						

Source: Calculation based upon the data of the *World Bank Development Report*

ANALYSES AND CONCLUSION

The measurement above is cursory. From these data, we can only grasp the basic trend and main features of the conversion of Chinese government behaviors. The numerical value we get is not accurate in fact, just having relative importance. First, the value are affected by the reform of revenue system and the adjustment of fiscal subjects, and the statistic data of Chinese fiscal income before and after 1986 are devoid of comparability. Second, the statistic data of China before 1981 and that of *World Bank Development Report* can not fit our target, so we have to use some succinct index to substitute the original index, which inevitably affects the accuracy of our measure. Besides, the data of the *World Bank Development Report* has the different approach with Chinese statistic data. Although there are some defects in our research, it still has particular academic value, which lies in that we attempt to measure the accommodating change of government behaviors in the marketization with a scientific method, and try to obtain a numerical value. All of these are never done before.

We can make some analyses according to the foregoing result.

1. The extent of Chinese government behaviors adapting to marketization has been rising steadily since the reform, which is consistent with the whole trend of Chinese economic marketization. The value of F0 changes from 5.4% in 1981 to 79.5% in 1996, an increase of 74.1 %.. But the pace of increase trends to descend as time goes by. This is because during the early stage of reform, the government behaviors are totally unfit for market economy, so a little change toward marketization can remarkably increase the extent of its adaptation to market economy. With the reform deepening and the extent reaching a higher level, only the substantial reform measure further could promote the degree of marketization improvement.

2. The changing process of government behaviors adaptation to marketization can be obviously divided into stages. We can roughly divide it into 3 stages. From 1979 to 1986 is the beginning stage, characterized by the sudden increase of extent of government behaviors adaptation to marketization. The value of F0 rises nearly horizontally and sharply from almost 0 to 64.2% within 7 years. The second stage is from 1987 to 1990, during the period the change of government behaviors nearly stagnates. F0 decreases 2 point instead of increase. The third stage is from 1991 to 1995, during which the extent of government behaviors adapting to market economy increases again. F0 reaches the highest point of 80.9% in this stage. In 1996 F0 decreases 1.6 point, though slight, the trend become different. But we still can not sure whether it means commence of a new stage because time is early for us to reach the conclusion. The characteristics of the stages of the government behaviors adaptation to market approximately parallel with that of economic authoritative departments with slight difference. But the difference just shows that there is a distance in the reform measures and the actual conversion of its behaviors.

3. The development of marketization reform in different aspect of government behaviors is unbalanced and they do not and cannot develop equally. In the burgeoning phase of reform, F2 and F3 decreased and increased dramatically, which on one hand reflects difficulties and conflicts of early reform, and on the other hand, reflects the features of Chinese reform. During early days of the reform, the most important measures of reform are to reduce the government control, which could be reflected from the rapid increase of market indexes. The decline of F2 reflects the increase of proportion of national budgetary investment, which illustrates that the development of Chinese market economy is under the support of government plan. The decline of F3 reflects the increase of proportion of price subsidy in fiscal income and GNP, which illustrate that the features of "buying reform with money" in the early phase of reform. Altogether, the decline of F2 and F3 shows that in the first stage of reform, the government took moderate principles and thought about the benefit of all aspects. The reform of this period is impelled and controlled by government.

4. Compared with the mature market economy countries, the level of government behaviors adapting to marketization still has big disparity. The mean F of the six developed market economy countries in1980s is 95.8%, 16 points higher than the current level of our country. This status shows that although the marketization of our country has obtained remarkable effect, there is a long way to go before reaching the goal of developed market economy.

REFERENCES

Chen Zongsheng. 1987. "On Reform of Economic Decision-making System", Fujian Forum(Issue 4).

Chen Zongsheng and Zhou,Bin. 1998. "Measurement of Marketization of China's Economic System", *Sournal of Social Sciences* (Summer).

Development Report of World Bank(1981—1993).Beijing: Chinese Financial and Economic Press.

Sheng Hong.1994 *Labor Division and Transaction.* Shanghai: Shanghai Sanlian Press.*Statistical Yearbook of China(1981—1993)*.Beijing: statistical Press of China.

Stigler, G. J.1975,1983. *The Citizen and the State*; *The Organization of Industry.* (Chinese edition,1996: *Industrial Organization and Government Regulation*).Shanghai: Shanghai Sanlian Press.

Zhou,Bin and Xie, Hui. 1997. "Research on the Reform of Government Administrative Departments of Industry", paper presented at the "Nankai Institute of Economics Academic Seminar Fortnightly".

ZhuGuanghua.1995. *Economic Functions of Government and System Reform.* Tianjin: Tianjin People's Press

MEASUREMENT AND ANALYSIS OF THE MARKETIZATION OF COMMODITY PRICE SYSTEM IN CHINA

After reform, the price reform has achieved remarkable progress. The price formation mechanism has been transformed from a highly centralized planned price formation mechanism to a market one. The traditional situation that the prices of both goods and service are exclusively controlled by the government has been changed and now most of the prices for commodities and service are formed in the market.

The marketization of price formation mechanism is propelled by the price reform, therefore, it is consistent with the price reform process. What on earth is the marketization of price formation mechanism like? To what extent is our marketization of price formation? To answer these questions, we need specific data, and take quantitative measurements and give a detailed analysis.

A BRIEF RETROSPECT OF THE PRICE REFORM PROCESS

In China, prices are highly-centralized planned before the 3rd Plenary Session of the 11th CPC Central Committee in 1978. This price formation mechanism had played an active role in the history, but its maladies revealed with the economic development process: the planned prices remained unchanged for a long time; they deviated from values and did not reflect the relations of demand and supply; the prices of agriculture products, raw materials were commonly lower than their value; production costs were not equally compensated. All these restricted the development of economy and the adjustment of production structure, meanwhile they imposed heavy burden upon the finance of the state. Under such circumstances the price formation started. The 18 years price reform course can be divided into five phases.

Initial phase (1979-1984)

This phase is characterized by "adjustment". Because the focal points of reformation were dealt with and safe measures were taken to guarantee success, the irrational price structure was straightened up preliminarily. In view of the situation of the inequitable price parities between industrial and agricultural products, the government raised purchasing prices for agricultural products by a big margin. Compared with 1978, the purchasing prices of the agricultural products increased by about 50% in 1984, and the price parities between them decreased by about 30%. Preliminary adjustment was also made with regard to the inequitable price parities between the fuels, raw materials and the manufactured goods. Compared with 1978, in 1984 the coal price rose by 38%, the prices of mineral products and raw materials went up by an average of 50% in metallurgy, chemical, material industry; the prices of some industrial consumption goods in light industry, textile industry and medicine industry varied, but remaining approximate the level; the prices of electronic products decreased by about 20%.

In this phase, some obviously unsounded prices were readjusted, which improved the production and operation condition and was beneficial to some products in some important industry. The reform achieved good results. But the readjustment was within the planned-price system. The problem of the rigidity of planned prices and constant changing of relative costs of all kinds of products could not be solved by the readjustment to some prices. The new price distortion emerged constantly. All industrial sectors vied for price adjustment and readjusted prices by all means, which made the state bureau of prices stranded. In this difficult situation, the government realized the importance of the marketization of price formation, which pushed the price reform forward.

Developing phase (1984-1988)

This phase is characterized by the combination of "readjustment" with "decontrol". The price reform was fully conducted in two aspects of administrative system and price structure. The market mechanism was introduced in to the price formulation and price administration. Three kinds of prices--the government-set price, the government-stipulated price and the market price--began to exist side by side. In this phase, the state monopoly in purchasing agricultural products was replaced by purchasing by means of a contract of fixed quotas. The prices of most the industrial consumer goods and non-stable foods were decontrolled, such as cigarettes, wines of famous brands, bicycles, radios, poultry, aquatic products, fruits, etc. The prices of industrial capital goods were formed under "two-track" planned price system. The restrictions of the 20% rise in the prices of goods over the plan were abandoned. The prices of all the small commodities were decontrolled.

In this phase, the price reform made great progress in the adjustment of both the price administration system and the price structure. But the reform was in complete and the government did not take the macro-control in time so that prices of some of the products hiked and were to some extent out of control. To make it worse the economy developed so fast that inflation occurred and panic purchase took place frequently. In the mean time, the "two-track" planned prices of important capital goods abetted such corrupted practices as "going through the back door" and "scalping the planned goods.". This phase was important to marketization of price formation but the economy was disordered this time. The government agencies had to take necessary measures to rectify the economic order.

Rectification phase (1988-1991)

Price reform of this phase centralized on dealing with inflation, rectification of the economic order and control of the general price level of retail goods. The macro-control ability of price and comprehensive tackling were enhanced. Price administration was reinforced and severe measures were taken to check the rise of prices, such as stabilizing the price level of the people's living necessities, halting arbitrary or disguised price hike of agricultural capital goods, fixing the ceiling prices of the key capital goods above the plan, straightening out prices in circulation banning exploitation by intermediate links, controlling and stipulating prices of the industrial consumer goods whose prices had been decontrolled, and regulating charges of city public utilities and services, etc..

The measures taken in this phase suppressed inflation and ordered the economy, and paved the way for further price reform. The rectification relied mainly on the means of planned administration, and so the marketization of price formation retrogressed in some aspects and there was a resurgence of thoughts and methods of planned economy.

Deepening phase (1992-1993)

This phase is characterized by "decontrol". The market price formation mechanism took shape tentatively. In 1992, Deng Xiaoping made a trip to inspect south China and made his famous remarks on China's economic reform. Influenced by his remarks, the price reform took a further step. The ratio of market prices increased sharply, above 20%. The market price occupied the leading position in price formulation. By the end of 1993, among the goods whose prices were set or stipulated by the government were only some of medicines, agricultural capital goods, salt, gold ornament, etc in retail goods; cotton, silkworm cocoon, flue-cured tobacco, etc. in agricultural products. Prices of grains and edible oils were decontrolled nationwide. Of the product materials, only the prices of only such goods were controlled by the government as some coal, electricity, crude oil, natural gas, a few of the chemical devices, mechanical and electrical equipment. While the prices of most of the planned steel, part of the iron ore, cement etc. was completely decontrolled.

Deng Xiaoping's remarks during his trip to the south restarted the process of marketization of price formulation. The reform of this phase resulted in that most of the prices were formulated in the market, which in turn could regulate the operation of the economy and very important to the marketization of the economy system. The decontrol of the prices of most of the capital goods got rid of the disadvantages of "two-track" price system. It is the decisive phase of the marketization of price formation course.

Consummating phase (1994-)

In this phase, hyperinflation took place in the economy, and to check the inflation is the first priority on the government macro-control agenda. Macro-control and the price administration were enhanced so as to keep the inflation low and to stabilize the people's life. In March, 1994 for instance, the State Council demanded the government at all levels supervise and check the prices of daily necessities and services specifically including: grain, oil, staple and non-staple food, articles of everyday, civil fuels, services, and so on altogether 20 different varieties. Prices of contract-purchasing grains and grain ration were determined by the government, so were of crude oil, finished oil. Prices of the steels, whether for basic construction or infrastructure and for military and agriculture use were stipulated by the government for they are most critical to the nation's economy and the people's livelihood. Prices of all the planned coals were decontrolled and formulated in the market, which further promoted the transformation of the price formulation mechanism.

Judging the situation, the government took back some of the pricing power, administered more effectively the goods which cannot be lessened or were not qualified for being lessened so as to change the situation of price disorder. It is the eligible improving price administration that pushed the marketization of price formulation forward.

THE SYMBOLS AND EVALUATION INDEXES OF THE MARKETIZATION OF PRICE FORMULATION

There are two meanings of the price formulation. Narrowly speaking, it means the manufacturer and the distributor of a commodity set the price according to the law of economy and to the relations of demand and supply. The current market adjustment price in China belongs to this category, in addition the state stipulated price has partial nature of marketization. Broadly speaking, marketization of price formation should also includes the prices controlled by the government because these prices should also be fixed according to the production cost, profits, demand-supply relations and the law of value. In this chapter, we research on the marketization of price formulation and its extent from the narrow point of view. The marketization degree of price formulation increases with the deepening of the price reform because the process of the price administration system reform is the course that the government lessens the pricing power constantly and let the price be formulated in the market and in the course of exchange.

Three Symbols of Marketization of Price Formation:

1. The manufacturer and the distributor $\geq$ r have the completed discretion to fix the price of their own. We use a to stand for this symbol, $0 \leq a \leq 1$. If the manufacturer and distributor have the complete pricing power, $\alpha = 1$; otherwise $\alpha = 0$. If the manufacturer and the distributor have incomplete or partial pricing power, $0 < \alpha < 1$.

2. Full competition in the course price formulation. b is used to indicate this symbol, $0 \leq b \leq 1$. If the price is formulated in a completely competitive marker, $b=1$. If there is no competition, the price is monopoly, $0 < b < 1$.

3. Prices regulate resource allocation and demand-supply relations. This symbol is represented by c. $0 \leq c \leq 1$. If prices play an active role in regulating the resources allocation as well as the demand supply relations, $c=1$; otherwise $c= 0$. When prices function only to some extent, $0 < c < 1$.

The Evaluation Index for Marketization of Price Formulation

The marketization of price formation was decided by three factors: the manufacture and distributor's discretionary powers in pricing, the price formulation in a complete competitive market and the price regulation of resources allocation and the adjustment to the demand-supply relations. These 3 factors make up the evaluation index of the marketization degree of price formation when they function jointly. This index is represented by r.

$$\gamma = \sqrt[3]{abc} \quad 0 \leq \gamma \leq 1$$

When $\gamma = 1$, the degree of marketization of price formulation is 100%. It is impossible in actual economy, for competition and monopoly co-existed in most economy system.

When $\gamma = 0$, prices are decided by the force beyond the market such as the price formation in the former countries of highly centralized planned economy.

When $0 < \gamma < 1$, some of the prices are formulated in the market and the others are still controlled by the government. The degree of the marketization of price formulation is reflected by the ratio variations of these two kinds of goods to total, respectively. This is the normal case in the actual economy.

Evaluation of the Marketization of the Current Three Kinds of Prices in China

There are three kinds of prices in China at present: the government-set price, the government-stipulated price and the market price. P_i denotes evaluation of them, i=1, 2, 3.

P_1: evaluation of the government-set price.
P_2: evaluation of the government-stipulated price.
P_3: evaluation of the market price.

The producer and the management have no discretion on the government-set price, therefore, a=0.

With regard to the government-stipulated price goods, the management and the producer may fix the price within the government-stipulated scope. This kind of prices is decided partly under competition and can regulate the relations of demand and supply to some degree. For the sake of convenience, we assume a, b, c=0.5.

$$P_3 = \sqrt[3]{abc} = \sqrt[3]{0.5^3} = 0.5$$

As for the market price goods, their price formation generally accords with the demands of the three symbols of marketization, that is a=b=c=1.

$$P_3 = \sqrt[3]{abc} = 1$$

MEASUREMENT OF MARKETIZATION OF PRICE FORMULATION

For the purpose of the evaluation of the marketization degree of price formation, goods and services are classified into four categories: retail goods, agricultural by-products, industrial capital goods and administrative and operational service fees. First, we measure the marketization of price formation for each price form of each category, then we use the results as weights to calculate the marketization degree of each category. Finally, we use the new results as weights again to work out the overall marketization degree of price formation in China. We evaluate the marketization degree on the basis of the first three categories for there is no statistical data for the last one.

1. We use R_j to denote the index of marketization of price formation for the last one.

$$R_j = \sum P_i X_{ij} / \sum X_{ij}$$

P_i denotes the marketization evaluation of the three price forms; i is the ordinal number of each price form; j is the ordinal number of each category; X_{ij} is the total goods value of each price form.

2. We denote the marketization of each category by R_k:

$$R_k = \sum P_j X_{jk} / \sum X_{jk}$$

k is the ordinal number of each category; X_{jk} is the goods value of each category.

3. R represents the synthetic index of marketization of price formation

$$R_j = \sum P_k X_k / \sum X_k$$

X_k is the goods value of each category.

EVALUATION OF MARKETIZATION OF PRICE FORMULATION IN CHINA (1979-1995)

The ratios of the three price forms are the crucial data for the evaluation. China's price bureaus survey these three price forms and their ratios since 1990. In order to evaluate the marketization degree since economic reform, we need to analyze and estimate the marketization degree of price formation of some important years (1979, 1984 and 1988) during 1979-1989.

First, let's ascertain the data of marketization in 1979. According to the price bureau' statistics, the ratio of the goods value to total is 97% whose prices were set by the government; that is 92.6% of agricultural by-products and 100% of the sales income of industrial capital goods. We assume the prices except the government-set price one were market-regulated. The ratios of market price to three categories are 3%, 7.4%, 0, respectively. If we work out the weights of retail goods, agricultural by-products purchases and sales income of capital goods we could estimate the marketization of price formation in 1979.

Table 4.1 Ratios of the Three Categories to the Total

	Retail goods	Agriculture by-products	Capital goods	Total
Amount of money (one hundred million yuan)	8033.52	3204.84	9753.69	20992.05
Proportion(%)	38	15	47	100

Source: The Former Department of Synthesis under the State Bureau of Commodity Prices

Notes: Of the information from the government price bureaus only the corresponding amounts of money of the three price forms of 1990: are available; they are not available in the following 5 years and only the ratios of them are announced. There fore, we use the ratios of the value of retail goods, agricultural goods and capital goods to total, respectively, as the weights to calculate the marketization degree of price formation.

The marketization degree of price formulation of 1979 can be calculated as follows:

$$R = 38 \times 3 + 15 \times 7.4 + 47 \times 0 = 2.25\%$$

Obviously the degree is very low.

From 1979 to 1984, the reform was characterized by "readjustment". The government mainly readjusted the purchasing prices of agricultural products and the price of raw materials. Readjustment to price parity and price difference improved the price system, which created favorable conditions for price decontrol. It can be regarded as the preparing period of the full price decontrol. The marketization went formation developed rapidly.

The ratio of market price went up. The prices of most of the industrial consumer goods and non-staple food were decontrolled. The limit of 20% rise was abolished for the industrial capital goods beyond the plan. The limit of small commodities is completely decontrolled. The three price forms began to stand side by side with the reform of price administration system. We appraise the marketization of price formation in 1988 positively because the reform decontrolled the prices and let the price be formulated spontaneously in the market. This means the marketization of price formation went further by a leap in 1988. We should assess the value of R in 1988 relatively high. Referring to the value in 1990, we can determine it. R is 54.5% in 1990 when the government was rectifying the economy order, therefore, it should be a bit more than in 1990. We make it 60%.

The course of marketization of price formation was interfered in when the government began to rectify the economic order and improve the economic environment in the fourth quarter of 1988. R value dropped a little during 1989-1990, but the marketization trends of price formation were already irreversible.

The marketization degree during 1990-1995 is calculated in Table 4-2.

Table 4.2 Ratio of the Three Price Forms in China, 1990-1995 %

Category	administration level	Ratio of government-set price						Ratio of government stipulated						ratio of market price					
		1990	1991	1992	1993	1994	1995	1990	1991	1992	1993	1994	1995	1990	1991	1992	1993	1994	1995
Retail goods	total	29.8	20.9	5.9	4.8	7.2	8.8	17.2	10.3	1.1	1.4	2.4	2.4	53.0	68.8	93.0	90.8	90.4	88.8
	central	16.3	11.9	3.3	2.5	3.5	4.0	5.4	2.8	0.2	0.4	0.4	0.5						
	province	9.7	5.6	2.2	1.9	3.0	3.6	8.6	4.7	0.6	0.6	1.6	1.3						
	city	3.8	3.4	0.4	0.4	0.7	1.2	3.2	2.8	0.3	0.4	0.4	0.6						
Agricultural by-products	total	25.0	22.2	12.5	10.4	16.6	17.0	23.4	20.0	5.7	2.1	4.1	4.4	51.6	57.8	81.8	87.5	79.3	78.6
	central	23.8	20.2	12.3	9.3	15.3	14.9	9.9	9.4	3.3	1.1	1.3	2.1						
	province	0.9	1.2	0.1	1.0	1.2	2.0	11.7	7.6	1.4	0.6	2.2	1.7						
	city	0.3	0.8	0.1	0.1	0.1	0.1	1.8	3.0	0.8	0.4	0.6	0.6						
Capital Goods	total	44.6	36.0	18.7	13.8	14.7	15.6	19.0	18.3	7.5	5.1	5.3	6.5	36.4	45.7	73.8	81.1	80.0	77.9
	central	33.4	26.7	14.5	10.4	10.7	11.5	12.5	11.2	5.6	3.4	4.0	4.8						
	province	8.5	6.9	3.1	2.4	3.4	3.5	5.0	5.6	5.7	1.3	0.9	1.4						
	city	8.7	2.4	1.1	1.0	0.6	0.6	1.5	1.5	0.2	0.4	0.4	0.3						

Source: *China Price Yearbook 1996*, p.388.

Note: The data of Inner Mongolia, Guizhou and Tibet are not available in 1994; the data of Hainan and Tibet are not available in 1995.

Table 4.3 R_k Value Calculated from Table 4.2 %

Category	R_k					
	1990	1991	1992	1993	1994	1995
retail goods	61.6	74.0	93.6	94.5	91.6	90
Agricultural by-products	63.3	67.8	84.7	88.6	81.4	80.8
Capital goods	45.9	54.9	77.6	83.7	82.7	81.2

To calculate R value from 1990 to 1995, we still use the ratios of retail goods, agricultural by-products purchase and sales income as well as that of industrial capital goods to the total as the weights respectively. (See Table 4-1)

Table 4.4 R-value Calculated from Table 4-3

Year	1990	1991	1992	1993	1994	1995
R	54.5	64.1	84.7	88.5	85.9	84.5

On the basis of the evaluation and calculation above, we get the following R value table (1979-1995), which reflects basically the process of marketization of price formation during these years.

Table 4.5 R-value in 1979-1995

Year	1979	1984	1988	1990	1991	1992	1993	1994	1995
R	2.25	15	60	54.5	64.1	84.7	88.5	85.9	84.5

According to Table 4.5, We draw the curve for marketization of price formation in 1979-1995.

Figure 4.1 Marketization of Price Formation, 1979-1995

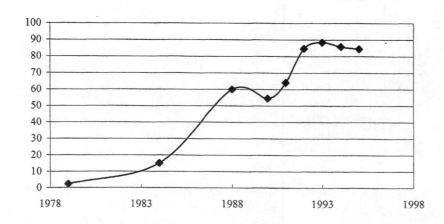

From figure 4.1, we know the curve has two peaks, which is consistent with the government's loose or tight policy in the economy system reform course.

Price reform varies greatly in different regions of China. In some places (Shenzhen, Guangdong Province for instance), prices are decontrolled in advance. The price reform of the coastal areas is consistent with the whole reform process while the inland regions lagged behind of China. The national statistical data roughly reflect the marketization process. In order to measure the marketization of price formation accurately, we surveyed comparatively the data from Tianjin, measured and analyzed in detail the marketization process of price formulation of this city.

MEASUREMENT OF MARKETIZATION OF PRICE FORMATION IN TIANJIN (1990-1995)

From 1992 to 1993, the price reform was in the deepening phase characterized by "decontrol". In these years, marketization of price formulation reached its highest degree. It helpful to further improvement of the price formulation mechanism to improve the price formation mechanism, measure and analyze the degree of the marketization of price formation in this particular phase is.

According to the goods value and the ratio of the goods value of the three price forms to retail goods, agricultural by-products and capital goods, we may work out the marketization degree of price formation of Tianjin from 1990 to 1995 by the designed equation for measurement of marketization. As the commercial and trade center in North China and one of the four municipalities directly under the Central Government, Tianjin is typical in terms of the marketization of price formulation. Refer to table 4-6~4-10 for specific data and results.

Figure 4.2 Marketization of Price Formation Process in Tianjin (1990-1995)

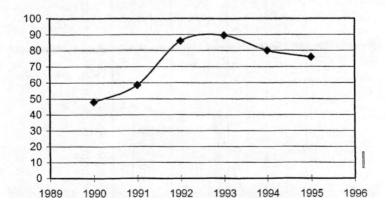

Table 4.6 Ratio of Goods Value of Three Price Forms to the Total Retail Goods and Marketization Degree of Price Formation (in 100 million RMB yuan)

Classification	total	government-set price		government stipulated price		market price		marketization degree
	(1)	amount (2)	Ratio (3)=(2)/(1)	amount (4)	ratio (5)=(4)/(1)	amount (6)=(1)-(2)-(4)	ratio (7)=(6)/(1)	(8)=(0.5δ(4)+(6))/(1)
Food	70.95	22.9	32.27			48.05	67.73	67.73
Clothing	30.09			2.43	8.10	27.66	91.9	95.96
Daily Articles	42.76	0.08	0.19	1.1	2.57	41.58	97.24	98.52
Cultural and recreation goods	12.57	0.88				12.57	100	100
Book magazine newspaper	2.24	2.01	39.29			1.36	60.71	60.71
Medicine and medical apparatus and instruments	10.05	2.01	20			8.04	80	80
Fuel	4.60	4.38	95.22			0.22	4.78	4.78
Agricultural capital goods	14.42					14.42	100	100
Total	187.68	30.25	16.12	3.53	1.88	153.9	82	82.94

Source: Tianjin Bureau of Commodity prices.

Note: Marketization degree is calculated in accordance with the formula

$R_J = \sum P_i X_{ij} / \sum X_{ij}$ and $R_k = \sum R_J X_{jk} / \sum X_{jk}$, so are those of other years.

Table 4.7 Ratio of Goods Value of Three Price Forms to Total Agricultural By-products and Marketization Degree of Price Formation (in 100 million RMB yuan)

Classification	total	government-set price		government price	stipulated	market price		marketization degree %
	(1)	amount (2)	Ratio (3)=(2)/(1)	amount (4)	ratio (5)=(4)/(1)	amount (6)=(1)-(2)-(4)	ratio (7)=(6)/(1)	(8)=(0.58(4)+(6))/(1)
Cereals	5.37	1.88	32.96			3.6	67.04	67.04
Cash crop	10.7	3.8	35.51			6.9	64.49	64.49
Bamboo & wood	0.03					0.03	100	100
Paints for industry	3.8					3.8	100	100
Poultry & livestock	7.12					7.12	100	100
Silkworm & cocoon	--	--	--	--	--	--	--	--
Dry & fresh fruit	3.74					3.74	100	100
Dry/fresh vegetable & spice	4.06					4.06	100	100
Medicine and medical material	0.09					0.09	100	100
Native & by-product	2.43					2.43	100	100
Aquatic product	2.04					2.04	100	100
Total	39.38	5.57	14.14			33.81	85.86	85.86

Source: See Table 4.6.

Table 4.8 Ratio of Goods Value of the Three Price Forms to Total Sales Income of Capital Goods and Marketization Degree of Price Formation in Tianjin (1992) (in 100 million RMB yuan)

Classification	total	government-set price		government stipulated price		market price		Marketization degree %
		value	Ratio(%)	value	ratio(%)	value	ratio(%)	
	(1)	(2)	(3)=(2)/(1)	(4)	(5)=(4)/(1)	(6)=(1)-(2)-(4)	(7)=(6)/(1)	(8)=(0.5*(4)+(6)/(1)
By product usage extractive industry	26.1	6.9	26.44			19.2	73.56	73.56
Material industry	124.9	19.4	15.53	0.8	0.64	104.7	83.83	84.15
Manufacturing industry	423.5	34.63	8.18	27.06	6.39	361.81	85.43	88.63
By industry coal mining and separation	--	--	--	--	--	--	--	--
Oil and natural gas exploitation	26.1	6.9	26.44		--	19.2	73.56	73.56
Ferrous metal	--	--	--	--	--	--	--	--
No-ferrous metal	--	--	--	--	--	--	--	
Building material selecting & nonmetallic ore mining and separation	--	--	--	--	--	--		
Salt	2.4	2.4	100	--	--			0
Other minerals	--	--	--	--	--	--	--	--
Logging and bamboo wood	--	--	--	--	--	--	--	--
City water producing and supplying	2.2	2.2	100	--	--			0
Paper making	4.9	3.9	79.59			1	20.41	20.41

Classification	total	government-set price		government stipulated price		market price		Marketization degree %
	(1)	value (2)	Ratio(%) (3)=(2)/(1)	value (4)	ratio(%) (5)=(4)/(1)	value (6)=(1)-(2)-(4)	ratio(%) (7)=(6)/(1)	(8)=(0.5*(4)+(6))/(1)
Textile	48					48	100	100
Electricity, vapor, hot water Producing and supplying	1.9							0
Petroleum processing	2.6					1.8	69.234	84.62
Cooking, gas and coal products	3.3							0
Chemical	56.9					51.2	89.98	89.98
Chemical fiber	2.7					2.7	100	100
Rubber	10.2					9	88.23	88.23
Plastics	8.1					8.1	100	100
Building material and nonmetallic products	13.1					13.1	100	100
Ferrous metal smelting and flattening	57.9					23.97	41.4	62.04
Non-ferrous metal smelting and flattening	4.8					4.8	100	100
Metalware industry	23.4					23.4	100	100
Mechanical industry	51					47.84	93.80	96.9
Communication and transportation facility	27.7					4.3	15.52	15.52
Electrical machine and appliance	22.3					22.3	100	100
Electronic and communication	26.9					26.9	100	100
Measuring and metrical instrument-making	3.9					3.9	100	100
Other industry	173.1					173.1	100	100
Total	573.4	60.93	10.63	27.86	4.86	484.61	84.52	86.94

Source: see Table 4-7

Note: Sales income of non-capital goods is not included.

Table 4.9 Marketization Degree of Price Formation in Tianjin (1992) (in 100 million RMB yuan)

	Value	Marketization degree
Retail goods	187.68	82.94
Agricultural by-products	39.38	85.86
Sales income of capital goods	573.4	86.94
Total	800.46	85.95

Note: Marketization degree of price formation is calculated in accordance with

$$R = \sum R_k X_k / \sum X_k,$$

so is the same with the other years.

Table 4.10 Ratio of Goods Value of Three Price Forms to Total Retail Goods in Tianjin and Marketization Degree of Price Formation (1993) (in 100 million RMB yuan)

Classification	Total	government-set price		government price		market price		Marketization degree
		value	ratio(%)	value	stipulated ratio(%)	value	ratio(%)	%
	(1)	(2)	(3)=(2)/(1)	(4)	(5)=(4)/(1)	(6)=(1)-(2)-(4)	(7)=(6)/(1)	$(8)=(0.5\delta(4)+(6)/(1)$
Food	83.13	2.61	3.1			80.52	96.9	100
Clothes	38.33					38.33	100	100
Articles of everyday	60.71					60.71	100	100
Stationery and recreation goods	13.89					13.89	100	60.7
Book, magazine & newspaper	2.45	0.96	39.3			1.49	60.7	89.98
Medicine and medical apparatus & instruments	11.48			2.3	20	9.18	80	2.8
Fuel	7.46	7.25	97.2			0.21	2.8	2.8
Agriculture capital goods	10.27					10.27	100	100
Total	227.72	10.82	4.75	2.3	1.01	214.6	94.24	94.74

Source: Tianjin Bureau of Commodity Prices

Table 4.11 Ratio of Goods Value of Three Price Forms to Total Agricultural By-products in Tianjin and Marketization Degree of Price Formation (1993) (in 100 million RMB yuan)

Classification	total	government-set price		government stipulated price		market price		Marketization degree
		value	ratio(%)	value	ratio(%)	value	ratio(%)	%
	(1)	(2)	(3)=(2)/(1)	(4)	(5)=(4)/(1)	(6)=(1)-(2)-(4)	(7)=(6)/(1)	(8)=(0.5&(4)+(6)/(1)
Cereals	7.05	1.77				5.28		75
Cash crop	13.7	4.86				8.84		64.5
Bamboo & wood	--	--	--	--	--	--	--	--
Paints for Industry	5.8					5.8		100
Poultry and livestock	8.77					8.77		100
Silkworm and cocoon	--	--	--	--	--	--	--	--
Dry and fresh fruit	4.43					4.43	100	100
Dry/fresh vegetable and spice	4.37					4.37	100	100
Medicine and medical material	0.05					0.05	100	100
Native and by-product	2.12					2.12	100	100
Aquatic product	1.39					1.39	100	100
Total	47.68					41.05	86.1	86.1

Source: see Table 4-10

Table 4.12 Ratio of Goods Value of the Three Price Forms to Total Sales Income of Capital Goods and Marketization Degree of Price Formation in Tianjin (1993) (in 100 million RMB yuan)

Classification	Total	government-set price		government stipulated price		market price		Marketization degree %
	(1)	value (2)	ratio(%) (3)=(2)/(1)	value (4)	ratio(%) (5)=(4)/(1)	value (6)=(1)-(2)-(4)	ratio(%) (7)=(6)/(1)	(8)=(0.5δ(4)+(6)/(1)
By product usage extractive industry	43.1	11.38	26.4			31.72	73.6	73.6
Material industry	153.62	16.94	11.0	1.29	0.8	135.39	88.1	88.5
Manufacturing industry	528.94	48.54	9.2	17.28	3.3	463.12	87.5	89.19
By industry coal mining and separation	--	--	--	--	--	--	--	--
Oil and natural gas exploitation	43.1	11.38	26.4			19.2	73.56	73.56
Ferrous metal	--	--	--	--	--	--	--	--
No-ferrous metal	--	--	--	--	--	--	--	--
Building material selecting & nonmetallic ore mining and separation	--	--	--	--	--	--	--	--
Salt	4.04	4.04	100	--	--	--	--	0
Other minerals	--	--	--	--	--	--	--	--
Logging and bamboo wood	--	--	--	--	--	--	--	--
City water producing and supplying	3.79	3.79	100	--	--	--	--	0
Paper making	7.22	5.7	79			1.52	21	21
Textile	58.6					58.6	100	100
Electricity, vapor, hot water Producing and supplying	3.41	3.41	100					0

Petroleum processing	4.30					3.01	70	85
Cooking, gas and coal products	5.19	5.19	100				100	0
Chemical	72.26					72.26	100	100
Chemical fiber	4.43	1.3				4.43	100	100
Rubber	12.95		10			11.65	90	90
Plastics	10.29					10.29	100	100
Building material and nonmetallic products	16.64					16.64	100	100
Ferrous metal smelting and flattening	73.53	12.5	17			48.29	65.67	74.34
Non-ferrous metal smelting and flattening	7.09					7.09	100	100
Metalware industry	29.72					29.72	100	100
Mechanical industry	64.77					60.24	93	96.51
Communication and transportation facility	35.18	29.55	84			5.63	16	16
Electrical machine and appliance	28.32					28.32	100	100
Electronic and communication Apparatus	34.16					34.16	100	100
Measuring and metrical instrument-making	4.95					4.95	100	100
Other industry	201.72					201.72	100	100
Total	725.66	76.86	10.6	18.57	2.6	630.23	86.8	88.1

Source: See Table 4-11

Note: Sales income of non-capital goods is not included.

Table 4.13 Marketization Degree of Price Formation in Tianjin (1993) (in 100 million RMB yuan)

	Value	Marketization degree
retail goods	227.72	94.74
Agricultural by-products	47.68	86.1
sales income of capital goods	725.66	88.1
Total	1001.06	89.5

Table 4.14 Ratio of the Three Price Forms to Total Retail Goods, Agriculture By-products and Sales Income of Capital Goods as well as Marketization Degree of Price Formulation

	ratio of government-set price						ratio of government- stipulated price					
	1990	1991	1992	1993	1994	1995	1990	1991	1992	1993	1994	1995
retail goods	32.4	26.3	16.1	4.75	4.1	5.4	14.5	10.8	1.9	1.01	6.9	9.8
agricultural by-products	18.7	18.8	14.1	13.9	--	--	33.9	19.2	--	--	--	--
sales income of capital goods	75.9	41.8	10.6	10.6	23.8	24.0	18.8	24.2	4.9	2.6	3.8	7.8

	ratio of government-set price						ratio of government stipulated price					
	1990	1991	1992	1993	1994	1995	1990	1991	1992	1993	1994	1995
retail goods	53.1	62.9	82.0	94.2	89.0	84.8	60.35	68.35	82.9	94.7	92.45	89.7
agricultural by-products	47.4	62.0	85.9	86.1	--	--	64.3	71.6	85.9	86.1	--	--
sales income of capital goods	5.3	34.0	84.5	86.8	72.4	68.2	14.7	46.1	86.9	88.1	7.3	72.1

Note: Tianjin Bureau of Commodity Prices does not survey the agricultural by-products purchasing since 1994.

Table 4.15 Marketization Degree of Price Formation in Tianjin (1990-1995)

	1990		1991		1992		1993		1994		1995	
	value	market-ization degree	value	market-ization degree	value	market-ization degree	value	market-ization degree	value	market-ization degree	Value	market-ization degree
Retail goods	148.73	60.35	169.19	68.3	187.68	82.9	227.72	94.7	303.37	92.45	373.78	89.7
Agriculture by-products	31.5	64.3	32.38	71.6	39.38	85.9	47.68	86.1	–	–	–	–
Sales income of capital goods	71.05	14.7	167.15	46.1	573.4	86.9	725.66	88.1	1101.7	74.3	1355.29	72.1
Total	251.28	47.94	368.72	58.53	800.46	85.95	1001.06	89.5			1729.07	75.9

Through the measurement of marketization of price formation of Tianjin during 1990~1995, we find that the marketization degree reaches its climax in 1992 and 1993, which was 85.95%and 89.5%, respectively, coming up to the standards of developed market economy countries (Ret Table 4- 16). Figure 4-2 shows that the marketization degree was about 50% in 1990 and 1991. It soared to 89.95% in 1992, rising by 27.42%, In 1993. It rose slowly by 3.55 percent, reaching 85.9%. In 1994, it went down abruptly by 11.25 percent to 78.22%. In 1995, it continued to decline by 2.75 percent to 75.47%. The price reform in 1992 advanced so impetuously that the price decontrol of such goods as contract purchasing grains, crude oils, finished oils, etc produced a succession of harmful effects. Summing up both positive and negative experience of a wide range of price decontrol since 1992, the government controlled again the prices of some commodities, which were of vital importance to the nation's economy and the people's livelihood. Prices were set again by the government of contracted purchasing grains and of part of the residents' grain ration, and so were those of all the crude oil and the finished oil beyond the plan. Sales prices were stipulated by the government with regard to chemical fertilizer produced in the seventeen large state-owned enterprises, and so were with the fourteen types of steel which were crucial to basic construction and production. Thus the marketization degree of price formation declined by a big margin. The dynamic trends of marketization of price formation reflect how our economy is transforming toward the socialist market economy system under which market price formation mechanism is consummating.

PROMOTING THE HEALTHY DEVELOPMENT OF MARKETIZATION OF PRICE FORMATION IN CHINA BY STUDYING THE EXPERIENCES OF THE DEVELOPED MARKET ECONOMY COUNTRIES

Marketization of price formation is one of the key targets of Chinese economy system transformation. To deepen the price reform, it is very important to study the experience of the developed countries for reference.

In market economy countries, market is not almighty. There are problems that cannot be solved by the market mechanism. The government should give full play to the fields in which market is out of work in order to ensure equation and efficiency. The 100% marketization of price formation simply does not exist. Take U.S. where laissez-faire economy is uphold most for example, its highest marketization degree of price formation is something like 95%. It is thus clear that the government also needs to control prices of some goods and services while that market mechanism gives its full play.

Scope and Guarantee System of Price Control in Developed Countries of Market Economy

Before 1970s, price controls were within the scope of general welfare and monopoly goods and services, such as electricity generating and supply, gas and thermos-supply, drainage, communication and post, railway transportation, domestic air transportation, harbor services, urban public traffic, toll of express way and bridge, cable television, public school and public hospital, etc. Prices of oil, gas, chemical fertilizer were once controlled by the government in some countries. Since 1970, privatization waves sweeps across the developed market economy countries, and price controls are loosening gradually, for example, price controls of communication and electricity are loosened in different degrees. Price controls are abolished or lessened in railway transportation, highway transportation and bus transportation. Clearly, employment of price controls varies constantly with the economic development in developed countries of market economy.

The guarantee system of price controls is composed of 3 aspects in developed countries of market economy.

1. Law. The price-controlling institutions, policy-making programs, pricing principles, determinants of price are clearly defined in the laws concerned. The price-controlling institution can impose fine upon the controlled enterprises for their illegal practices, suspend their business licenses and even prosecute as a public prosecutor.
2. Information announcing. It includes publication of the operation situation of the controlled enterprises and price control principles and methods of the government, which creates favorable condition for society supervision.
3. Consumer's self-protection consciousness. Inhabitants in developed countries enjoy high living standards and have experienced a long democratic course, so they have strong consciousness of self-protection, which may reinforce the social supervision and self-decline of the controlled enterprises.

Price Controls in Developed Countries of Market Economy

In these countries, the government controls prices by legislation which embodies thoughts of competition protection and monopoly opposition. In the U. S. A, the Cleton Act (1914) has a prohibitory rule against direct or indirect price discrimination, which is beneficial to competition and unfavorable to monopoly. The Federal Trade Committee supervises the implementation of this rule. The Webster Export Act (1918) provides against hindrance to competition and against domestic price monopoly. Robison-Whiteman Law (1936) prescribes an unlawful price in the market. Many laws were introduced concerned with pricing, anti-price deception and anti-price monopoly, such as fair Dealing Act, Consumer Credit Act. Resale Price Act, Act of Restricted Trading Behavior, Act of Competition Financial Service Act, etc. These laws provide that the producers are forbidden to set the minimum price: the store must put the goods on sale with the prices clearly marked; newly stocked goods must not be discounted. Prices can not be raised deliberately with monopolist methods. Otherwise, the business concerned will be punished severely. The government set up special institutions--Fair Dealing Office and Monopoly & Integration Committee--to enforce these laws. In Germany, prices in which the government does not interfered are administered by the Cartel Bureau. It is whose responsibility to protect competition visas controlling prices. For instance, criteria are provided in Anti-Restriction of Competition Act to judge whether a firm monopolizes the market: if a firm sells more than 33% of the goods in the market, or if its sales income in the previous year is over 250 million DM, or if 3 firms cover 50% of the market or their sale income is above 100 million DM each in the last year, or if 5 firms cover 66% of the market, they will be under supervision by the government. If price monopoly does exist in the business or range of their price increase or decrease by as high as 30%, they will be punished. The punishment include monopoly rescinding; confiscation of monopoly income; exposure in the newspaper. To counter monopoly and protect competition in conformity with legal provisions is the compulsory means to assure the marketization of price formation in the market economy countries.

The Marketization Degree of Price Formation in Developed Countries of Market Economy

As a market economy country, USA emphasizes on the full play of market. The government administers and regulates the prices only in the less competitive fields when necessary. Such fields include agricultural products, electricity, subway, taxi, postal service, telephone, cable television, tap water, coal gas, tickets for museum, rent of the state-owned houses, products for military use, etc. The proportion of the price controlled industry in the economy declines with the privatization wave since 1980s. Estimated at 5-10% while the marketization degree of price formation is 90-95% in U.S.A.

In Japan, prices are controlled of energy by the government including electricity, oil, coal, gas, etc; of transportation including railway, plane, bus, taxi, highway, ocean liner, etc; of communication including postage, telegraph, telephone, etc; of charges of culture, education and healthcare, including lectures in national and public university, TV programs broadcasting, medicine, consultation fee, hospitalization expense, medical treatment of social insurance, etc.; of charges of public utilities, including water, public housing, land, public baths, hygiene, etc.; of monopoly of rice, cigarette, salt, etc.. The proportion of the government- controlled prices is 18% to the total consumer goods.

In Germany, the current price control system is set up according to the requirements of the social market economy. There are three basic principles: (1) Market priority. In market economy, the essence of the government's price policy is to ensure that the firm can set prices freely according to the market situation. (2) The least direct intervention. The government will not intervene with the market until there is monopoly in the price formation. (3) The government's appropriate intervention. The government controls prices of some goods and services which is vulnerable the prices or charges of public services supplied them or of the industries monopolized by the government. It is the Federal government that sets directly in accordance with the cost-compensation principle all the charges concerning post, telecommunication, railway transportation, etc. The charges are generally set directly by the state government with regard to technical supervision, state-run TV or radio broad casting, public hospital and sanitary facilities. Charges are set directly by the city (or town) government regarding such services as water and electricity supply, long distance heating supply, credentials granting, urban traffic, waste water processing, garbage disposal public facilities supply, etc. Goods and services which are directly controlled by the government covers some 10% in the market, and marketization degree is 90% or so in Germany.

In Italy, 37 prices are controlled or supervised by the special institutions at different levels. Prices of 18 kinds of goods and services is administered by the ministry price committees, they are: electricity, telephone, car insurance, charges of TV station, railway transportation, gas of daily life, civil airplane, inland water transportation, highway fee, post and telecommunication, sugar, basic medicine, petroleum, newspaper, home-made cigarettes, two kinds of matches, etc. The prices or charges of five kinds of goods and services are administered by the provincial price agencies, they are: water, hotel, loaf, whole milk powder, and out-camping. The prices or charges of five kinds of goods and services are controlled by the city price agency, they are: urban traffic, coach, funeral and interment fee, entrance ticket for museums, etc. The prices of nine kinds of goods and services is supervised by the ministry level price committee: gas for bus, coal gas, beef, cooked wheaten food, daily-use medicine, diesel oil for heating, petroleum for plane and bus, etc.21.4% of the consumer goods and services are controlled by the government, and the marketization degree of price formation is 75.9%.

In France, the government normally controlled the prices of products from monopolized state-owned firm. Based on the pricing principle of marginal cost and the law of value, the government determines the prices, taking into consideration the firm's balance of revenue and expenditure and the targets of restraining inflation. The government controlled goods includes: some energy, such as coal, electricity, gas for civil use; the state monopolized products, such as tobacco, alcohol, matches, etc, Transportation, post and telecommunication services such as railway, civil aviation, urban public traffic, post telecommunication, etc; most of the medical products medical charges, education charges, rents, products for military use, etc. The purchasing prices of agricultural products are uniformly decided by EEC Credit interest rates are also controlled by the government covers 15% of the total and the marketization of price formation is 80-85%. In U.K., the Labor Party government carried out a stringent policy to regulate prices. After The Conservative Party came into power the government try hard to deregulate the prices. But in some monopolist industries, prices are still controlled by the government such as coal, hydroelectric power, steel, oil, aviation, railway transportation, shipbuilding, etc. The value of goods, whose prices are regulated by the government, covers 18.5% of GDP. The marketization degree is some 91.5% of price formation.

Table 4.16 Marketization Degree of Price Formation in Developed Countries of Market Economy

	USA	Japan	Germany	Italy	France	U.K.
Marketization degree	90~95	82	90	75.9	80~85	91.5
Control degree	5~10	18	10	24.1	15~20	8.5

To sum up, in developed market-economy countries, their existed not only the principles, ways and means to promote the marketization of price formation, but also ways and measures to administer prices among which many can be used by us.

1. To counter monopoly and protect competition; to counter price deception and ensure fair trade. Law and statutes concerned are made and appropriate supervisory and guarantee measures are taken for this purpose.
2. Do not intervene in the competitive goods and services so that prices of them are formulated in the free market.
3. To control or administer prices of public or monopoly goods to protect the consumers' rights and interests.
4. To promote the standardization and legalization of administration on the basis of laws and statutes.
5. To control prices by means of readjusting to supply-demand relations and of restricting profit margin. The pricing principles and determinants of prices are prescribed in the laws concerned, and firms are required to make their operation information public for the sake of social supervision.

In China, there is neither a perfect legal system, nor a standardized administration and mature administration thoughts and principles. It is beneficial for us Chinese to use for reference the experience of developed market--economy countries when we push our economy reform forward.

PROBLEMS AND SUGGESTIONS

Great progress has been achieved in marketization of our price formation with the price reform going on. So far as price administration is concerned, the marketization of our price formation has approached or attained the level of the developed countries of market economy. Exploring it thoroughly, we find that the following problems concerning the marketization degree of price formation in China.

1. The performances of our pricing subjects are not standardized, and the laws and statutes with regard to market order as well as price formulation are imperfect. In recent years, China has expedited the reform of economy system. Laissez-faire attitude is taken to prices and this made the trade and pricing disordered in many fields where deception and faking are rampant. Some people think it is a matter of

course to reap illegitimate super-profits. The decontrolled prices can only be formulated by the market mechanism when they are under the circumstances of competition protection and monopoly opposition, legitimate management protection and fake and deception opposition, legitimate profit earning protection and illegitimate super-profit objection.

2. As a result of 18 years reform, the market mechanism is already playing a dominant role in the price formation of goods and services, but the price reform lags behind in the production factor field. The deepening of price reform urgently requires accelerating the reform of factor price. Marketization of factor price formation is the inherent character of socialist market economy and vital element to resource allocation, and it is essential prerequisite for the price of material products to be formed rationally and to play effective roles. When prices of goods and services are decontrolled, they fluctuate with the demand-supply relation. If the prices of production factors are not marketized, and such factors as funds, labors, technology, lands, etc., cannot flow freely, such the automatic regulation mechanism of demand and supply will be out of work in the market price formulation, that is, the mechanism cannot help form rational prices nor regulate the resource allocation effectively. Accordingly, the marketization of price formation of goods and services is restricted by that of production elements. Now, the prices of factors are actually situating, two-track precipitate: the government-set price and market price. The marketization degree of price formation of goods and services declines in this situation.

3. Broadly speaking, the price formation lacks standardization and legalization with regard to the goods and services controlled by the government. The combination of equality with efficiency cannot be attained; there is not a feasible and scientific pricing method to reflect the actual supply and demand. As a result of the unreasonable pricing formation, some firms violate law and regulation, illegally overcharging for their goods or services. In developed market-economy countries, the basic pricing principle of the controlled prices is permitted cost plus permitted profit. In order to shorten the time different of price readjustment and to increase the firms' efficiency, readjustment coefficient of inflation and of compulsory reduction of cost is included in the readjustment equation. A set of laws and statutes are made to safeguard the controlled firms' pricing.

4. In calculating the marketization degree of price formation, the ratio of the government-set price and the government stipulated price is calculated according to the current price. If revised according to the market price, the ration of them will be higher and the marketization degree is accordingly a bit lower.

5. The administrative and operational service fees are usually excluded in the calculation. In fact, the government-set price ratio in these charges is rather high, such as, transportation, postage, rent, gas of daily life, water, tuition of universities and colleges. In the developed market economy countries, these fees are also included in the statistics. If we also take consideration in the marketization of these charges, the marketization degree will be lower.

To sum up, we come to know that there is a gap in the marketization of price formation between China and the developed countries. Disregarding the elements we discussed above, our marketization degree of price formation is 60-70%. There is along way for China to consummate the marketization of price formation.

From the conclusion we draw above, we propose: first, to expedite the reform of marketization of factor price formation, and thus promote the marketization of good and service price formation; second, to enact price law and other corresponding decrees to the price Act of P. R. C to counter monopoly and standardize the market order; Thirdly, to standardize pricing of government controlled goods and services and make it standardized and legalized, equally and efficiently, as well as reflect the demand-supply relation and the law of value. Fourthly, Competitive goods and services which are now controlled by the government should be decontrolled when necessary. Let the prices be formulated in the market, thus increase the marketization degree of price formation and accelerate the transformation from planned economy to market economy. Finally, for the sake for international comparison, service fees should be included when calculating the marketization degree of price formation.

REFERENCES

Chen Zongsheng. *"Inflation and Enterprise System Reform"*. *Shanghai Finance* (No.11). 1994.

Chen Zongsheng.*"A Study in Institutional Change of the Restoration of Price Control"*. Economic Research Journal (No.11). 1997.

Chinese Commodity Price Yesrbook,1996. Beijing: Chinese Press of Commodity Price.

Commodity Price of China. All the issues from 1991 to 1996.

Jia Xiuyan. *"Principles on Price Theory"*. Tianjin: Nankai Univesity press. 1990.

Price Theory and Practice. All the issues from 1981 to 1996.

Chapter 5

MEASUREMENT OF THE MARKETIZATION PROCESS OF THE LABOR FORCE IN CHINA

After more than ten years of reform and opening to the outside world, especially after the 14th National Congress of the Communist Party of China, China's labor force market has, by and large, shaped up and has made considerable progress. The phenomenon can find specific expressions in the following four aspects: (1). The subjects of supply and demand have been established; the freedom of employing and being employed has been increased, (2). The flow of labor force is becoming active day by day and the scale of this flow is becoming more extensive. (3). The marketization of labor salary is becoming higher, and it is becoming an effective means to adjust the supply and demand of labor force. (4). Various market mechanisms and social security guarantee systems have been or are being gradually established which provide a powerful backing for the development of the labor force market.

According to the theory of labor force market economics and the features of the development and evolution of China's labor force market, we set up the indicator system of measuring the degree of maturity of China's labor force market on the basis of statistical data and some investigation data on hand. After careful selection and arrangement, we chose the following four indicators: the degree of flexibility of job selection; the freedom of labor force's flow; the employer's liberty to choose an employee; the degree of marketization salary.

Our survey includes over ten typical units and individuals. They are: Tianjin Northern Talent Market, Tianjin Labor Force Market, Tianjin Personnel Bureau, Head offices of big corporations which are in Tianjin, large and medium-size enterprises in Tianjin, Tianjin Education Committee, the Distribution Offices for Graduates from different universities or colleges, enterprises with exclusive investment and some Chinese staff who have been working in an American company for several years.

Some reference coefficients are indispensable for us to measure the degree of maturity of labor force market. (In the course of reforming the traditional planned system of obtaining employment, China's labor force market formed). Under the planned economy system, neither the laborers nor the employing units had the power to make their own decision to choose an occupation or to select employees: once a laborer was distributed to a unit, he would have few opportunities to change his job. Moreover, salaries were formulated by the state's unified plan and therefore, it failed to reflect the situation of labor force's supply and demand and to mirror the economic performances. So, under the traditional planned economy system, market did not really exist. We can regard this period as the starting point for our investigation of labor force's market-transformation process.

To what stage can we say that the market has "matured" or has "reached its peak"? There is no exact criterion for this question. However, we can choose a country as a reference in which the development of the labor force's market is comparatively mature in the world. We take the United States as an example.

REFERENCE COEFFICIENT: LABOR FORCE MARKET OF THE U.S.A.

America's labor force market consists of the buyer of labor force (employer) and the seller of labor force (employee). The objective of the employer is to seek the maximum of profit. They take marginal labor productivity as the norm of labor force's disposition and management. In labor force market, every laborer with ability to work enjoys the equality to obtain a job, regardless of their identities. The only difference lies in the fact that they have varying competence or they have different education backgrounds. They can look for and get jobs in different professions occupations and areas according to their own skills, preferences and habits. The relationship between employers and employees is characterized by pure exchange. The employer can fire the employee, while the employee is free to choose jobs, working time, working places and is entitled to hand in his resignation. Labor force is modulated by price system and can flow freely among different departments or occupations. The state does not interfere in the specific distribution of labor force market.

In the U.S., employers and employees get in touch with each other by means of staffing advertisements, employment agencies, offices of distribution or the personnel division of enterprises. Both sides exchange such information as price and applicants' quality by way of job application, interview and passing on messages by acquaintances, etc. They reach final agreement on the basis of mutual selection and consultation. Flow results entirely from the behavior taken by both employers and employees who are driven by their own interests.

As far as the evolution of salary of labor force's market is concerned, it is decided by the supply and demand situation of the labor force market. In enterprises, employers make their own decisions concerning the way of salary distribution. The government does not meddle with the private affairs of the enterprises.

In modern developed countries, labor force market is a comparatively perfect social system. It includes such problems as labor force's job-selection and salary allocation which have immediate influence on the supply and demand of labor force. Moreover, it includes such questions as social security, job training and safety and hygiene of jobs. These issues are indispensable parts of labor force market's operation. America's *"Labor*

Law" clearly stipulates the items and scope of social security and the way by which payment of various insurance premium is made, etc. Among these regulations, America's old-age insurance belongs to mandatory insurance and consists of social old-age insurance and retirement insurance. The insurance premium is undertaken by the government, employees and enterprises.

Has the America's labor force market been completely marketized? Here, we will not discuss the identity and distinction between America's labor force market and that of other western countries that have relatively advanced labor force markets. We assume that the degree of America's labor force's marketization is 100%, then in the range between 0% to 100%, we will make a research concerning the developing process of China's labor force market. In addition, labor force marker is a dynamic system that is constantly changing. When the supply of labor force exceeds the demand, labor force will have less freedom to choose a job; on the contrary, when the demand of labor force exceeds the supply, labor force will have more liberty to select an occupation. In order to give a brief explanation, we suppose that China's labor force market is in a static state with a balance between supply and demand.

DEVELOPMENT OF CHINA'S LABOR FORCE MARKET

The development of China's labor force market can be divided into four phases:

1. The period from 1979 to 1985 belongs to the phase of emergence. In this period, China's urban and rural labor force markets were at an embryonic stage. In 1985, the premier of the State Council expressed clearly in his comments on some interior news references that the government would support and set up labor force market.

2. The period from 1985 to 1988 belongs to the phase of development. In this period, urban economic reform was rapidly carried forward. In 1985, state enterprises carried out a policy called "direct contact between work and payment" in order to invigorate the recruitment system; in 1986, the State Council promulgated "*A Notice of Four Regulations about the Reform of Labor System*", to popularize labor contract system in the country, and established security system for the unemployed people; in 1986, the Standing Committee of the National People's Congress adopted "*Law of Bankruptcy of Enterprises in the People's Republic of China(trial implementation)*"; in 1987, the State Council wrote instructions on a report about the development of labor force market which was submitted by Labor Personnel Bureau and referred it to those concerned; in 1988, the first conference of the 7th People's Congress passed "*Law of Industrial Enterprises Owned by the Whole People in the People's Republic of China*". This statute stipulates that the enterprises owned by the whole people are independent production units, which enjoy the right to distribute, the right to employ and fire the employees. Besides, exchange of technical personnel and flow of qualified personnel have experienced obvious development.

3. The period from 1989 to 1990 belongs to the phase of stagnation. In this period, because of economy retrenchment, rationalization of economy and the influence of old structures, the labor force market found itself basically in a condition of stagnation and took a wait-and-see attitude.

4. The period from 1991 up to now belongs to a period of consolidation. During these years, China has selected "market economy" as its basic pattern. The 3rd conference of the 14th Central Committee published programmatic document about China's market economy-"Decisions about the Establishment of Socialist Market Economy System", in which the term of "unemployment" was first used in the documents of Communist Party In this period, labor force market was making great progress. Throughout the whole country, there were more than 20,000 labor force markets organized by various departments in different ways. In 1994, "Law of Labor the People's Republic of China" was passed, published and was put into effect all over the country in1995. The implementation of this law provides law guarantee for the operation and improvement of the labor force market. The recent important task of the "Labor Law" is to practice labor contract. In this way, the function and task of labor force market are greatly increased.

THE INDICATORS AND MEASUREMENT ANALYSIS OF THE PROCESS OF THE LABOR FORCE MARKETIZATION IN CHINA.

As we have mentioned above, during the research of the process of labor force marketization in China, we choose four indicators to analyze:

a. the degree of freedom for labor force to choose a job;
b. the freedom of labor force to circulate;
c. the liberty of units to employ working staff,
d. the degree of marketization of labor salary.

Now, on the basis of these four indicators, in accordance with the four phases that cover the four main years of 1979, 1985,1990 and 1995, we will analyze and measure the process of marketization of China's labor force.

Degree of Freedom for Labor Force to Choose a Job.

Labor force is the principal subject of labor force market. Therefore, whether labor force can enter labor force market freely and look for a job freely and independently is a main sign showing whether the labor force market has been formed and well-developed.

Labor force's job-selection includes three aspects: newly-generated labor force making his first selection; employed labor force who wants to change his job and unemployed labor force who wants to find a job. Owing to the complexity of the latter two problems, we will look into them in our discussion concerning the freedom of circulation of labor force. A general conclusion can be drawn from the investigation into the object of study of newly-generate labor force making his first selection. Because of the restriction of China's system of registered permanent residence, job-selection of newly-generated labor force is divided into two aspects: urban newly-generated labor force and rural newly-generated labor force.

Freedom of Job-Selection of Urban Newly-Generated Labor Force

Each year, China's urban newly-generated labor force can basically be divided into four groups: {a} urban newly-generated labor force; {b} labor force who transfer from rural area to permanent urban residence; {c} university graduates and graduates from secondary specialized schools; {d} others.

With the deepening of economic system reform, freedom of job-selection for labor force has been increased. When the system of labor contract of the enterprises owned by the whole people is carried out, the freedom of job-selection of urban newly-generated labor force, of labor force who transfer from rural permanent residence to urban permanent residence and of other kinds of labor force and basically the same. Therefore, when we analyze the free job-selection of urban newly-generated labor force, we can divide them into two categories which include urban newly-generated labor force (not including graduates from universities and from secondary specialized schools) and graduates from universities and from secondary specialized schools.

A. As to the first category, i.e. urban newly-generated labor force (not including graduates from universities and from secondary specialized schools), the method of measuring the freedom of job-selection in 1979,1985,1990,1995 is shown as follows:

a. In 1979, because of the non-existence of the labor contract system, we do the measurement according to the proportion of self-employed workers in the newly-generated labor force as a whole. It can be expressed by the following formula:

$$a_{79} = \frac{\text{number of urban newly - generated self - employed workers}}{\text{number of urban newly - generated workers}} \times 100\% = 3.16\%$$

b. In 1985 and 1990, if we do the calculation according to the annual rate of signing contracts of newly-generated labor force, the rate comes into two categories: {1}. rate of signing contracts in economic units owned by the state and in collective ownership; {2}. rate of signing contracts in joint-ventures, self-employed units and other economic units. Then take the number of the working staff as weight number to calculate the weighted average, we work out, the degree of the freedom of urban newly-generated labor force's job-selection. The rate of signing contract in "joint ventures", in self-employed units and in other economic units is 100%. The rate is of the

economic units of collective ownership and units owned by the whole people
is obtained by the annual statistical data in *Statistical Yearbook of China* The
result is 23.3% in 1985 and 22.35% in 1990.

c. In 1995, the labor contract system for the whole staff was practiced, so the
degree of the freedom of labor force's job-selection is 100%. Urban newly-
generated labor force included some armymen transferred to civilian work.
At present, this group of people relies mainly on national planned
distribution, free job-selection being subsidiary. However, with the market's
development, the degree of freedom of this group of people's job selection
has been strengthened, leaving state's planned distribution gradually
becoming a kind of ensuring measure. Because of the scanty number of this
group of people, it can be overlooked.

B) In 1979, urban graduates from universities or from secondary specialized schools
were distributed by the state's plan. With the reform of education system and the
stimulation given by market mechanism, the in traditional planned distribution system
has changed. It has evolved to a new style; government distribution departments and
schools provide information of employing units for the students and arrange the meeting
of supply and demand. Then both sides will have negotiations to select jobs or
employees. The government acts as the middleman. This, to a certain extent, gives more
freedom to students to select a job. Therefore, the transition from planned distribution to
free job-selection has been realized.

According to the survey of Tianjin Talent Market, Tianjin Education System and
Tianjin institutions of higher learning, China's graduates allocation has, on the whole,
experienced the following process of evolution.

a. In 1979, allocation plan was built by National Education Committee. The degree
of graduates' job-selection is zero.

b. In 1985, most of the graduates were distributed by the plan given by National
Education Committee, a few number of students were distributed by the plan
which was first made first by schools according to market demand and then was
examined and assigned by National Education Committee. Considering the
difference between 1979's distribution system and that of 1985,we suppose that
the degree of freedom of graduate's job-selection in 1985 is 5%.

c. In 1990, 70% of the whole graduates were distributed by the plan given by
National Education Committee, 30% of the graduates were distributed by
school's plan. For example, in Nankai University, only the students in four
departments were distributed by school's plan. They are the department of
history, philosophy, physics and mathematics. School's plan was made
according to social demand, but the meeting of supply and demand and mutual
selections were not actually realized. In this case, the degree of freedom of
graduates' job-selection in 1990 can be supposed as 20%.

d. In 1995, graduates relied mainly on free job-selection, national planned allocation being subsidiary. The units which belong in national allocation plan are as follows: a). In order to meet the need of key departments or crucial units such as national defense industry, national security units and units in remote places, every year, an allocation plan that a certain proportion of graduates should be distributed to the above units was made and given to institutions of higher learning by the National Education Committee. If the plans had not been completed, all of that year's graduates' allocation schemes would not be approved. This part constituted 5%. In recent years, because the working condition and salary are satisfactory, the plan is very easily to be completed. B) In order to meet the need for education, farming and forestry production, factory, mine, medical and health work, the government makes it a rule 90% of the normal university's graduates should be distributed within education system, 10% could find jobs outside education system; 10% of the medical and health college's graduate must work in medical units which belong to some factories or mines, while 90% could find jobs according to their own desire; 90% graduates from agriculture or forestry colleges should work in agriculture and forestry units, while the rest of the graduates could look for jobs freely; considering that some of the graduates allocated in accordance with the government's requirement into the above-mentioned systems still had free job-selections, so it is very difficult for us to estimate the percentage. We suppose that it is 50%. Therefore, normal university's graduate's degree of freedom of job-selection is about 55%; medical colleges, 95%; agriculture and forestry schools, 55%. National plan must be completed, otherwise, these allocation plans mentioned above would not be approved.

According to the statistics of graduates from institutions of higher learning and secondary specialized schools recorded in *Statistical Yearbook of China* in 1996, we arrive at Table 5.1

Table 5.1 Number of Graduates from Institution of Higher Learning and Secondary Specialized School in 1995 (in 10,000)

	Secondary Specialized Schools	Institutions of Higher Learning	Total μ	Degree of Freedom of Job-Selection n %
Agriculture	4.9915	3.2975	8.2890	55.00
Medicine and Health	9.0855	5.5711	14.6566	95.00
Normal University	24.9415	17.3797	42.3212	55 00
Other Things	44.8982	54.2914	99.1896	95.00
Total	83.9167	80 5397	164.4564	

Therefore, in 1995, the degree of freedom of job-selection of graduates from universities and secondary specialized schools is expressed by the following formula:

$$a_{95} = \sum_{i=1}^{4} \mu_i n_i / \sum_{i=1}^{4} \mu_i \times 100\% = 82.69\%$$

(Note: The calculation method we adopt is all by the weighted average method. Notes to formulas hereafter, will be omitted.)

According to this analysis, we get Table 5.2 which reflects the degree of freedom of China's urban newly-generated labor force's job-selection.

Table 5.2 The Degree of Freedom of Urban Newly-Generated Labor Force's Job-Selection.

	1979	1985	1990	1995
Urban Newly-Generated Labor Force(10,000)	688.5	502.3	340.0	270.0
Labor From Rural Residence to Urban Residence(10,000)	70.8	150.2	118.0	220.0
Other Things(10,000)	109.9	72.6	159.0	20.0
Total(10,000)	869.2	725.1	617.0	510.0
Degree of Freedom of Job-Selection(%)	3.13	23.3	22.35	100
Graduates from Universities and Secondary specialized Schools(10,000)	33.4	88.5	168.0	164.46
Degree of Freedom of Job-Selection(%)	0	5	20	82.69
Degree of Freedom of Urban Newly-Generated Labor's Job-Selection(%)	3.01	21.31	21.85	95.78

Degree of Rural Labor Force's Free Job-Selection

Before investigating the degree of rural labor force's free job-selection, we should first have a look at the change of reference. In our previous analysis, the degree of freedom of urban labor force's job-selection has as its starting point the distribution made by government in a unified way under the system of planned economy. However, under the traditional system, cities and rural areas were ruled separately by the government. As to the rural labor force's job-selection, the government has no definite regulations. In this respect, the degree of rural labor force's free job-selection can be described as 100%. However, the case is not really so. Compared with the marketized job-selection of urban labor force, rural labor force's job-selection is facing many obstacles. Some of these barriers derive from social system, for example, the separate administration of cities and rural areas, and some of them derive from traditional mode of production.

With the increase in agricultural productivity and owing to the fact that government loosens up on the administration for farmers, a great number of rural surplus laborers begin to turn into non-rural laborers, thus becoming the main body of supply for non-rural labor force market. Among them, some enter urban labor force market, and some are melted into the non-rural productive labor in rural areas, such as village and township enterprises, self-employed units and private enterprises.

To those rural laborers who have come into urban labor force market, they are still confronted with some obstacles. The principal obstacles come from the fact that city government prohibits some urban units to hire farmers as workers because of the city's own pressure of job-distribution. It can be expressed as follows: {1}. every year, urban activities of recruitment only open doors to those who have urban-registered permanent residence, while rural labors can not enter. {2}. in some cities, some professions are not entitled to recruit rural labor force. {3}. when the pressure of urban job-distribution becomes higher and higher, city government will make a provisional decision, to the effect that some rural laborers who have found jobs in the cities would be fired or checked up. In addition, discrimination against rural laborers still exists in urban labor force market. For example, to reduce the salary of rural labor force, to extend working hours, to ignore the working condition and safety of rural labor force. The obstacles and discrimination mentioned above make the rural laborers find jobs in harsh, dirty and dangerous trades. Rural labor force has limited opportunities to find jobs in cities. Because of our limited data, we can not draw an exact conclusion concerning this kind of limitation. However, we will think it over together with our research of the degree of freedom of rural labor force's job-selection.

Do the rural labor force that tries to find jobs in village and township enterprises and in rural private enterprises face obstacles? Theoretically speaking, the obstacles should not exist. However, in fact they do exist. The reason lies in the fact that the development of rural market economy is restricted by the backward rural economic system, therefore, it bears a striking flavor of clan and small-scale production. As a result, because of the limitation given by clan or rural officials, some labor force will be treated unfairly when they try to work in the non-rural department in countryside. This phenomenon will undoubtedly influence the degree of rural labor force's free job-selection in the non-rural fields.

Every year, some rural labor force finds jobs in cities and township enterprises, rural self-employed or private units. According to the analysis mentioned in last few paragraphs, in order to measure the degree of rural labor force's free job-selection, the proportion of this group of people in the whole rural labor force can be regarded as one aspect to study the freedom of rural labor force's job-selection. Most rural people who are engaged in agriculture are doing it voluntarily. However, because of the existence of barriers, farmer's outdated traditional mode of thought of employment and farmer's ill-informed situation, this voluntary behavior is limited by some factors. Therefore, we suppose 50% farmers in the year of 1985,1990 and 1995 make their choices according to their own will. That is to say, to this group of labor force, the degree of freedom of job-selection is 50%.

According to *Statistical Yearbook of China.*, we get Table 5.3

Table 5.3 The Degree of Rural Labor Force's Free Job-Selection

	1979	1985	1990	1995
Rural Labor(10,000)	31237	37065	42009.5	45042
Laborers Working on a Public Project in Cities(10,000)	200	1000	2000	3566
Labor in Village and Township Enterprises(10,000)	2914	6979	9265	12862
Labor in Rural Self-employed or Private Enterprises(10,000)	0	0	1604	4521
Degree of Freedom of Job-Selection(%)	9.97	21.50	30.60	44.30
Agricultural Population(10,000)	28132	30351.5	33336.4	32334.5
Degree of Freedom of Job-Selection(%)	0	50	50	50
Degree of Freedom of Rural Labor's Job-Selection(%)	0.99	34.33	39.18	46.68

Summing up the analysis of Table 5.2 and Table 5.3, using the weighted average method we get Table 5.4 which displays the degree of freedom of the whole country's labor force's job-selection.

Table 5.4 The Degree of the Whole Country's Labor's Job-Selection (%)

	1979	1985	1990	1995
The Degree of the Whole Country's Labor's Job-Selection	1.06	34.04	38.83	47.40

The Degree of Labor Force's Free Flow

The degree of labor force's free flow is another important index to analyze the degree of labor force's marketization. The flow of labor force is an inevitable outcome of two steps: the free employment of units, labor force's free job-selection, in other words, two-way selection.

Degree of Urban Labor Force's Free Flow

With the development of industrialization and market economy, a person's social role is not a static one any more. It finds itself in a constant flow. As far as jobs on which people rely for a living is concerned, thanks to the development of technology and the constant change of mode of production and living style, the category of jobs are accordingly changing. However, this is only a part of the changing of jobs, the change of job of laborers' occurs more frequently. A laborer may work in different economic units, just as what Karl Marx has said, "large-scale industry's innate character is a decisive factor affecting the change of labor, the change of jobs and the all-round flow of workers".

A series of statistical data indicates that, in the countries with flourishing market economy, personnel in specific fields are highly mobile. On the average, in American personnel in specific field changes his positions for about twelve times his whole lifetime. In Japan, a country that carries out lifelong employment system, personnel in specific field changes his position for 10.2 times throughout his whole life. However, in China, this kind of flow remains only once in a person's whole life. According to news reports, in 1988, 30.73% of China's personnel in specific field had the intention to change their jobs, but in fact, only 2-3% of them achieved their aims. The fact that trained personnel failed to circulate made it impossible to adjust the distribution of qualified personnel and to overcome the imbalance between supply an demand. According to the survey, in 1993, 65% of the country's talented people are technical staffs. They swarmed in the units of industry, health, education and government organizations. Departments under the Party's Central Committee and the State Council possess 72% of the whole country's students with master degree and 47.5% of the whole country's talented people with high-ranking titles of technical or professional posts. According to the sample survey organized by the National Science Committee, in China, rate of utilization of personnel was only 60%, namely, to let 3440,000 people lie idle. China's Science Academy's investigation in 1992 shows that the rate of waste of engineers and technicians in large and medium-scale state enterprises reached 52.3%

With the enactment of labor contract system and the emergence of labor force market, labor force became more and more mobile. According to 1996's *Statistical Yearbook of China*, in 1995, 39.05% labor force of the whole employed people in the country registered in the market to change their jobs. 18.5% of them were successful. Compared with that in 1988, the rate of success was obviously raised.

Modern western countries with market economy always adopt the system described as follows: to fix labor relationship with charters or contracts, to break the limitation of identity, to advocate equal competition. This system make it possible for enterprises to govern and use their labor force efficiently, to provide guarantee for effective disposition of social labor force, to bring about a great advance in enterprises and to keep the whole market economy functioning efficiently. The main distinction between traditional society and modern society lies in the fact that the former is a society of identity, while the latter is a society of contract. The society of identity will inevitably result in the contract society. Nowadays, China's labor contracts system aims at breaking the limitation of identity and providing system of guarantee for labor force to flow freely. Therefore, we choose the signing rate of labor contract as the index to measure the present degree of labor force free flow in China.

$$\text{Signing Rate of Labor Contract} = \frac{\text{Total of Urban employees under Labor Contract}}{\text{Total of Urban Employed People}} \times 100\%$$

By the end of 1995, according to the regulation of "Labor Law", 43,960,000 laborers in China's urban state enterprises have signed labor contracts with their employers. This number accounts for 39.04% of the total number of the whole workers. Other non-state economic units such as "foreign-funded" enterprises, individual operation and private units have also signed labor contracts in accordance with the regulations and relevant documents. This shows that China has made further progress on its way to transfer from planned economy to market economy.

Labor contract is only a prerequisite of the free mobility of labor force. Actually, the flow of labor force is also restricted by many objective or artificial factors. The objective factor includes three aspects: a. the existence of new jobs. B. limitations of practical conditions for the labor force to flow. C. law's influence on labor force's flow. For example, although the China's residence-registration-system is becoming weaker to certain extent, it is still a factor which restrains the flow of labor force. As a result, many cross-regional flow of labor force is limited by the residence-registration-system. Another factor, which creates restriction on the flow of urban labor force, is the system of public ownership of houses. Many laborers regard the problem of having a house as the principal prerequisite of flow. Consequently, many people can not move because of the problems of houses, although they are eager to change their jobs. In addition, another factor comes from the fact that there is no unity concerning the policy of social security. From one place to another, employees have to pay pension in different proportions. This brings trouble to both employees and units. Many people are stuck in the original posts because their pension can not be transferred. The factors mentioned above occur mainly in cities and towns, so the rate of labor force's flow in cities and towns is relatively low. According to some statistical data, the annual rate of flow of labor force in different kinds of units in cities and towns is less than 10%, among which the rate of flow of the state-enterprises is lower than the average. However, in the countries with market economy, the rate of flow usually reaches 20-30%. These factors make it difficult to measure the flow of labor force with a specific quantity, so we will investigate the degree of labor force's free mobility in terms of the signing rate of labor contract.

Two types of economic units are under our investigation when we try to discuss the degree of urban labor force's free flow. {1} State economic unit {2} Non-state economic unit. Table 5.5 can be drawn according to the statistical data.

Table 5.5 Degree of Urban Labor Force's Free Flow

	1979	1985	1990	1995
Number of staff and workers in State Economic Units(10,000)	7693	8990	10346	11261
Signing Rate of Labor Contract(%)	0	3.70	13.26	39.04
Number of Staff and Workers in Economic Units of Collective Ownership(10,000)	2237	3324	3549	3147
Signing Rate of Labor Contract(%)	0	2.20	8.10	37.40
Number of Staff and Workers in Other Economic Units(10,000)	37	494	835	2939
Signing Rate of Labor Contract(%)	100	100	100	100
Degree of Urban Labor 's Free Flow(%)	0.40	7.02	16.90	49.07

Degree of Rural Labor Force's Free Mobility

In China's rural areas, man-made limitation of labor force's mobility is less than that in urban areas. Therefore each year, there are tens of millions of rural people flowing outside their own provinces or regions. According to statistics, at present the annual cross regional flow of labor force reaches one hundred million, which constitutes 20% of the whole rural labor force. Among these people, every year, about 300,000,000 people are cross-provincial labor force. However, at present, several reasons make it premature for rural labor force to transfer or flow in large-scale. They are:

a. China's labor force market is still in a developing stage.
b. Market mechanism has not been entirely formed.
c. People are not well-informed about the labor market, so the state of "market with no real communication and flow" still exists.
d. The isolation mechanism between urban areas and rural areas does exist.
e. Rural labor force is under-qualified.

In order to measure China's rural labor force's free flow, we should know that the factors which have influence upon the rural labor force's free job-selection and the elements which affect the rural labor force's free flow are almost the same. So, we adopt the value of the degree of labor force's free job-selection and get Table 5.6.

Table 5.6 Degree of Rural Labor Force's Free Flow (%)

	1979	1985	1990	1995
Degree of Rural Labor Force's Free Flow	0.99	34.33	39.18	46.68

According to the analysis of the degree of urban and rural labor force's free flow, synthesizing list 5 and list 6, we get the degree of the whole country's labor force's free flow which is expressed by Table 5.7.

Table 5.7 Degree of the Whole Country's Labor's Free flow (%)

	1979	1985	1990	1995
Degree of the Whole Country's Labor's Free flow	0.85	27.32	33.40	45.31

Degree of Employment Unit's Free Recruitment

We can analyze the degree of employment unit's free recruitment from three aspects: (1). recruitment system of non-state economic units. {2}. recruitment system of state economic units {3}. recruitment system of urban governments and institutions at all levels.

1. The non-state economic units mentioned here still refer to "foreign-funded' enterprises, private and self-employed economic units, etc. These units themselves result from the operation of market system. As far as the method of using labor force is concerned, the starting point is the maximum of profit, i.e., the complete market behavior. As a result, we think that degree of the non-state economic unit's employing system is 100%.

2. Degree of state economic units' employing system is very complicated. Under the traditional planned economy, state enterprises follow state's plans and have all members in the society employed as their objective. This behavior results in an inefficient hording of a great quantity of labor force. In the course of shifting to market economy and the adjusting the structure of production, the first problem lying ahead of state enterprises is how to cast off the burden of redundant personnel. If an enterprise wants to follow market principles and to proceed from the considerations of benefits, it will have to cut down surplus personnel. However, out of concern for social stability, the government demands that enterprises digest and absorb these superfluous personnel. Examining the issue from this angle, state enterprises' recruitment is still under the control of the government and they have no power to make their own decision to fire and cut down on personnel.

Since the 1990s, state enterprises began to carry out labor contract system. Till 1995, state enterprises had carried out labor contract system for all staff members. Contract relationship can be described as a kind of market relationship, to the effect that both sides have right to establish and terminate labor relationship in terms of the contract. However, up to now, the system of establishing and terminating a relationship according to the contract has not been formed in state enterprises. The practice of labor contract still fails to extricate itself from the formalistic characteristic.

Because of the complete lack of power to fire workers, state enterprises had to adopt flexibly the job-waiting method to solve the problem of redundant personnel. Enterprises can, according to their own situation of production, decide the number of job-waiting workers and the level of subsidy to the job-waiting workers. In fact, to a certain extent, this flexible method provides enterprises with some power to employ workers according to their own will.

According to the analysis mentioned above, at present, when measuring the enterprises' free power to employ working staff, we should mainly take the enterprises' free power to fire working staff into consideration. According to our survey and the measure of the two degrees of freedom mentioned above, we suppose that in 1995, the degree of state enterprises' free recruitment is 50%. The degrees in other years, were calculated according to the ratio between the number of fired people in each year in Tianjin to that of in 1995, see Table 5.8 .

Table 5.8 Degree of Urban State Enterprises' Free Recruitment in Tianjin

	1979	1985	1990	1995
Number of Fired workers(10,000)	0.40	0.63	0.80	28
Degree of Urban State Enterprises' Free Recruitment	0.70	1.10	1.50	50

In Tianjin, in 1995, the number of fired workers accounted for 14% of the whole number of state enterprises' staff. Published In the 151st issue in 1997 of a magazine called "General Survey of Central Plain's Market" are the proportions of the number of job-waiting workers in the whole members in seven cities in 1996 in China. The proportions are as follows Shanghai 14%; Guangzhou 5.8%; Shenyang 23%; Fuzhou 27.5%; Zhengzhou14.8%; Chengdu 20-30%; Lanzhou 12.4%. The arithmetic mean of these seven cities is 17.5%. In 1995, in Tianjin, the degree of state enterprises' right to fire workers is 14%. Considering the fact that the right of state enterprises to fire worker in 1996 is more powerful than that of 1995, so we can safely use 14% as a representative number and use it to measure the degree of the whole country's state enterprises' right to fire workers.

The management system of urban units of collective ownership is basically similar to that of enterprises owned by the whole people, so we can consider these two kind of units together.

Degree of Free Recruitment of Government Organizations and Institutions

With the implementation of the reform and opening policy, China's government and institutions adopt the system of inviting application for jobs to recruit new cadres. The practice of this kind of system creates necessary social environment for the equal competition and rational use of talented people. In this way, it is easier to select qualified people than before.

In August 1993, *"The Temporary Regulation of Government Office Workers"* was promulgated, and this symbolizes that China's personnel management system has stepped into a new stage of legality. The examination of the employment of government office workers consists of two parts: written exam and interview. The exam aims at testing the examinee's common basic knowledge, proficiency of professional knowledge, other professional quality and working ability, which are required by a certain occupation. The work of examination and recruitment is done by the employing units in terms of the unified requirement given by the responsible institutions. Because the examination system to recruit government office workers is still in its primary stage, it is not perfect. Therefore, we suppose that in 1995, the degree of government organization's free employment of cadres is 50%. We can refer to government organizations for institutions' employment system in 1995. Before 1990, the degree of free employment of government offices and institutions was similar to that of state enterprises, so their degree of freedom can be obtained in the light of state enterprises.

According to the analysis mentioned above, we get the degree of China's labor force employing unit's free employment that is shown in Table 5.9.

Table 5.9 Degree of China's Employment Unit's Free Employment

	1979	1985	1990	1995
Number of staff and Workers in State Enterprises and units of Collective Ownership(10,000)	7903	10161	11279	11474
Degree of Free Employment(%)	0.70	1.10	1.50	50
Number of Staff and Workers in Non-State Enterprises(10,000)	37	494	835	2939
Degree of Free Employment(%)	100	100	100	100
Number of staff and Workers in Government Organizations and Institutions(10,000)	1599	2153	2616	2934
Degree of Free Employment(%)	0.70	1.10	1.50	50
Degree of Labor Employing Units' Free Employment(%)	1.09	4.91	7.08	58.47

Marketization Degree of Labor Salary

Marketization Degree of Urban Labor Salary

China's salary-allocation system has experienced a process of gradual vicissitude since 1978's reform, from the former system of planned distribution to present disposition system, which is decided by the market.

Under the traditional planned economy, central government set a nationally unified standard of salary by means of some administrative measures. The increase of salary is also determined by government. As to enterprises' salary, the government carried out arbitrary budget constraint and the enterprises had no power to distribute salary. Every staff and worker in the units of collective ownership "sit in his right seat" according to his wage scale determined by administrative organizations. There is no direct connection between the withdrawal of enterprises' wage fund and the production and management results of the enterprises. The wage fund was guaranteed by government regardless of the enterprises gain or loss. However, when enterprises were deficient in money, the same policy was still carried out. In this way, the enterprises could have stable yields despite drought or excessive rain, and in the whole country, there was the allocation system of serious egalitarianism. Basically, salary had no influence on the demand and flow of labor force. This kind of allocation system dampened the laborers' enthusiasm and lowered the social production efficiency.

With the practice of market economy, a series of reforms have been carried out in connection with the system of salary allocation. The salary is drawn up mainly according to three points as follows: a. the enterprises' efficiency and benefit; b. average salary of other enterprises of the same trade; c. the demand and supply of labor force in the market. At present, China's labor force's salary can be divided into three categories:

State Economic Units

State economic units include state enterprises, government organizations and institutions. Before the 1990's, state economic units' salary allocation system was characterized by intensive unanimity. With the further development of the reform and opening policy, labor contract system and government office worker system were carried out one after another, Great varieties begin to appear in state enterprises' salary allocation system. Therefore, with all the statistical data, we can get the proportion of workers' bonus in the total amount of workers' salary as a whole in state economic units Then, we use this newly-obtained data to measure the degree of marketization of workers' salary in state economic units. After some research, we find the degrees of salary' marketization in 1979, 1985 and 1990 are 5%, 25.40% and 27.50% respectively. The measurement of the degree of salary's marketization in 1995 is as follows:

a. State Enterprises: Before 1990's, state enterprises' salary was distributed according to the number of the people. Since 1990's, salary has been allocated according economic performances. State enterprises can determine their total wages on the premise of "two below" The government no longer makes any unified arrangement of working staff's salary adjustment. With the development of socialist market economy, the right of free distribution enjoyed by enterprises has been exercised more and more thoroughly. An enterprise can adopt different styles of salary distribution according to the various concrete situations of the enterprise. As far as the interior structure of enterprises' total salary is concerned, several categories can be formed: standardized salary, piece rate salary, bonus, subsidy and so on. Standardized salary and subsidy belong to comparatively stable income, while bonus has close contact with enterprises' economic performances. We regard the proportion of bonus in the total salary as workers' marketized salary. After some calculation, in 1995, in state enterprises, 70% of the workers' income belong to marketized income.

b. Government Organizations. In 1993, "*Provisional Regulations of National Government Office Worker*" was published and it established the salary system with stress on posts and ranks. The salary standard is fixed according to government office worker' title, rank, number of years of his tenure in the office and length of service. Salary consists of four parts: {1}. basic salary {2}. salary related to specific work posts {3}. subsidy which is given according to one's length of service {4}. bonus. The government raises the salary standard of government office workers in a planned way, according to the development of national economy and the alteration of price index of living expenses. According to national regulation, government office workers enjoy local subsidy and other kinds of allowance. In form, China's present system of government office worker has already been connected with that of western developed countries with market economy, but there are still some inadequacies. We suppose that the degree of marketization of this kind of system is 70%.

c. Institutions: According to different sources of funds, the salary management can be divided into three types: {1}. salary provided totally by government. {2}. differential appropriation {3}. money earned and allocated by institutions themselves. Market adjustment function has been adopted, allocation system has been transformed, a brand-new salary system, which conforms to the characteristic of institutions, has been established. The new salary system makes the following regulations: in institutions whose salaries are totally provided by the government, 70% of the workers' salary are fixed; in institutions whose salaries are appropriated differentially by the government differential, fixed salary amounts to 60% of the whole; in institutions who responsible for their own gain and allocation of salary, fixed salary only constitutes 50% of the whole income. Government encourages the institutions whose salaries are totally provided by the country to gradually transform their salary system to the system of differential appropriation. In the meantime, government urges that institutions, whose salaries are appropriated differentially by the government, change, step by step, into institutions that are responsible for their own gain and distribution of salary. Then, the institutions can step into markets and realize marketization. Generally speaking, salary of staff and workers in institutions can also be divided into three types: {1}. basic salary. {2}. all kinds of allowances. {3}. bonus. The adjustment of basic salary follows the country's unified regulations. In our analysis, we only consider bonus the income of marketization. According to the investigation, the degree is about 40%.

On the basis of the above-mentioned analysis, we can take the total number of staffs and workers in different kinds of units as weighted number and do some weighted average, then we have the results: the degree of marketization of workers' salary in state economic units in 1979,1985,1990,1995 are 5%, 25.40%, 27.50% and 62.98% respectively.

Urban Economic Units of Collective Ownership

Before the reform of salary system, salary income of urban economic units of collective ownership is the same as that of the state economic units. After the practice of the system of labor contract for whole staff and workers in 1995, salary income of urban economic units of collective ownership is similar to that of such non-state economic units as "joint ventures' and self-employed units.

Foreign-Funded Enterprises and other Non-state Economic Units.

Generally speaking, such non-state economic units as joint ventures aim at pursuing the maximum profit. Their economic behavior belongs to strategies of marketization, i.e. laborer's salary is determined by the situation of supply and demand in the labor force market. Therefore, we can suppose that the degree of marketization of such non-state economic units as joint ventures is 100%.

According to the above analysis, using the weighted average method to deal with item 1, item 2,and item 3, we get Table 5.3.10 in which the measure value of the degree of marketization of China's salary is shown.

Table 5.10 Degree of Marketization of Urban Labor Force's Salary Income.

	1979	1985	1990	1995
Number of Staff and Workers in State Economic Units(10,000)	5675	6482.30	7416.80	8155.30
Degree of Salary's Marketization(%)	5.00	25.40	27.50	62.98
Number of Staff and Workers in Economic Units of Collective Ownership(10,000)	2237	3324	3549	3147
Degree of Salary's Marketization(%)	5.00	25.40	27.50	100
Number of Staff and Workers in Non-State Economic units(10,000)	37	494	835	2939
Degree of Salary's Marketization(%)	100	100	100	100
Degree of Marketization of Urban Labor Salary(%)	5.44	28.98	32.63	78.80

Marketization Degree of Farmer's Income

Since the practice of the reform policy, the sources of China's farmers' salary have got great varieties. On one hand, a great number of enterprises of village and of township appear rapidly and attract the attention of lots of surplus labor force; on the other hand, because the country loosens up on the control of farmers' actions, many rural labor force free themselves from farm work and begin to be engaged in various kinds of work, such as livestock husbandry, sideline production, building industry and service trades. Farmers' income began to include not only pure agricultural income, but also non-agricultural income. Moreover, the latter accounts for a proportion which becomes larger and larger. We regard the proportion of farmers' non-agricultural income in the total income as part of the degree of marketization of farmers' income. Among agricultural income, grain is the main source of agricultural income, and the quantity of income obtained from grain has a direct connection with the degree of freedom given by the government to the grain's price. Therefore, to measure the degree of marketization of agricultural income, we regard the degree of freedom given by the government to the grain's price as an index. Then, by calculation, we can get the degree of marketization of farmer's income. It can be indicated in Table 5.11.

Table 5.11 Marketization Degree of Farmer's Income

	1979	1985	1990	1995
Agricultural Income (yuan)	131.55	298.28	510.86	996.51
Degree of Marketization(%)	1.30	15	60	89
Non-Agricultural Income (yuan)	14.95	69.42	146.49	483.98
Degree of Marketization(%)	100	100	100	100
Degree of Marketization of Farmer's Income (%)	11.4	31.05	68.90	92.60

Note: The data concerning the degree of freedom of grain's price comes from one of this research's question's sub-subject which deals with the measure of the process of price's marketization

Combining Table 5.10 and Table 5.11, we can get the data of the degree of marketization of China's labor salary income which can be seen in Table 5.12.

Table 5.12 Degree of Marketization of the Whole Country's Labor Salary

	1979	1985	1990	1995
Urban Labor Force(10,000)	10019.5	12808	14730	17346
Degree of Marketization(%)	5.44	28.98	32.63	78.80
Rural Labor Force(10,000)	31237	37065	42010	45042
Degree of Marketization(%)	11.40	31.05	68.90	92.60
Degree of Marketization of Salary Income(%)	9.95	30.52	59.48	88.76

Summing up the above-mentioned analysis, we can get the measure values of individual indexes which are used to measure the process of China's labor force's marketization. Among them, the degree of labor force's free job-selection is a, the degree of labor force's free flow is b, the degree of employing units free recruitment is c and the degree of marketization of labor salary is d, the arithmetic mean of the four indexes is the comprehensive value of the degree of China's labor force's marketization. It can be supposed as e:

e=(a+b+c+d)/4

Table 5.13 The Measure Value of the Process
for Marketization of China's Labor Force (%)

	1979	1985	1990	1995
A compounded Measure of the Process of Labor's Marketization	3.24	24.20	34.70	60.00

Therefore, we can draw a rough conclusion. Although the labor force market can into being rather late in China, the speed of its development was not slow. The scope and degree of labor force market's function have been gradually strengthened. Labor force market system plays a fundamental role in distributing the source of labor force and it has been an important section of the development of socialist market economy system.

In western countries which have high degree of marketization of labor force market, such as the United States, there is a series of comparatively consummate social security system which together with the labor force market, forms a complete network, for example, insurance system for old people, insurance system of medical treatment, insurance system for the unemployed, insurance system for industrial injury, accommodation fund, maternal hygiene etc. These indicate that the social nature and marketization of social security is bound to follow the rapid development of social nature of productive forces. However, the development of China's social security system has not kept pace with the labor force market. At present, only the insurance system for old people is a comparatively mature system. Every year, an enterprise hand in to the insurance company the insurance premium which constitutes 24% of the total salary of a employee; 20% of the insurance premium is handed in by the enterprise, 4% is handed in by employee. Other kinds of social security system have not been practiced. Some are just on trail.

Although China's labor force market is experiencing a very rapid development, many problems still exist. For example, {1}. government imposes too much interference on the administration of labor force market. {2}. the development of the function of market adjustment is unbalanced {3}. China's household-register system has a great influence upon labor force's job-selection and flow. {4}. the imperfect social security system restrains the process of labor force marketization.

SOME SUGGESTIONS ON POLICIES

At present, in order to promote the process of marketization of China's labor force, to establish a labor force market which can be depicted as "unified, open-minded, competitive and in good order", and finally to achieve the aim of adjusting the allocation of labor force source by adopting market mechanism, it is necessary to deepen and improve current reform. For this reason, we put forward some proposals concerning the policies:

1. Deepening the reform of salary system and set up scientific and logical systems to determine and restrain salary.

Salary reflects the value of labor force. As the principal part to require labor force, enterprises should, according to the degree of distinctness of property right relationship, correctly handle the relationship between the distribution according to labor and the distribution according to capital. At the same time, enterprises should establish mutual control system between these two kinds of distribution systems by making a trial implementation of yearly-pay-system to managerial people and by salary's being determined by collective discussion. On what has already been achieved, in the light of their own traits, enterprises can set up a basic salary system whose main focus is on salary system of post-skill. According to the degree of scarcity in labor force market in a certain post and the actual contribution made by a laborer in particular, the enterprises can fix a reasonable salary standard for an individual laborer. The country can gradually form a balanced rate of market salary through several measures. {1}. Establishing and adjusting the minimum wage standard; {2}. Making the directory line for salary increase {3}. Strengthening the collection and control on individual income tax {4}. Setting up system of salary defrayal {5}. Standardizing the conduct of salary defrayal; {6}. Protecting legal income and banning illegal income {7}. Adjusting income, which is too high and ensuring the basic necessities of people who have low salary.

2. Strengthening government's macroeconomic regulation to counteract the weakness of market regulation.

During the period of system transformation, labor force market is an incomplete market. On one hand, it is impossible for labor force market to break away from China's unique history and national condition which are characterized by several traits: (1) China is still in the primary stage of socialism. (2). China has a large population. (3). There still exists a large difference between urban areas and rural areas. On the other hand, it is still influenced by the long-drawn-out planned system. In addition, at present, the peculiarity of China's labor market makes it impossible to depend on market regulation only. A perfect system of macroeconomic regulation must be established and it is necessary to strengthen the macroeconomic regulation on the labor force market's operation. As far as China's current situation is concerned, we should make every effort to improve the following aspects: (1). In the process of advancing the "two fundamental transformations", government should strengthen the effective regulation of the cross-regional flow of rural surplus labor force and promote the arrangement of state enterprises' surplus staff and workers. (2). Strengthen the regulation upon the irrational disparity and gap in salary distribution among regions, occupations and industries as well the sharp gap among different society members and ensure the healthy development of social economy. {3}. Establish and make perfect labor regulations and effectively solve the chaotic problems which appear during the labor force market's operation such as tort, illegal intermediary and default of salary.

3. Accelerating the reform of social security system and accommodation system, and gradually establish basic condition to promote labor force's flow.

At present, China's social security system is not perfect. Generally speaking, as far as such social security systems as accommodation, unemployment and medical treatment are concerned, staff and workers in state enterprises can enjoy more favorable conditions. As a result, a gap emerges between state enterprises and non-state enterprises. This gap becomes a guiding factor of the interest which is not in tune with the requirement of labor force market's development and therefore, hindering the reasonable flow of labor force. It is necessary to eliminate these obstacles of systems by adopting the principle of marketization. According to the prerequisite of equality, the society should provide essential guarantee for the laborers to deal with the risk that they will encounter in employment market. In this way, the social security system and house allocation system can transfer from one step to another, i.e. from the stage of unified allocation determined by units to more flexible process of development. As far as the reform of social security system is concerned, urban and rural enterprises security system should be unified on the basis of the combination of society-fund and individual's account. The integration of insurance system for old people should be promoted by combining the reform of the planned distribution of old-age pension with the reform of social security system. It is also indispensable to break the bounds between different employing units and different systems of ownership, and to gradually carry out a new old-age pension system which adopts unified regulation, criterion and management. For labors of different kinds in cities and towns. Insurance system for the unemployed should be expanded to all the urban enterprises' staff and workers. The system of the collection and management of fund should be improved. Ensure the necessities of life for unemployed staff and workers and at the same time, paying special attention to the issue of reemployment of these groups of people.

4. Besides the three problems mentioned above, we should do some corresponding adjustment concerning some other systems and policies such as labor contract system and household registration system. It is true, these problems can not be solved at one go, and there is a long way for us to go before resolving all these problems. However, we believe that, with correct policies, appropriate measures and active endeavor of the whole society, the objective of establishing a modern socialistic labor force market system will definitely be achieved.

REFERENCES

Chen Zongsheng: *"Unemployment, Unemployment securities and labor force market"*, Tianjin Social Sciences, 6th issue, 1994.

Chen Zongsheng, Gao Guoli, *"The 'wave' of the countryman along the coastal areas and the policies on the 'wave'"* Tianjin Social Sciences, 3rd issue, 1995.

Chen Zongsheng, Gao Guoli, *"An investigation into the 'wave' of the countryman who are looking for jobs in the cities"*, Material for Economic study, 4th issue, 1995.

Li Zhong. "Some Different Kinds of Judgments on the Degree of Market-orientation of China's Economy", Developments of Economics, 9th issue, 1996.

Research Institute of Rural Development in China Social Sciences Academy, and The Assembling Unit for the Investigation of Rural Social Economy in National Statistics Bureau: *Report on the Development of China's Rural Economy in 1995 and Analysis of Its Tendency of Development in 1996.* China Social Sciences Press, 1996.

Research Group of the Rural Economy Research Center in Agriculture Department. "*The Influence Imposed on Farmers, Agriculture and the Sending-out Regions by the Rural Labor Forces' Looking For Jobs in Cities and Corresponding Countermeasures*", *in Management of Labor Economy and Labor Force Sources*, 2nd issue, 1997.

Ronald Iranberg and Robert Smith, translated by Pan Gongsheng, etc. "*Contemporary Labor Economics---Theory and Public Policy*", China Labor Press, 1991.

Song Changqing. *"Elementary Analysis on the Development Situation of China's Labor Force Market"* in *Analysis on Market and Population*, 1st issue 1996.

Statistical Yearbook of China (1996). China Statistics Press, 1996.

Sun Shangqing. "Report of the Development of China's Market.(1995)". China Development Press, 1995.

Chapter 6

THE PROGRESS AND MEASUREMENT OF CHINESE FINANCIAL MARKETIZATION

Financial marketization is "finance deepening" in the western countries. There's much in R. I. Mckinnon and E. S. Shaw's theory on finance deepening that we can learn .In his book *Finance Deepening in Economic Development*, Shaw believes: Traditional economic theory has ignored the relationship between finance and economy. In fact, financial sectors are closely linked to the development of economy, deep finance has a positive effect on economy, and while shallow finance has negative effect upon economy. Whether the finance of a country is in the state of deepening or being restrained can be measured by the stock and flow of its financial assets, the scale and structure of its financial system and the price of its financial assets. The economy in which the finance is deepening has many features as follows: the categories and time limits of financial assets increase; so does the ratio of financial assets to national income or visible material wealth; the flow of financial assets depends more on national savings than on financial revenue and international capitals, and the velocity of flow of money decreases too; the scale of financial system extends, the number of financial institutions increases, and the function of which becomes more and more professional; the interest of financial price reflects more accurately the opportunity of investment's substituting for consumption. The real interest becomes higher and the difference between interests becomes smaller. Financial restraining has many characteristics opposite to the above-mentioned. It cuts down on the earning rate of national financial assets, thus depressing their demands. Obviously, the only strategy that fits and promotes the development of socialist market economy is to carry out financial marketization. But the truth is just the opposite: financial institution lags behind other sectors slightly. Therefore the year of 1996 may be a crucial or turning year to the financial marketization in China. On April 1st of the same year, China proclaimed that interest marketization would be its goal in the future. On May 1st and August 23rd, the interest rate was lowered twice. The president of People's Bank of China (BPC) spoke publicly that China would develop "direct financing" and realize the free convertibility of RMB under current account, which indicates that the capital market in China is already on the way of gradually opening to the outside world.

China has already been on its long road to financial marketization, how to measure and estimate the degree of which since 1980's is a big problem that is crucial to our goal of financial marketization. When we are practising market economy under public ownership conditions in a densely populated country, we can hardly find any experience of other countries similar to ours for our reference. Thus the best way is to draw lessons from the countries that have developed market economy.

THE PROGRESS OF CHINA'S FINANCIAL
MARKETIZATION SINCE 1980'S

Economic Monetization and the Rapid Increase of China's Aggregate Financial Assets

First of all, China's economic monetization synchronizes with her reform and opening. Monetization means monetized economy expands towards the field of non-monetized economy such as economy in kind and barter trade. The progress of monetization is an important sign of a developing country's level of economic development. A certain research report points out that economic reform leads to monetization through at least five channels as follows:

A. through increasing transactions of habitants and enterprises;
B. through introducing the system of production responsibility in rural areas, which brings thousands of peasants who need cash to make a deal in the markets;
C. through the emerging of many rural and small town enterprises during reforms; and cash is one of the main transactional mediums for these enterprises that are not included in the plans of central government;
D. through the rapid growing of self-employed economy and private economy;
E. through the speedy increasing of free markets. (Yigang, p. 132-133, 1996)

Obviously, monetization certainly brings about the continuous increase for demand to cash. When planned economy occupies the leading position, peasants, self-employed businessman and township enterprises cannot build up their own business reputation, the only efficient way which makes business transactions go on successfully is to accumulate cash balance rapidly. The reform of rural system, especially the carrying out of system of production-responsibility, brings thousands of peasants into markets, and because they sell their agricultural products directly to government and get cash as payment, the aggregate of cash by which government buys grain from farmers sharply increases. In 1978, there were 72.1percent of farm products that were liquidated through bank account transference, only 27.9 percent of which were paid in cash. From 1979 to 1983, the average proportion of payment in cash by which government bought farm products increased rapidly. The percentages of 1979, 1980, 1981, 1982, 1983 are respectively 33.7, 40.2, 46.6, 52.3, 60 respectively. (ditto, p. 137,) This is a typical example of great demand for cash brought about by the reform of system in rural areas which is related to monetization. In the economy of many coastal provinces, the vigorously developing township enterprises have occupied "half of the country", even "two thirds of the country", the great cash demand brought about by this is more striking. The progress of monetization makes the chain of monetary circulation longer and more complicated, it enables money to circulate among various economic units without flowing to government directly. On the other hand, new monetized sectors absorb much currency, which deposits into social economic lives, thus lowering the velocity of currency. In the years of reform and opening, money supply of our country has showed an average yearly increase at extra-normal speed, which is explained by following statistics: between 1978 and 1995, our country's average annual growth rate of GNP is 9.7%, whereas the average rate of inflation is 7.5% yearly. The average growth rate of broad money (M2) is 25% and in 1995 it is as high as 29.5%, In June 1996, the aggregate of broad money is up to 6,813.2 billion yuan. (*Securities Market*, issue 46,1996, p 16; *Shanghai Security Newspaper*, July 16th, 1996, front page). According that the principle that the growth rate of money supply is equal to that of GNP plus the rate of inflation, we reached a conclusion that our country's yearly money supply increased excessively. But before 1988, this didn't result in serious inflation, even between 1988-89 and between 1993-95 when two relatively big inflation occurred, the level of inflation is fairly low compared with that of some developing countries in the world. The reason is that our country's newly-born monetized sectors and rapidly increasing sectors absorb much excessive money supply. Meanwhile it proved that we have big demand for money supply. Just because of above-mentioned reasons, the rate of our broad money supply compared with GNP has been showing a one-way increase for 17 years. In 1978 it is 0.32; in 1985 it is 0.60; in 1992 it is above 1.0; in 1995, even after 3 years of austerity, it is still 0.93(Calculated according to the numbers in *Shanghai Securities Newspaper*). Compared with other countries in the world, the increase in China is striking. For example, in 1990, the same ratio in U.S.A is 0.67; Korea 0.57; Taiwan 1.48; Japan 1.89; whereas in India it is 0.37 in 1978, In 1990 it is 0.47(ditto, p. 131).

That the ratio of broad money to GNP increases continuously proves the progress of our country's financial marketization. But this ratio is not the better the higher. For example, in American, it is only 0.67 in 1990, but in Japan it is as high as 1.89. Which is more proper depends mainly on money demand. In un-monetized countries, it depends on the level of monetization, while in monetized countries, it depends on the prosperity and depresses of economy, people's habit of consuming and saving, etc. In China the ratio is relatively higher mainly because newly-born monetized sectors absorb much excessive money, whereas in planned economy system these sectors didn't transact with cash. The phenomenon itself proves the development of our financial marketization, and that the ratio of M2 to GNP increases continuously is an important macro-indicator to measure the level of our financial marketization. Although the ratio of M2 to GNP is high, cash circulation has been lowered in recent years, which indicates that the government's deflation policy has greatly restrained the demand for cash.

The ratio of financial assets to GNP is another important evidence measuring the progress of financial marketization. In our country it also shows a one-way increasing trend since reform and opening too. In 1978 it was 0.94; in 1994 it was up to 2.14; by the end of June 1996, it was about 2.35. Obviously, its rapid increase is mainly because of the increase of the aggregate stock of our financial assets. The owner of financial assets, the change of structure of national savings, and the pluralistic development of financial variety, and financial instruments are the important factors of the increase of the aggregate financial assets.

Before economic reform, there was barely any other kind of financial asset than cash in circulation and deposits. Since reform and opening, China's financial assets has developed from single bank assets to marketization and pluralistization, At present, China's financial assets mainly include cash in circulating, deposits of financial institutions, loans of financial institutions, valuable securities (bond, stock, etc.). Circulating cash is the owner's right of credit on central bank. Financial institution's loan is mainly the bank's right of credit on enterprises. Valuable securities are the tools for direct financing, which reflects investor's right of credit, stock right and other kinds of ownership. Between 1981 and 1996, our country issued a total of 479.44 billion yuan of government loans, 31.40 billion yuan of government investment and investment corporate loans, 118.30 yuan of financial institution loans, 173.83 billion yuan of enterprise loans, face value of 12.00 billion yuan of A shares and 179.6 billion yuan of wholesale deposits. 1996 is a year in which stock and bond developed by leaps and bounds, until the end of October, we had issued government loan worth of 220 billion yuan. It is estimated that the market price of the aggregate stock had approached 980 billion yuan (China Security Control Committee, 1995; *China Securities Newspaper*, 13/11, 12/12/1996)

Although in China the varieties of financial assets have developed in the direction of pluralistization and the structure has changed, the main parts are still the deposits and loans of bank and other financial institutions. The ratio of bank and financial institution's deposits and loans to the aggregate financial assets in 1978 was 93%; 1986, 87%; 1991, 84%; and 1995, 83%.

The main reason is that money market and capital market is opening relatively slow, so many financial instruments which have no other fields to move about have to crowd in the banks, thus resulting in the abnormal structure of China's financial assets. This can be seen from following table; the main body of China's saving has changed radically since 1980's. The main source of saving changes from government and public enterprise in the past to common inhabitants now. For example, in 1978 the aggregate of saving was 133.05 billion yuan, and the inhabitants' saving was 21.06 billion yuan, occupying 16.2%; whereas the deposits of enterprises undertakings and government totaled 108.99 billion yuan, which occupied 83.8%. Until the first half of 1996, urban and rural inhabitant's savings totaled 3546 billion yuan, which occupied 64.7%; whereas, the deposits of financial institutions, enterprises and undertakings totaled 1932 billion yuan, occupying 35.3%.

Table 6.1 The Ratio of Financial Assets to GNP in China Unit: 100 million yuan

Items	1978	Ratio to GNP	1991	Ratio to GNP	1996	Ratio to GNP
Cash in circulation	212.0	0.06	3177.8	0.15	8910	0.14
Aggregate deposit of Financial Institution	1300.5	0.36	18079.0	0.83	67500	1.07
Habitants' deposits in Urban and rural areas	210.6	0.06	9107.0			
Enterprises' deposits (including fiscal and financial institutions)	1089.9	0.30	8972	0.42		
Aggregate loan of financial Institutions	1890.0	0.52	21021.5	0.97	61000	0.97
Balance of national debt			1141.6			
Balance of enterprises bonds			331.1		820 (in 1995)	
Balance of financial bonds			123.1			
Stock market price			452.4		9800	0.156
Aggregate financial assets	3417	0.94	46404	2.14	148030	2.36

Source: *China's financial yearbook*, 1993; The data of 1996 was estimated according to the numbers in Dai Xianglong's speech (*Securities Times*, 12/12/1996)

That the ratio of financial assets to GNP increases continuously reflects the fast development of China's financial marketization. But 90% of financial assets in the form of deposit and loans of bank and other financial institutions is an abnormal structure that is surely embodied by enterprise construction of liabilities. Enterprises' obtaining fund mainly depends on the loans of bank and other financial institutions, making it very difficult to obtain fund from direct financing, such as bond and stock. Enterprises rely on banks excessively, which also shifts risk on to banks. So if we don't change the structure of financial assets, we cannot change the abnormal relationship between banks and enterprises and the enterprises' management pattern of high debt and high cost.

The Opening Level of Chin's Capital Market

The main part of China's financial assets is the deposit and loan of bank and other financial institutions, even until 1995, this part still occupied 93% of the aggregate financial assets. This feature decides the main financing channel of enterprises that is through banks, in the indirect way of financing such as the loan of bank and financial institutions, whereas the direct financing way such as bond market and stock market is still in the subsidiary position. According to the statistics of related sectors, in present capital operating, the aggregate indirect-financing occupied about 90%, the aggregate direct-financing (stock, bond) occupied about 10%, among which the most representative kind is stock. In 1994 the ratio of aggregate stock market price to GNP (securitization) is only 6.76%, if we deduct uncirculated state-owned stock and cooperate stock, the ratio is about 1.83%. Whereas in abroad, such as in U. S. A, it is 70%; in France, it is 136%, in Germany, it is 97%; in Korea it is 149%; in Malaysia, it is 119% (*Economic Reference Newspaper* 28/7/1996, He, Xiaolin, etc.). But we must note that 1996 maybe a critical year in the history of development of China's capital market when both stock issuing and listing and government loan issuing all broke the historical record. Until November 1996, The securities exchanges in Shenzhen and Shanghai listed 183 new stocks a year, a 40% increase compared with that in 1995. In 1996 we issued 220 billion yuan government loan which is equal to 67 percent of the accumulated balance of the 330 billion yuan government loan issued between 1981 and 1995. The stock market price totaled about 980 billion yuan, capital stock totaled 113 billion. But circulating stock A occupied only 21.68 percent of total capital stock, even when added with foreign-owned B stock listed at home and H stock listed in Hong-Kong, the total three occupied only 35.04 percent of total capital stock (*Securities Market*, 1996, issue 47, Zhang Bo). Estimated according to these, total circulating stock market price is about 350 billion yuan at most. Estimated further, Until Nov.11th, 1996, Chinese government loan balance (counted by nominal value) and circulating stock value totaled about 900 billion yuan, occupying 13.5 percent of GNP of that year's (estimated by the growth rate of 10%. In 1995 GNP was 5765 billion yuan). Even when estimated according to total stock market price 980 billion, the total market price of stock and bond occupied merely 24 percent of GNP. This ratio is much lower than that of Southeast Asia countries and western developed countries. Calculated according to the numbers of Table 6.1.2, in seven regions such as Hong Kong, Indonesia, Korea, Malaysia, the Philippines, Singapore, and Thailand, the average ratio of stock market price to GNP is 148.25% in 1993. In German, Japan, England and America, it is 75%. Let's have a look at the ratio of stock market price to GDP, the average of the above seven newly-industrialized east-Asia countries is 30,25%, and the average of German, Japan, England and America is 74%, the weighted average of the two group is 52.13%. Take the ratio of securitized capital in particular, the weighted average of eleven countries the (of two economic developing levels) is 111.63%, whereas that of China is only 14.4% (the ratio of 980 billion yuan to GNP 6780 billion yuan in 1996). If we add up the ratio of stock to GDP and the ratio of bond to GDP, the weighted average of 11 countries according to two levels is 163.76%, whereas that of China is merely 24%(20% in 1995), that is, China's level of direct financing through capital market is merely equal to 0.15percent of that of western developed countries and newly-industrialized countries. This number shows the opening level of China's capital market, and it is also the most important evidence of China's financial market.

Table 6.2 11 Countries' (or Regions') Stock, Bond Market Price in 1993

Region	M2		Bank Assets		Stock Market Price		Bond Market Price	
	US$	%	US$	%	US$	%	US$	%
China	519	88	547	128	41	9	47	11
Hong Kong	119	109	200	182	385	352	6	5
Indonesia	69	48	85	59	33	23	13	9
Korea	139	42	229	69	139	42	138	42
Malaysia	54	88	60	93	220	342	35	54
The Philippines	22	42	28	51	40	74	24	43
Singapore	51	92	92	167	133	240	38	70
Thailand	98	79	118	95	130	104	10	8
Average		73.5		105.5		148.25		30.25
German	1184	65	2766	145	463	24	1587	83
Japan	4633	111	6338	150	300	71	2887	68
Britain	885	96	2101	223	1152	122	311	33
America	4013	64	3471	55	5224	83	6993	112
Average		84		143.25		75		74

Source: Yi Gang *The Analysis and Policy Implication of China's Financial Structure*, Academic Report of China Center For Economics Research, Beijing University, 1996, 10.

The above analysis and data have a pessimistic sense, which is also proven by the speech given by Yin Tieyan, vice president of PBC, about China's capital market. He points out that China's capital market is still in the period of developing. "The opening of capital market in China must advance steadily."(*Securities Market*, 1996. Issue 48. p. 12).

If we look at the present situation of China's capital market, we find that it actually has many deficiencies. First of all, the scope of market is too small. The main channel through which enterprise obtains fund is through banks. This indirect financing has many shortcomings that are be coming more and more obvious. For example, it aggravates enterprises' interest burden, which results in enterprises' excessive dependence on banks, therefore it prevents banks from reforming themselves, and it keeps society from efficiently allocating its funds, thus leading to bad benefit of funds etc. All these show that development of direct financing is of great urgency. Overheated situations in securities market recently indicated that Chinese government has on this point agreed with specialists in economic fields, although they still have disagreements on the speed of opening. Some people have this view: If China's securitized ratio increases from 6.76% in 1994 to 30%, the direct financing stock market price realizing in a year will be 1,500 billion yuan, whereas circulating stock market price at present are merely about 350 billion yuan. Bond listing issued directly by enterprises is also too few, and most of the bonds have a short time-limit. The longest time-limit of bonds in U.S.A. is as long as 40 years, even 100 years. But in our country, enterprises' benefit and reputation are fairly low. So it is almost impossible for them to issue long-term bonds.

Second, China's capital market lacks unity because of the existence of disintegration and closing. At present China's listing corporations total stock capital can be roughly divided into three types according to whether they circulate or not. (1). Circulatable stocks. RMB normal stock-A stock, foreign-owned stock listed at home B stock, foreign-owned stock listed in Hong Kong-H stack, foreign-owned stock listed in New York-N stack. (2). Uncirculating stocks, national stocks, founder corporate stock, social corporate stock, foreign corporate stock, (3). Stock that has conditions to circulate, labor-owned stock, i.e. stocks held by internal employees. Stocks that are not circulating create a great deal of noncirculatable stock that can be transferred or added with more shares. It is a big problem as to how to put the noncirculatable national stocks and corporate stock on the market to let them circulate, to handle stock assets flexibly, to promote the restructuring of property rights. It is also a big problem as to how to form a unified market, to make stock A and stock B on the same track and attract foreign capital to list in the market judging from the present situation. These two problems will not be easily solved in a short time. Although there exists the problem of endurance extent of China's stock market, the fundamental problem is the ideology. The government and the fundamental problem of whether the circulatable national stock belongs to "capitalist" or to "socialist", and the problem of whether it is privatized or not to sell national stocks to individuals. Therefore, the first step now is to make circulate the part of national stock that can be transferred or added with more shaves, together with the founder corporate stock and social corporate stock. If the stocks can enter the market of stock A, the market of stock A will be expanded twice. Obviously, even this will not be easily realized within one or two years.

Third, the system of securities law is not perfectly established at present, Security Law, regulation of fund management have not been drawn up till now; there are many deficiencies in supervising money and in regional government behavior, this brings speculative atmosphere and relatively great fluctuation into stock market, This has something to do with shareholders' direct scalping and the lack of big fund institutions' operation, which all need further improvement of law. From the developed countries' experience, we can find that investment fund is an important source that sustains security market. From 1950 to 1993, American investment fund assets increased about 4000 times. In 44 years In 1970, the investment fund assets were no more than 47 billion, but by the midst of 1994, they were up to 2000 billion, the variety of funds being 6300 In Japan the variety is 1250, total assets being 245 billion. In Hong Kong, there are 338 kinds of fund, with a total fund assets of 15.6 billion dollars. But in China there're only 122 kinds of fund and securities that belong to fund, at present most of them are small in scale, and only 25 kinds of them were listed formally. So at present it is of great urgency for us to develop investment fund.

Besides, It is still a problem for foreign capital to enter China's capital market. Although we have adopted many favorable measures to attract foreign capital, all of the measures are for capital entering enterprises (production or commodity circulation), many people still have worries about foreign capital's entering CCM. Although we now have many branches of foreign-owned banks, they cannot deal in Renminbi business. Definitely foreign capital cannot directly enter nominal stock market. But many evidences show that ice has been broken. It is not rare for foreign capital to take over Chinese enterprises' stock capital. Regulation of China-foreign cooperate fund will be issued, which will attempt to open our stock A market to foreign capital. In 1996, our government has sanctioned four foreign capital banks to deal in Renminbi business in Pudong. At any rate, attracting certain foreign capital into China's capital market has more advantages than disadvantages.

The above-mentioned analysis adumbrated many disadvantages of CCM. But, if we look back on its developing course, we still find it has made a great progress, and has a promising future.

Interest Marketization

The marketization of interest, which is the most important lever of macro-economy, basically means that interest level is decided by as the supply and demand of financial market. In market economy countries, central bank merely proclaims discount rate towards commercial banks. The market interest in the short-term financial market in which commercial bank are the main participants are complete "free market interest". On the other hand, government's adjustment of discount rate still depends on market. From this view, the change of discount rate is still "directed by market". For example, American discount rate often lags behind market interest. If we take the above principle as the direction of China's interest marketization, we will discover that at present, China's interest situation has quite a distance from the goal of setting up interest system whose main body is the interest in short-term fund market, and from the goal of carrying out relatively flexible floating interest rate. Even though Bank of China permits commercial bank to have certain loan-interest floating range, under the conditions of long-term bondage of planned management system and government-owned banks' controlling the whole country, it is very difficult for floating interest to float. Usually, it is practiced according to the up-limit of floating interest, and the exception is rare. There is no competition among government-owned banks, meanwhile rural cooperative foundation and people-to-people financing services seize the opportunity to enter, therefore there exists " one country, two systems " phenomenon in the interest rate field, which cannot embody principle of fair play. The most radical consequence is that interest rate level cannot accurately reflect capital price and relationship between fund supply and demand. Developed market economy countries control their central bank's loan size by adjusting discount rate (the interest rate of rediscount of central bank) and legal reserve ratio, but in China, up to now it is the government who determines the loan size of all banks. This indirectly reflected Chinese interest has not, in complete sense, played its role as market lever.

But, looking back on the change of interest level since reform and opening, we can prove that it actually advances in the direction of marketization, what is more, its steps may be speedier in the near future.

Before 1979, interest rate had been frozen for about 20 years, it was firmly controlled on a fixed level much lower than that of equilibrium.

Since 1980's although interest rate was not completely decided by the market, its marketization became deeper and deeper. The writer summarized it as follows: the government began to realize that interest rate is the most important lever of macroeconomics, and it began to use interest rate to influence aggregate demand and supply. Since April 1, 1980, people's Bank of China adjusted interest rate 16 times, which is a strong evidence. Before August 14, 1987, interest rate was relatively low. Since 1988, the growth of monetized economy began to slow down, but social economy wasn't able to absorb the great quantity of the over-supply of money, so the pressure of inflation began to become bigger, thus making interest rate rise accordingly. After July 11th, 1993, the interest rate, together with the guaranteed-and-subsidizing interest rate, of loans three years up began to be upside down, that is the interest the banks paid to the customers was higher than the interest the bank received from the enterprises, interest rate reached unprecedented peak. Since May 1996,interest rate was cowered twice. After August 23 the interest rate returned to close to the level of 1992 and 1987, The following table is the data of the interest rate of one year's fixed-term lump-sum deposits and lump-sum withdrawals, it shows the change.

All in all, we have made great progress in regulating economy through the lever of interest rate during the 1980's. Public marginal propensity to save, enterprise cost, profit of bank and income of government all change with the level of interest rate. The waxing and waning of macro-economy alter with the rise and fall of the level of interest rate. For example, after Deng Xiaoping's speech in his tour to the south at the beginning of 1992, economic overheating began to appear in China. As we greatly raised the interest rate in May and July in 1993, the phenomenon of economic overheating immediately disappeared. But the following three years of tightening policy made lots of state-owned enterprise overburdened. On May 1, and August 23, 1996, as central bank again lowered the interest rate twice, the macro-economy went out of the stalemate in the third quarter. It is estimated that twice lowering interest rate may make the state-owned enterprises depending on bank loans save over 100 billion yuan; the profit of enterprise may rise gradually. In fact securities market has the most sensitive and enthusiastic response to the falling of interest rate. Fund has the property of chasing the highest profit; it is estimated that lowering the interest rate push at least over 150 billion yuan circulating fund into stock market, so share index in Shanghai and Shenzhen was always pushed to record high. From the beginning of 1996 to the end of November 1996, the share index in Shenzhen rose about 365%, ranking the first in increased volume of securities all over the world in 1996, the share index in Shanghai also rose about 134%. It is believed that with the development of the marketization of interest rate, its function of regulating the macro-economy and the micro-economy in China will be more and more notable.

Table 6.3 Adjustment-Interest Situation Survey

Date of adjustment	85.4.1		85.8.1		88.9.1		89.2.1		90.4.15		90.8.21	
	Before	After	Before	After	Before	After	Before	After	Before	After	Before	After
Interest level (%)	5.76	6.84	6.84	7.20	8.64	8.65	11.34	11.34	10.98	10.98	8.64	8.64
Adjustment range	+1.08		+0.36		+1.44		+2.7		-0.36		-2.34	

Date of adjustment	91.4.21		93.5.15		93.7.11		96.5.1		96.8.23		96.8.23	
	Before	After	Before	After	Before	After	Before	After	Before	After	Before	After
Interest level (%)	8.64	7.56	7.56	9.18	9.18	10.98	10.98	9.18	9.18	7.74		
Adjustment range	+1.08		+1.62		+1080		-1.08		-1.071			

Table 6.4 Comparison between Interest Level and Inflation Level in 1996

Date	January	February	March	April	May	June	July	Before 8.23	After 8.23
Interest Level (%)	10.98	10.98	10.98	10.98	9.18	9.16	9.18	9.18	7.47
Inflation level (%)	7.6	7.7	7.7	7.4	6.50	5.9	5.8		
Real interest level(%)	3.38	3.28	3.28	3.58	2.68	3.28	3.38		

Source: " *Security Market Weekly*" Issue 34, p.7, 1996.

The Relative Independence of Central Bank, the Marketization of the Regulating Way and the Marketization of the Trade Behavior of Other Financial Enterprises

Although the problem of the independence of the central bank has been being discussed endlessly almost when it came to this world, the central bank is relatively highly independent in most of the countries that have developed market economy. Within the limits of right endowed with by law, it independently carries out monetary policy and is beyond the intervention of the government. Judging by its economic activity exercise, it is an economic entity. The function of management of the whole country's financial enterprises was added to the central bank, but its main activities do not aim at profit.

The central bank is not only the most important department of adjusting economy in those countries that have developed market economy, but also the head of financing, so if we research the Chinese economic marketization, we must research the pattern of central bank.

America Federal Reserve System (FRS) enjoys relatively high independence, which is the most typical one in the system of western central banks. Its features are:

1. FRS is under the control of the law of FRS. FRS can take action independently by the authority of the congress. It does not need the sanction of the president. It has power to the monetary policy independently and to decides by itself to take measures and to wield polices. It is responsible and accountable to the congress. FRS does not belong to the president and other government department. The president can not give order to FRS without the authority of the congress. The Treasury can not intervene in the monetary policy of FRS.

2. FRS does not have the duty to give long-term to support the Treasury financing (including issuing bonds). The Treasury's money- raising can only be fulfilled through issuing government bonds on opening market.

3. FRS is divided to 12 districts. In every district there is a bank of FRS, whose capital belongs to every member bank, that is, every member bank purchase the stocks of the bank of FRS it participates in, the amount being equal to 6% of each member's total paid-in capital and public accumulation fund. So this kind of central bank has, in nature, has the quality of private share capital.

4. Seven directors of the council, the highest decisive department in FRS, are appointed by the president for a term of 14 years with the agreement of the Senate and none of them can be re-appointed, A person must be changed every two years, Staggering the change and the presidency makes the president not be able to change most of the members in the council of FRS system during his (or her) term. This in form restricts the possibility of the president's total control over the board of FRS system.

On the contrary, people's Bank of China didn't have the function owned by central bank until 1984, but still is not the same as the central bank in the west. It is more like a department of government. In March 1995, "*Law of People's Bank of China*" was formally adopted by the National People's Congress and was promulgated and put into effect. This means that China has its first central bank law. This endowed the bank with two functions: the first is that under the leadership of the state council, PBC makes and carries out monetary policy stabilizes the currency value and promotes the development of economy; the second is that PBC supervises and administers the financial department, looking from the content of the law, it is still a government department managing financial organization but I think there are two points in the law worthy of special notice. The first is that it definitely stipulates that PBC has right to independently carry out monetary policy under the leadership of the state council, beyond the intervention of other government department, local government, social group or individual, namely, PBC is endowed with the relatively independent and centralized financial leadership. The second is PBC does not permit government to overdraw, In this way, the possibility of government's excessively issuing circulating currency, which will lead to currency inflation, is rooted out by law. This stipulation ought to be viewed as the important step toward setting up the system of central bank in the true sense in China, it also shows that our system of central bank will be made perfect with the development of the market economy. The system of central bank in countries that have developed market economy may be our last or partial goal.

ESTIMATION OF MARKETIZATION LEVEL OF CHINA'S FINANCE

From the above-mentioned comprehensive summary of China's financial marketization since 1980's, we can see that the factors of marketization play a more and more important role in the increase of China's total financial asset, in the increase of the portion of direct financing and in the structure and change of currency supply. To estimate the level of financial marketization is to judge how far the factors of marketization influence the area of finance. Here we define 2 indexes to estimate and measure. One is the change of proportion of negotiable securities in total amount of financial asset. From it we can see the change of the structure of the total amount of China's financial asset and the increase of the proportion of direct financing in China's capital market, because the negotiable securities is the tool of direct financing; the other is the influence of the floating interest rate in the graded interest rate determined by government on the structure and amount of loan, which is related to the structure and amount of money supply, in the whole society. See the table below.

Table 6.5 Proportion of Valuable Securities to Chinese Financial Assets Unit: 100 million yuan

Item / Time	Valuable Securities					Cash	Deposits	Loans	Aggregate Financial Assets	Ratio of Valuable Securities To financial Assets
	Total	Nation-owned bonds	Enterprises bonds	Financial Bonds	Stock					
1985	50	50				1000	4273.03	5905.51	12994.44	0.4%
1990	1267.42	234.16	126.37	70.55		2600	13029.3	16541.3	33438.02	3.8%
1995	7631.04	3591.3	364.35	1675.19	2000	7885.3	15955.4	56327.53	117799.27	6.5%S

Notes: (1) Stock in 1995 is calculated according to face-price, including shares B, H and N, whose circulating value is about 200 billion, estimated according to market price.

(2) In 1995 government bonds include exchequer bonds, fiscal bonds, special construction bonds, special national bonds, value-guaranteed bonds, oriented government bonds, national investment bonds, and national investment cooperate bonds.

(3) In 1985 the value of valuable securities is the estimated according to closing balance.

(4) Source: "*China Finance yearbook*" in 1992,1996,1986.

Table 6.6 Ratio of Floating-interest-rate Loan to the Aggregate of Loan Unit: 100 million yuan

Time	Item: The name of Financial institution	Floating range of floating-rate	Loan controlled By floating rate	The aggregate of loan	The ratio of floating rate to total loan
1985	Rural credit cooperatives	Loan to rural credit cooperatives is determined by provinces.	399.96	5905.51	6.8%
1990	Rural credit cooperatives	Add 60% to the loan rate of Professional banks Above 60% must be ratified by The people bank above level	1413	16541.3	8.54%
1995	Rural credit cooperatives	Add 60% to the loan rate of Professional banks Above 60% must be ratified by The People bank above level	5234.2	56327.53	12.7%
	Urban credit cooperatives	Add 30% to the loan level of Professional banks Above 30% must be ratified by The People bank above level	1929		

Notes: (1) What was executed in 1995 is "deposit-loan floating rate table of credit cooperatives" proclaimed on July 11th, 1993.

(2) Generally, loan of rural credit cooperative is classified into to collective agricultural loan, township enterprises loan and farm loan.

(3) Source is the same as table 6.4

In the two lists ahead, the first index, namely the change of proportion of negotiable securities in the total amount of financial assets, reflects the gradual change of enterprises' financing in the direction of direct financing, but also reflects the change of fiscal policy of government, that is loan is not obtained by overdrawing, but is obtained by borrowing from people directly. So it is a very important index. The second reflects that the rate is changing gradually in the direction of marketization, for example, after 1993, floating rate has already expanded to urban credit cooperatives and the amount of loan dominated by floating rate was enlarging. Then we get magnitudes at every time point of China's financial marketization by taking the average of the two index they are, namely, 3.6% in 1985, 6.15% in 1990, 9.6% in 1995.

From these magnitudes, we can see that the level of China's financial marketization is relatively low. This is the outcome of government's control. For fear of financial chaos and inflation, the government enforces firm administration and control in the area of finance, for example, firmly prohibiting individuals from opening banks; to firmly forbid individuals from to raising money; to put limitation on foreign capital from coming into China's capital market and to firmly restrict financial department from altering loan interest without approval. Those make the reform of marketization in the area of finance fall behind the progress of marketization in other economic areas. But in view of stabling finance and economy, of preventing financial disturbance to reach the goal of reform, this is suitable for present circumstances in our country, for example, the financial crisis in south-east Asia in summer and autumn in 1997 did not influence China much, this is just because China didn't open its capital market to foreign capital and that RMB was not freely convertible. But it should be pointed out that the progress of marketization in China's financial area just quickened its steps in 1996.

In a word, from the 1980's China's financial marketization has stepped onto a right track. The achievements are obvious. But there is a long distance away from the developed market economy countries.

The introduction of China's financial marketization, the measure index and level of estimation made in the section can be used as the reference to observe the future progress of China's financial marketization.

REFERENCES

Chen Zongsheng *Inflation and Deepening of Enterprises' Reform,* Published in *Shanghai Financing*, issue 11, 1994

China Finance Yearbook in 1992, 1996, 1985, China Financing Publishing Press.

E. S. Shaw: *The financial deepening in economic development*, Edition in Chinese, published by Sanlian Bookstore in Shanghai, 1988.

Yi Gang *Money, bank and financial market in China 1984-1993*, Published by Sanlian Bookstore and People's Publishing House in Shanghai, 1996

Chapter 7

THE MEASUREMENT OF REAL ESTATE MARKETIZATION IN CHINA

We define the real estate marketization as the allocation of house estate and land estate resources by means of market mechanism, i.e. the real estate commercialization. In China, REM in a true sense began in 1978 after the reform and opening to the outside. What is the maturity degree of China's real estate market now? That is the main topic we shall study in this chapter. Here we only study the urban real estate market, without involving the real estate market in the countryside. Meanwhile, because residential house real estate occupies an important proportion of the whole real estate industry (in general, about 50%), and the non-house real estate as fixed assets has participated in the marketization of relevant industry and section, in our analysis, emphasis is put on the residential house marketization to reflect roughly the whole REM course.

THE BASIC FRAMEWORK OF CHINA'S REAL ESTATE MARKETIZATION

During the economic development course of human society, along with the development of market economy and the advance of the urbanization, the pattern of specialized commercialization of the development and management of real estate was gradually formed and real estate industry became an independent industry. Therefore, we can say that the real estate development and management is the inevitable result of the social and economic progress, and the objective requirement of the market economy operation. However in China, under the planned economy system, urban real estate was "state-owned" and "state-managed". The urban land was developed and utilized free of charge. Urban real estate development and construction were monopolized by the state. The non-house real estate (i.e. operational real estate) invested by the state were appropriate to the enterprises and the administration units at no cost; residential houses were directly distributed as material to the employees welfare, the government just collected a symbolic rent at a low level. The whole real estate economy was a product economy pattern; the process of supply and demand was non-monetarized. The adjustment function of price didn't exist. One word in all, the real estate economy was completely non-commercialized and non-marketized. It was until the reform and opening that REM process started with the reform of real estate economic systems, especially the reform of urban housing systems.

The basic connotations of China's REM are as follows:

1. To form subject of property rights by clarifying the property rights and the subject of the property rights;
2. To establish the transaction relationship of effective supply and effective demand by transform the material allocation to the monetary allocation;
3. To transform the single function of value-recording of price to cost-checking and adjustment function;
4. To set up and make perfect the law and regulation systems and intermediary services systems to assure the orderly operation of real estate market.
5. The clarifying of property rights is the prerequisite for real estate transfer and circulation.

Real estate is a special kind of resources and asset, to which many types of rights are attached, for example, dominium and jura in realiena. In these right, there are ownership in a wide sense that includes ownership, occupation, disposition and use; and there are still some ancient or modern forms of right forms such as lease, mortgage, superficies, predial servitude, pawnage right, neighborhood relationship, space right, etc. All these rights form a complicated rights bundle. Among all these rights, ownership, usage and management rights are the basic rights of market subjects, which constitutes the bases of the real estate market transactions. If property rights are not clear, the cost of negotiation, signing and execution of real estate transaction contracts will be extremely high, which shall form a real estate resource allocation mechanism of high-transaction-cost and low-efficiency; Sometimes tort and infringement of the legitimate rights and interests may take place. In China, on the one hand, the tort manifestation is the loss of state-owned real estate revenues; on the other hand, the rights and interests belonging to the enterprises and individuals can not be compensated for or be realized.

The effective supply of real estate is the supply from which the real estate suppliers can get normal profits. The effective demand of real estate is defined as the demand that the demanders have desires and have purchasing powers. The formation of effective demand and effective supply determines the possibility of real estate market transaction. Presently there exist many channels of real estate supply in China. The investors can be divided into several kinds: the government's direct investment, the real estate developer (including foreign-funded investment), enterprises' and units' direct investment, private investment, collective investment, etc. The multiplicity of investment now has formed. The effective demand for real estate consists of investment demand and consumption demand. The consumption demand can be further divided into citizen income (wage) effective demand and credit-backed effective demand. The basic economics principle tells us that, the market will not reach equilibrium until the supply equals the demand. In China, at present, the effective demand is insufficient, which restricts the growth of the real estate market and the development of the entire real estate industry.

Price is the core of market mechanism. In real estate market, the transaction of property rights and the balance of supply and demand cannot be accomplished without the lever of price. Supply and demand affects price; price adjusts supply and demand. When the price becomes the main method of allocating resources, the real estate market is born. Under the traditional planned economy in China, real estate "management" was non-marketized, the price mechanism did not exist at all. The so-called residential house price is only the instrument to record investment; and the houses in circulation stage are given out without any charge. Therefore, setting up a reasonable price system and adjustment mechanism is the main contents and symbol of China's REM.

Market economy is the legality economy. Market operation needs the safeguard of perfect law and regulations, so does the real estate market. Under the planned economy system, there were few laws and regulations on real estate, and none on real estate market. Thus stipulating of laws and regulations on real estate market is also a main content of China's REM.

As to the intermediary service system, it is an important component of modern market economy, it is also the necessary content of China's REM.

In summary, the basic framework or basic contents of China's REM are as follows: to gradually form market subject by clarifying the property rights; to set up effective supply and effective demand mechanism to realize monetized transaction; to perfect the price mechanism and build up the core of market adjustment; to establish and to improve the law and regulation system and intermediary service system to ensure the orderly market operation.

THE RETROSPECTION OF CHINA'S REM COURSE

China's REM course parallels with the reform of China's real estate economic system, especially China's urban residential housing system. The course of reform is also the advance of marketization. By recalling the course of REM, we can not only understand the contents and the present situations of China's REM more deeply and more concretely, but also grasp the development course of China's REM more easily.

The First Stage: Theoretical Breakthroughs and Exploring Phase (1978-first half of 1987)

There were many malpractices with the traditional housing and land use system: the low rent' inadequacy for the maintenance cost; shortage of housing; unequal distribution; serious land waste; the loss of state-owned land revenue, etc. All these had severely restricted the development of our economy and had aroused the concerns of theoretical circles and relevant sections. Deng Xiaoping suggested that individual citizen be allowed to build their houses; urban citizen build or purchase houses by themselves; that the rent should be adjusted according to the actual housing price, etc. With Deng's thoughts being the turning point, the theoretical circles began to fervently approach and discuss the commodity nature and the commercialization of housing, theory of rent of socialist land and land property rights theory, etc. A series of important breakthroughs had been achieved, which afforded the theoretical basis and guiding ideology for the reform experiment with real estate system and the REM.

In 1979, the State Urban Construction Bureau appropriated some fund from the state-subsidized housing construction fund to Shanxi and Guangxi Province. Xi'an, Liuzhou, Nanning and so on were selected to be the first group of cities where the government built the houses and sold them to the individuals at the construction-cost price. In1982, the State Counsel selected four cities, Changzhou, Zhengzhou, Siping, Shashi, to make experiment with "one third housing sale pattern", i.e., the government, the enterprises and the individuals each bore one third of the housing price. In October 1984, the State Counsel authorized the expansion of the experiment scope where the state-owned houses were sold with discount or subsidy. By the end of 1985, 27 provinces, 160 cities and 300 towns began to sell public houses with subsidy, all these were the valuable explorations of the commercialization of housing. From 1986, according to the "second time distribution" theory put forward by the theoretical circles, under the guideline of "raising rent, increasing wage, transforming the implicit subsidy to the explicit subsidy, transforming the material distribution to the monetary distribution", the reform of the public housing rent began. Many cities, such as Yantai, Bangbu, Tangshan, made such experiment, especially, Yantai and Bangbu established the Housing Savings Bank; some other cities established the real estate credit department under each specialized banks. From then on, China's real estate financing started and developed

As to the reform of the land using regulations, in October 1980, the State Counsel ratified collecting urban land use fee. In 1983, Fushun city began this experiment: the urban land was classified into four ranks, the fee standard ranging from 0.2 to 0.6 Yuan per square meter. In 1984, Guangzhou levied land use fee on development zone, new construction projects and land involving foreign-funded projects. In 1987, Chongqing followed suit. So the experiment with land paid for use spread out among urban zones. (In 1988, the State Counsel promulgated the temporary rules of urban land use tax, substituting the land-use tax for the land-use fee.

As to the real estate development industry, in September 1980, Beijing Housing Construction Office hung up the signboard of Beijing Urban Development Company. That is the prelude to real estate comprehensive development. In 1984, the State Plan Committee and the Urban Construction & Environment Protection Department promulgated "The Temporary Regulations of Urban Construction and Comprehensive Development". From 1985 and on, development corporations in every province entered their peak period, a great number of development companies with government functions began switching to be enterprises' characteristics; the sources of investment funds became diversified. During this stage, the real estate transactions tended to be active, all kinds of real estate transaction forms sprang out.

The Second Stage: The Start of REM (second half of 1987-1991)

To satisfy the need of real estate transaction expansion, beginning from 1988, all cities and counties began to set up real estate transaction organizations and standing real estate transaction market. At the end of 1988, in order to push on housing reform and curb the inflation, the government put forward the reform scheme of "selling houses with discount but not subsidy". The pattern was adopted mainly by small towns. From 1989, a new reform scheme was put forward, i.e., for the newly built houses under new system, selling them first, leasing them second, and encouraging individuals to buy and build houses. Many large cities, such as Beijing, Zhengzhou adopted this scheme. In 1990, Shanghai announced its housing reform program, which was the symbol of a new situation of "full scale, multi-respects, comprehensive and supporting reforms", especially the establishment of housing-public-accumulation-fund system explored a new feasible channel of collecting housing construction fund. From 1991, the Housing Reform Leading Group of the State Counsel ratified the housing reform schemes of 24 provinces and autonomous regions and cities directly under the State Counsel. From then on, the housing reform was smoothly carried forward in China.

From the second half of 1987, the state government authorized Shanghai, Tianjin, Shenzhen, Guangzhou and Hainan to be the experimental areas where the right of land use be transferred with pay. On November 26, 1987, Shenzhen municipality first transferred a piece of residential land through open bidding. On December 10, it again transferred the very first piece of land by auction. This was the true beginning of China's land marketization.

On April 12, 1988, the first session of the seventh National People's Congress passed the "*Constitution Amendment of the People's Public of China*", which provides that "the right of land use can be transferred according to the provisions of law". This acknowledges the legal basis for paid-for transfer of urban land. After that, a series of laws, regulations and ordinances on land transfer were promulgated successively. As a result, the first land market characterized by the monopolistic transfer by the government, and the second market characterized by the transfer, lease, and mortgage of the right of use of land constitute the basic framework of Chinese urban land market.

The Third Stage: The Fluctuating Stage of REM (1992-1993)

In 1992, the housing reform progressed on full scale. The housing reform organizations were established. The enterprises took the lead in pushing on housing reform, the main plan being to sell the public houses at a preferential price and to raise rent by a big margin; real estate management was transformed to enterprization, socialization and specialization; the housing public accumulation funds system was carried out in all China. In 1993, the aim of the housing system reform was to establish three-level housing foundations and to issue housing bonds to raise housing construction funds. At the end of this year, the government put forward the "Anju Project" (ordinary and comfortable housing project), and began to practice it, thus the construction of economical and suitable houses for the middle and low income families developed quickly.

After Deng Xiaoping's speech on his south trip was published in the spring of 1992, real estate industry became a hot spot of China's economic development. The investment of real estate increased at a high speed till the first half of 1993. By the end of July 1993, the state-owned real estate development organizations amounted to 29625. Many local governments excessively set up economic development zones, sanctioned the transfer of land beyond the plan, most of the land was transferred by means of allotment or agreement, this attracted a great deal of speculative capital to flood into the real estate industry. The speculation resulted in the rapid increase of real estate price. The investment structure of real estate lost its balance, the supply of ordinary housing was insufficient, while the luxury housing, villas, and office building were in excess of the demand. Many people thought that the real estate industry was overheated and tend to become real estate bubble. In the second half of 1993, the government began to take macro-regulation measures to control the scale of investment on fixed assets, to adjust the real estate revenue, to change the distribution of real estate investment, to rationalize the real estate market behavior. The effect of the macro-adjustment was swift and apparent: the real estate market contracted notably; the increase rate of investment slowed down; the real state price gradually became stable, and the market order became better. But many speculative real estate companies got into trouble, even went bankruptcy. To China's real estate industry, 1993 is the turning year with historic significance, because the real estate market transformed from the abnormal mess in relatively rational, and reasonable direction.

The Fourth Stage: The Reasonable Advance of REM (1994---)

From 1994, the housing reform developed in depth. The government designed the basic framework of new urban housing system, and made perfect some policies and regulations on partial property rights of reformed housing and the connection of selling price of public house etc.

In July of 1994, "The Urban Real Estate Management Law of People's Public of China" was promulgated, which was a key turn in real estate market's becoming rationalized. Under the government's macro--adjustment, the real estate market went past the depression, absorption and digestion period, and then began to resuscitate. The ordinary housing developed by leaps and bounds. The real estate market system became complete; property management market and intermediary service market appeared. The real estate financing was gradually deepened; mortgage now are widespreading; the components of real estate price are rationalized. The housing consumption amount included in employees' wages is raised gradually. The housing marketization advances steadily. Especially now the government advocates the houses being new consumption item and new economic growth pole, which will induce the more rapid advance of REM.

The above brief retrospection indicates that the China's real estate industry has made many breakthroughs in not only market principals, the relationship of supply and demand, the price formation mechanism, but also in the law and regulation system and intermediary service system, etc. The mechanism has changed greatly. The marketization course has started. In addition, as an industry, the scale of China's real estate industry has made great advances, especially the housing industry, which occupies one half of the entire real estate industry, develops more rapidly. At present, the urban housing space amounts to 3,000 million square meters, which can be converted into assets value of 3,000 billion yuan, twice the real value of national industrial assets. In view of this, some people suggest that real estate industry should be Chinese pillar industry or quasi--pillar industry, that housing industry should be the new consumption center and new economic growth pole. Therefore the research into and promotion of China's REM has great theoretical and practical significance on the development of China's real estate industry, and on deepening the research into socialist market economy theory, and accelerating the development of national economy.

THE INDEX SYSTEM OF MEASURING THE CHINA'S REM

The REM degree discussed above means to what extent the real estate resources are allocated by market, i.e., the maturity degree of the real estate market. As the substitute for and vicissitude of a system, the REM initiates the disequllibrium of the entire system structure, including the disequllibrium of real estate system itself and other system structure. Therefore, the smooth advance of the REM not only depends on the improvement of real estate system itself, for example, the definition of real estate property rights, the rationalization of price mechanism, the normalization of transaction forms, the improvement of the government's macro--adjustment measures, the establishment of the real estate financing institutions, etc., but also depends on the innovation and creation of systems outside real estate industry, for example, wage system, investment system, bank credit system, enterprise system, social security system, so on so forth. Therefore to estimate the maturity degree of real estate market needs both "hard" quantitative indices and "soft" indices which reflect the perfect degree of legal system, the distinctness of property rights, the qualities of government administration services and so forth. Here we mainly concentrate on the former and make a quantitative analysis.

Owing to the heterogeneity of real estate, each piece of real estate is a unique market, so strictly speaking, there exist no nationally uniform real estate market, but only local ones. From the point of reform, by making a static analysis of the transformation from welfare housing allocation and the system of land use free of cost to the gradual marketization of the real estate, we give, in this chapter on China's REM, a brief description of how the real estate market, starting from scratch, gradually developed. Also the description affords an important industrial case for analyzing China's national economy marketization.

Centering on the basic framework of China's REM, taking the REM of developed countries (districts) as contrast, assisted with the analysis and prediction of development trend of China's real estate market, selecting several indices, having calculated and synthesized, we reach a proportioned figure which roughly reflects the general trend of China's REM from 1986 to 1995. In addition, we take the REM of Tianjin as a typical case.

We select seven indices: the privacy rate of urban houses, the proportion of housing expenditure, the ratio of housing price to household yearly income, real estate financing depth degree, the multiplicity of real estate investment, the index of land transfer marketization, and the index of housing price marketization.

The Privacy Rate of Urban Houses

In foreign countries, the privacy rate of urban houses (PR) is defined as the proportion of the number of suites owned by urban families to the total number of urban suite housing. In China, the rate of complete suite housing is lower, only about 50%, so it is not appropriate to count private houses by the unit of suites. We adopt the rate of floorage of private houses to that of total housing to calculate PR. The calculation formula is as follows:

$M_1 = H/P$
M_1: the privacy rate of urban houses
H: the floorage of urban private houses
P: the floorage of urban housing

At present stage in China, the ways of privatizing houses are purchasing, self--building, inheriting and donating. The former two are the primary ways. In commodity economy society, house is individual's property as consumer goods, and its management must be commercialized. At present, in China, the housing privatization, whether through purchasing or by self-building, is accomplished by selling and buying under certain legal conditions. Purchasing is the direct transaction of housing real estate; while self--building is done through a series of markets, for example, building material market, construction market, land and labor market etc. This process indicates that the property rights of the two parties of the transaction are distinct; that the subjects of property rights or subjects of market are definite; that the relationship of supply and demand and the function of price are clear. So the PR index can comparatively give a complete reflection of the basic contents of China's REM, and it is one of the most important indices to measure the degree of China's REM. However, because of the high value of housing, it is difficult for the middle and low-income families to buy or build a house at one time, the lease market also exists. Even in the developed market economy countries, the private housing rate is only about 60%, not 100%.

The Proportion of Housing Expenditure (PE)

The proportion of housing expenditure is the ratio of housing expenditure of urban family to their living expenses. The specific contents of housing expenditure vary in countries. There are three main types:

1. The housing expenditure refers only to rent, which seems to be too narrow;
2. Referring to not only rent, but also water, electricity, fuel, and other fees such as furniture and equipment services etc., which seems too wide;
3. The housing expenditure mainly consists of rent, but also includes expenditure for water and electricity fees.

We consider the third type most appropriate. So we take it as the measurement criterion in this chapter (We also list the former two to be the reference in the following calculations). The calculation formula is:

$$M_2 = Y/C$$

M_2: the housing expenditure proportion
Y: Monthly housing expenditure of urban family
C: Monthly living expense of urban family

It seems that there is no direct link between EP and REM from the surface. But under the traditional housing system in China, low rent system is practiced. Housing expenditure takes a small percentage in living expenses. The housing rent is so low as to be neglected. Along with the growth of the housing market, on one hand, the housing allocation is gradually changing from material to monetarized, which leads to the gradual rise of rent; on the other hand, the marketization of the housing investment requires that the cost of building houses match the rent of houses. Therefore the housing expenditure level is gradually getting close to the market rent level. This process reflects that in China the real estate lease market mechanism has been formed and marketization is advancing. Through the lease transaction, property rights are clear, leasing subjects are definite, parties of both demand and supply exist; the corresponding laws and regulations and intermediary services are being gradually improved. The price of leasing housing--rent, which constitutes housing expenditure, has been formed and will gradually rise to the market level with the continuously advancing of marketization process.

With the development of the economy and the increase of the income, the Engel's coefficient, standing for the food expenditure proportion of family, will become lower, and the expenditure on durable consumer goods (for example, house) will increase to finally reach a stable level in a mature market economy. So the EP index can reflect the change of income elasticity of demand for houses, the change of consumption structure and industrial structure, thus indirectly reflecting the proceeding of the REM. Therefore we consider it one of the indirect indices measuring the China's REM.

The Ratio of Housing Price to Household Yearly Income (PI)

The ratio of housing price to household yearly income means the ratio of the market price of a middle-level suite house to a family's yearly income. It should be pointed out that when computing this ratio, the authors of many articles take individual employee's yearly income or yearly salary, or a couples' yearly income as yearly in come, which results in high ratio of housing price to household yearly income. This method does not fit the international practice and has no comparability. The calculating formula is:

$$M_3 = A/I$$

M_3: the ratio of housing price to household yearly income
A: the sum market price of a middle-level suite house
I: the yearly income of urban household

It seems that the PI index has no direct link with the REM, but the housing price and family income as effective supply and effective demand are the prerequisites and basic contents of China's REM. The ratio of the housing price to family income is analogous to the housing expenditure ratio, which indirectly reflects the marketization and monetization degree of the houses which were originally allocated as welfare in kind. In addition, the reasonable ratio of housing price to household income reflects the balance of supply and demand or the equilibrium in housing market. Whether the market can reach equilibrium automatically means whether the market mechanism is perfect or not. From this point of view, the ratio of housing price to the household income can be one of the measurement indices to reflect the housing marketization degree.

The Real Estate Finance Depth Degree (FD)

The real estate finance deepening degree can be described as the ratio of real estate financial assets (including credits, bonds, and stock) to the GNP (gross national products), or ratio of the sum of real estate loans to the total loans from banks (or financial organizations). We select the latter to compute this index. The calculation formula is as follows:

$$M_4 = R/F$$

M_4: the real estate finance depth degree
R: the sum of yearly real estate loan
F: the sum of yearly loans from banks or financial organizations

A mature real estate market must coexist with developed real estate finance organizations. Sometimes the real estate finance is called "the second finance". At the end of 1982, the ratio of housing mortgage debts to GNP in Swiss was 64%; in the U.S.A., 28%; France, 28%; Canada, 36%; Japan, 15%(Zhu Tianxun, 1990). Thus we can see that real estate finance plays an important role in the national economy. During the course of China's REM, either the form of effective demand or that of effective supply needs the support of finance, especially the effective demand for houses is inseparable from the support of the housing consumption credits. Therefore, the real estate finance deepening degree is one of the important indices to measure China's REM.

The Multiplicity of Real Estate Investment (MI)

The multiplicity of real estate investment is the proportions of the various sources of real estate investment. There are several types of funds sources, state, collective economy, foreign-funded economy, individual investment, etc. In this chapter we take the proportions of investment by different investors to the total real estate investment as the multiplicity index. At the same time, we adopt some auxiliary indices, for example, the proportion of the number of development corporations with different ownership, the different housing floorage completed by economy of different ownership. The design of this index is directed against the sole housing investor under traditional planned economy system, in which the government or state--owned enterprises undertook all the housing construction, and the government practised autarky, non--commercialized or non--marketized management. In China, this is one of the main obstacles to current REM. In order to cultivate the competitive mechanism, this situation must be broken and the multifarious investors are needed. So the multiplicity of real estate investment can be used to estimate the China's REM degree. We use M5 to represent this index, the calculating method is introduced in the next section.

The Marketization Index of Land Transfer (ML)

The marketization index of land transfer refers to the proportion of land transferred to total market transaction, which is an index directly reflecting the REM degree, and certainly fits in with the basic framework of China's REM.

There are two categories and four kinds of methods to transfer land by the government: free allocation and paid-for transfer; the latter can also be divided into three kinds, i.e., transferred by agreement, open tender and auction. The marketization degree of the three types increases in sequence. Transfer by auction is complete market transaction, commonly adopted in Hong Kong and other foreign countries. Since the reform and opening, the urban land is basically transferred through being paid for. So we adopt this index to reflect the China's REM degree. The calculating formula is as follows:

$M_6 = K/L$

M_6: the marketization index of urban land transfer

K: the accumulated area of transferred urban land

L: the area of urban land area ought to be used with pay

The Marketization Index of Housing Price (MP)

The marketization index of housing price refers to ratio of the floorage sold at market price to the total amount of floorage that takes part in the transaction in the market. In China, at present, housing prices include the market price of commercial residential buildings, the cost price of ordinary and comfortable (Anju) housing, the discounted price or standard price of public housing, etc. Different types of housing price reflect different marketization degree. Here we take the proportion of commercial residential buildings sold at market price as the measurement basis. The calculating formula is as follows:

$M_7 = W/D$

M_7: the marketization degree of housing price

W: the yearly completed floorage of urban commercial residential

D: the total yearly completed floorage of urban housing

THE MEASUREMENT AND COMMENT OF CHINA'S REM

Measurement of Classified Indexes of REM in China

In order to measure China's REM, first, we use relevant, first-hand data to make basic calculation of each index specified in the above section, then we re-calculate and rectify some indices on the basis of the first calculation by taking the REM of developed market economy countries (districts) as reference and by analyzing and predicting the development trend of China's REM. In this way, we can get the real marketization degree of China's real estate which can be compared with that of the rest of the world.

Measuring the Privacy Rate of Urban Houses (M1)

By the end of 1994, the total urban housing floorage (P) in China was 2913.77 million square meters, among which the private housing floorage (H) amounted to 795.21 million square meters. According to the formula $M_1 = H/P$, we can get the value of M_1 in 1994:

$M_1 = 795.21/2913.77 = 32.45\%$

(Other data are listed in Table 7.1.1)

In Tianjin in 1994, the value of M_1 was: $M_1 = 10338/65.973 = 16.49\%$, (other data are in Table 7.1.2)

We have pointed out before that owing to the nature of housing, even in mature housing market, the privacy rate does reach 100%. So we don't think that we can directly use the above results to reflect the REM degree. The causes are: A. There exist several kinds of housing ownership, for example, individual owned, units or organizations owned, state-owned and so forth; B. In an economy society, the middle-and-low income class, especially the poor cannot afford to buy houses, so they can only rent the public or welfare houses supplied by the government; C. Even the complete commercialization and marketization of housing management include sale and lease, that is to say, selling market coexists with the leasing market. In fact, the housing privacy rate in general in developed countries is 50%-70% averaging about 60%(See Table 7.3). Therefore, we think that taking 60% as the standard or aim of China's housing privatization rate is feasible in a long time in the future, and it accords with the China's realities. The adjusted M_1 or the REM degree expressed by the housing privatization rate is: $M_1' = 32.45\%/60\% = 54.08\%$ (See Table 7.1). In Tianjin, $M_1' = 16.49\%/60\% = 27.48\%$, (See Table 7.2 for REM degree in other years)

Table 7.1 Privacy Rate of Urban Houses in China

Year	Total Housing Floorage (P) 10,000 Sq. Meter	Total Private Housing Floorage (H) 10,000 Sq. Meter	Private Rate $M_1=H/P(\%)$	REM Extent Reflected by M_1 $M_1'(\%)$
1986	145539	30106	20.69	34.48
1987	158363	33698	21.28	35.47
1988	176850	41184	23.29	38.82
1989	190840	47535	24.91	41.52
1990	199553	48362	24.24	40.40
1991	216450	65368	30.20	50.30
1992	239549	70544	29.45	49.08
1993	259580	79521	30.63	51.05
1994	291377	94564	32.45	54.08

Source: Construction Ministry, *Urban Construction Statistical Yearbook*, 1986--1995

Measurement of the Housing Expenditure Proportion M_2

According to the formula M2=Y/C and the average monthly housing expenditure of urban family (Y)and the living expenses (C), we estimate that the housing expenditure proportion M_2 (%)from 1992 to 1995 are 2.14%, 2.51%, 2.77%, 2.93% respectively (See Table 7.4). In Tianjin, M_2 of 1992, 1994, 1995 are 1.5%, 1.68%, 2.34% respectively (See Table 7.5).

What is the appropriate proportion of housing expenditure that reaches the standard of marketization? According to the situations of the developed market economy countries or districts where housing market is mature, the suitable proportion of housing expenditure is between 13-20%(See Table 7.6). Based on the actual situations of China, we think 15% is the reasonable rate of housing expenditure. Thus, the adjusted housing expenditure proportion or the REM reflected by this index in 1995 is: $M_2'=2.93\%/15\%=19.53\%$ (others in Table 7.4)

In Tianjin, the 1995's proportion $M_2'=2.34\%/15\% =15.6\%$ (others in Table 7.5)

Table 7.2 Privacy Rate of Urban Houses in Tianjin

Year	Total Floorage(P) 10,000 Sq. Meter	Total Private Floorage (P) 10,000 Sq, Meter	Private Rate M_1=H/P (%)	REM Degree Reflected By M_1 M_1' (%)
1990	5553.0	779.0	14.03	23.38
1991	5722.6	792.4	13.85	23.08
1992	5872.0	808.4	13.77	22.95
1993	6020.9	832.1	13.82	23.03
1994	6349.13	1047.09	16.49	27.48
1995	6597.3	2096.38	31.70	52.83

Source: *Tianjin Statistical Yearbook* China Statistics Press, 1993, p 246; 1994 p112; 1995, p107
The data of 1995 is from the general survey of urban housing in 1995 in Tianjin.

Measurement of the Rate of Housing Price to Household Yearly Income M3

In the formula M3=A/I A is the price sum of a suite, which is the price per space square meter multiplied by the area of that suite. It should be noted that not only the area of each suite is different, but also the average area per suite varies in different period in the same county or district. According to the "People Residence Report of The People's Public of China", the aim of urban housing development in China is that the average area per capita is 12 square meters by 2000. So let's assume that there are 3.28 people per family, a suite with an area of 60 square meters can realize the aim. We think it reasonable that the average suite area level is 60 square meters, which fits in with China's realities. The household yearly income(*I*)equals the average yearly income per capita multiplied by persons per family. Therefore, using the relevant data of 1995, we can compute the rate of housing price to household income, i.e., M3 = A/I = $(1612\times60)/(4282.96\times3.28) = 6.99$. The result indicates that an average household can buy a suite of 60 square meters with 6.99 years' income. (Detailed data are listed in Table 7.7).

In Tianjin, the value of this index in 1995 is:M_3 = A/I = $(2119.43\times60)/(4929.53\times3.23) = 7.99$.

Table 7.3 Housing Privacy Rate In Some Countries (Districts)(%)

Country (District)	1978	1980	1981	1983	1984	1985	1986	1987	1988	1989	1990	1991	1992	1993
Britain	55		51.1				62		64		67			
Hong Kong			27.9						54.46	53.92	53.01	53.01	53.01	53.4
Japan	60.4		62.1		71.4				61.3					59.8
France		46.7							52		54.4			
Taiwan					77.34	77.56	78.58	77.76	79.02					
Singapore		55		78										
U.S.A.		59	65.3											
Canada			56											
Australia			70.1											
Norway		50												

ource: Yearbook of Hong Kong Economy, Hong Kong Economy Herald Co 1989-1992.
Observation group of State Economic System Reform Committee and social security system: Japanese Housing: Survey, Policy, and Legal Organization, Housing And Real Estate,1995,Vol.4.
'earbook of Word Economy , China social Sciences Press 1992,P87;
'earbook of Taiwan, Economy Daily Press 1991,P141 others from Zhu, Tinactin's book "Housing Finance", Reform publishing House, 1990; Real Estate Economy issue 5.1989.

ource: *Statistical Yearbook of China*, China Statistics Press,1993, P286-288; 1995, P262; 1996, P282-295.

Table 7.4 Average Monthly Housing Expenditure of Urban Family in China (%)

Year	1985	1986	1987	1988	1989	1990	1991	1992	1993	1994	1995
I.Rate of Rent to Living Expenses	0.96	0.90	0.88	0.71	0.73	0.73	0.73	0.86	1.04	1.01	
II.Rate of Housing Expenditure to Total Expenses							1.87*	2.14	2.51	2.77	2.93
III. Rate of Residency to Total Expenses						4.76		5.96	6.63	6.77	7.07
Marketization degree (M$_2$)		14.80	13.86	12.40	12.47	12.47	12.47*	12.47	12.47	16.73	19.53

Note: We select "II" to compute the housing expenditure proportion, "" and "III" are listed to be reference.

Table 7.5 Monthly Housing Expenditure of Urban Family in Tianjin (%)

Year	1990	1991	1992	1993	1994	1995
Monthly Rate of Housing Expenditure to Living Expenses	0.84	0.88	1.5		1.68	2.34
Monthly Rate of Residency Expenditure to living Expenses			5.73	5.77	5.01	5.70
Marketization degree M$_2$			10.00	11.20		15.60

Note: We select to calculate the index value is listed to be reference.

ource: *Tianjin Statistical Yearbook*, China Statistics press 1993, P234--237; 1994, P122-127; 1995,P122.

Table 7.6 Housing Expenditure Proportion In Some Countries And Districts(%)

Country (District)	1980	1984	1985	1986	1987	1988	1989	1990	1991	1992
Japan (Worker Family)*	14.97					19.56	19.56	19.38	19.30	
Britain (Housing Expenditure)			16.39	16.80	16.31	17.52	17.14	17.91	19.39	17.42
U.S.A. (Housing Expenditure)*			14.5	14.23	14.26	14.09				18.23
U.S.A (ResidencyExpenditure)			26.51	26.28	26.55	26.75				
Hong Kong (Rent +Water Fee)*			13.17	13.34	12.99	13.16	13.48	13.12		
Taiwan (Rent +Water Fee)*		13.13	13.64	14.06	14.27	14.38	14.28			

ource: * *Yearbook of World Economy*, China social Sciences press 1991,P603

Overseas Chinese Yearbook, China social Sciences press 1994,P650

Yearbook of Taiwan Economy Economics Daily Press,1991,P867

**International Statistical Yearbook*, China Statistics Press 1995;P610,613; yearbook of world Economy, China social Sciences press 1993,XIII,P133;

Others are from Cai Derong" China Urban Housing--Theory, practice and Reform", P24.

However, what is the reasonable ratio of housing price to household income according to the standard of marketization? In 1990, the Human Residence Center of the United Nations, together with the World Bank, made a housing survey of the cities in 52 typical counties (districts) in various geographic zones with various income levels. The survey indicates that the average ratio of housing price to household yearly income in 52 countries (districts) is 5. In Japan, this ratio also fell to about 5 recently. (Chai Qiang, 1997)

We take 5 as the reference of the ratio of housing price to household income to estimate the China's REM degree. Thus the adjusted value of this index in China in 1995 can be expressed as $M_3' = 1 - (6.99-5)/5 = 60\%$.(Other data are in Table 7.7)

In Tianjin, the adjusted M_3 in 1995 is: $M_3' = 1 - (7.99-5)/5 = 40\%$.

Measurement of the Real Estate Finance Depth Degree (M_4)

In 1994, the loan of the state banks (F) amounted to 3,160,290 million yuan, among which the real estate credit (R) was 74,496,73 million yuan. According to the formula $M_4 = R/F$ the degree of the real estate finance depth (M_4)= 7449673/3160290 = 2.36%. Taking the housing consumption credit into account, we redress M_4 to be 3%. Similarly, the 1995's M_4 is: M_4= 88300/3939340 = 2.24%, which can be redressed to be 3%(Source: Construction Ministry "*Statistics of the Development of Nation-wide Real Estate in 1994*"; "*The Analysis of Real Estate Development in 1995*" *Statistical Yearbook of China.*, China Statistics Press, 1995-1996.

Owing to the lack of data, we cannot compute this index of Tianjin, but we think the level of the degree of real estate finance deepening in Tianjin is close to that of the national level. We list some substitution data in Table 7.8 as reference, from which we discover that the degree of real estate finance deepening in Tianjin (M_4) is 2.75%, 6.75% in year 1994, 1995 respectively (See Table 7.8).

In developed market economy countries where real estate market is mature, the degree of real estate finance deepening is about 30% (See Table 7.9, 7.10). The degree China's is about 20% Then the adjusted value of this index in China or the REM degree in 1994, 1995 is: $M_4' =3\%/20\% =15\%$.

In the same way, in Tianjin, the adjusted value in 1994 is: $M_4' =2.75\%/20\% =13.75\%$; in 1995, $M_4' =6.23\%/20\% =31.15\%$.

Table 7.7 The Ratio of Housing Price to Urban Household Yearly Income In China

Year	Average Price of Commercial Residential Housing(Yuan/M²)	Average Yearly Disposable Income Per Capita (Yuan)	Average Persons Per Family	Ratio of housing Price to Household Yearly Income	Marketization Degree Reflected by the Ratio of Housing price to Household yearly income M₃(%)
1988	503	1192.12	3.63	6.97	60.6
1989	573	1387.81	3.55	6.98	60.4
1990	703	1522.79	3.50	7.91	41.8
1991	756	1713.10	3.43	7.72	45.6
1992	996	2026.59	3.37	8.75	25
1993	1209	2577.44	3.31	8.50	30
1994	1194.12	3496.24	3.23	6.25	75
1995	1612	4282.95	3.28	6.99	60

Note: The area of a suite is assumed to be 60 square meters, the price in 1988-1990 is the price of the commercial residential housing; the yearly income in 1988-1991 is the yearly real income per capita.

Source: *Statistical Yearbook* of China, China Statistics Press. 1989-1996; Real Estate Department and Information Center of Construction Ministry Compilation of the Data of the Development of China Real Estate 1986-1995; The Analysis of the Development of Real Estate in 1995.

Table 7.8 The Degree of Real Estate Finance Deepening in Tianjin

Year	Credit Balance of Financial System (10,000 Yuan)	Accomplished Investment On Real Estate Development (10,000 Yuan)*	Degree of Real Estate Finance Deepening M_4(%)	REM Degree M_4' (%)
1994	9319300	256571	2.75	13.75
1995	11139500	694364	6.23	31.15

Note: "*" because the total real estate loan in Tianjin is not available, we use accomplished
investment on Real estate development to substitute for it, obviously, this will overvalue the
degree of finance deepening, however, since we didn't take housing credit into consideration,
we didn't think we overvalue the degree much.

Source: *Yearbook of Tianjin Economy*, China Statistics Press.1996, P537, P538.

Table 7.9 Rate of Real Estate Credit To the Total Credit In Hong Kong (%)

Year	1987	1988	1989	1990	1991
1.Credit For Building, Real Estate Development And Investment	10	11	15	14	14
2.Credit For Individual To Buy Houses and For Units "who have individuals participate in their plan"	2	2	2	2	2
3.Credit For Individual To By Other Housing or Building	15	15	15	17	20
4. Real Estate Credit=1+2+3	27	28	32	33	36

Source: *Yearbook Of Hong Kong Economy*, 1992, Hong Kong Economy Herald, Part 4,P127.

Table 7.10 Rate of Real Estate Credit to Credit Assets from Commercial Banks of U.S.A.

Year	1985	1986	1987	1988	1989	1990	1991	1992	1993
Rate (%)	15.88	16.90	19.00	20.86	22.50	23.86	24.86	24.87	24.81

Source: Zhao Zhanping, Pan Gongsheng *"Issues on the Development of the Housing Finance
Market in our country"*, China Real Estate Financing Vol. 1,1996.

Measurement of the Multiplicity of Real Estate Investment (M_5).

Under the traditional planned economy, housing was not commodity but welfare, the
housing investment was accomplished by the state only. From the experience of
developed countries who have mature real estate market, the proportion of state
investment to the total hosing investment is determined by the housing security service
offered by the government for the low-income class. In the U.S.A., the number of the
low-income class who can get the housing subsidy is no more than 20%of the total
population. In Japan, the government only supplies 13%of the total housing. According

to the framework of China's housing reform, the state, enterprises and individual each bear 30% of housing investment, we think it is appropriate to set the state housing investment at 30%. The calculating process of marketization is as follows: if the state investment is 100%, the marketization degree is zero; if the state investment is 30%, then the marketization degree is 100%; using the linear interpolation method we can compute the REM degree reflected by the multiplicity of housing investment (See Table 7.11, 7.12)

As for Tianjin, owing to the absence of data, we use completed housing floorage as a substitution. In 1995, the completed housing floorage is 4869.3 thousand M^2, among which 3782.3 thousand M^2 is completed by state economy, ratio of the state is about 77.7% (Source: *Yearbook of Tianjin Economy*, 1996, P540) thus the marketization degree of investment (M_5) is about 31.86%.

Table 7.11 Composition of National Urban Housing Investment

Year	Total Investment (100million Yuan*	Investment By State-owned Units (100 million Yuan)	Proportion of Investment By State-owned Units(%)	Marketization Degree of Housing Investment M_5 (%)
1986	327.11	242.85	74.23	36.81
1987	368.24	256.97	69.78	43.16
1988	458.67	292.33	63.73	51.81
1989	400.51	253.49	63.29	52.44
1990	498.33	370.19	74.29	36.73
1991	640.99	494.77	77.19	32.59
1992	1013.54	793.44	78.28	31.03

Source: *Statistical Yearbook of China*, China Statistics Press 1987-1993.

Measurement of the Marketization of Land Transfer (M6)

In the formula M_6 = K/L: K is the accumulated area of land transferred by the government with pay; L is the area of land ought to be used with pay. Because the lack of direct data of "L", we adopt indirect method. Since 1991 in China, the urban construction land is divided into ten kinds: residential land, public service land, industrial land, warehouse land, external transaction land, road and plaza land, municipal utility land, green land, and special land, according to the new statistical method on urban land use. It is reasonable to assume that 1/3 of the residential land, 1/2 of the public service land and all the industrial and warehouse land should be used with pay. Thus according to the formula M_6 = K/L, we can calculate the degree of land marketization in Tianjin and in China (See Table 7.13). Also owing to the lack of data, we substitute Tianjin's data of 1993, 1994, 1995 for the corresponding national data. In fact, Tianjin is a typical Chinese city and its situations are very similar to the national level.

Table 7.12 Urban Housing Floorage Completed By Different Ownership and Their Proportion

Year	Total	State-owned Economy	Collective-owned Economy	Individual Economy	Pooling Economy	Share-holding Economy	Foreign-funded Economy	Oversea Chinese Economy	Others
1994	3393180000 M²	17203.08	2332.07	12268.00	183.88	770.62	653.33	418.46	102.36
	100%	50.7%	6.87%	36.15%	0.54%	2.27%	1.93%	1.23%	0.30%
1995	374891000M²	17713.62	3286.38	13333.9	183.5	1255.62	927.62	676.62	112.20
	100%	47.25%	8.77%	35.57%	0.49%	3.35%	2.47%	1.80%	0.30%

Source: *Statistical Yearbook of China, China Statistics Press 1995 1996.*

Table 7.13 Land Marketization Degree in Tianjin and China

	Year	Area of Transferred Land (10,000M²)	Accumulate Area of Transferred Land(10,000M²) K	Area of Land Ought To Be Used With Pay(10,000M²) L	Marketization Degree of Land $M'_6 = K/L(\%)$
Tianjin	Before 1991		676.53	16907	4
	1992	400	1076.58	17137	6.28
	1993	980	2056.58	17380	11.83
	1994	750.63	2807.21	17320	16.21
	1995	613.56	3420.77		19.75
China	1987	15.73	15.73		
	1988	389	404.73		
	1989	625	1029.73		
	1990	948.2	1977.97		
	1991	1020	2997.93	606022	0.50
	1992	21890	24887.93	657615	3.78

Source: Construction Ministry ,Statistical Report of Urban Construction,1991-1995; Yearbook of Tianjin Real Estate Market,1994—1997 Nankai University Press.

Measurement of the Marketization Index Housing Price (M_7)

According to the formula $M_7 = W/D$, in which D stands for the urban housing floorage of China or Tianjin completed by different kinds of economic units, and W is the floorage of commodity housing. We compute the marketization degree of housing price in Tianjin and China in Table 7.14.

Table 7.14 Marketization Degree of Housing Price in Tianjin and China

	Year	Floorage of Completed Urban Housing (10,000M²) D	Floorage of Commodity Housing (10,000M²) W	Marketization Degree of Housing (M7) W/D(%)
China	1986	19392.80	3437.10	17.72
	1987	18539.95	4021.40	21.69
	1988	20232.55	5462.79	27
	1989	15637.67	4822.92	30.84
	1990	17182.05	4195.94	24.42
	1991	18556.55		
	1992	23140.22	4968.40	21.47
	1993	27606	7253.9	26.28
	1994	33931.80	11368	33.50
	1995	37489.10	12219	32.60
Tianjin	1994			
	1995	486.93	343.18	70.48

Source: *Chinese Statistical Yearbook*, 1987-1996 *Tianjin Statistical Yearbook*, 1995-1996 *Yearbook of Chinese Urban Construction*, 1988-1989, Construction Ministry (1995,1996); *Yearbook of Chinese Economy*, 1991-1996.

The Synthesis and Comments of the Indices Value on China's REM

We have calculated out the values of each index on China's REM above, whereas we still need to synthesize the values of different indices into one number to reflect the China's REM extent as a whole. There are three methods that can be chosen: the first is the simple arithmetical average method, which is simple but cannot take the weight difference of each index into account; the second is the classified weight arithmetical method, i.e., dividing the seven indices into three kinds--building estate market, land estate market, and real estate market, whose weight is 0.25, 0.25, 0.5 respectively. This seems more reasonable in weight, but the results is very similar to the first kind; the third method is AHP (Analytical Hierarchy Process), which is complicated with many parameters, and the result is close to the former methods. So we finally adopt the simple arithmetical average method. The calculation formula is:

$$M = (M_1' + M_2' + M_3' + M_4' + M_5' + M_6' + M_7')/7$$

The values of the whole REM degree of China and Tianjin are listed in Table 7.15.

The results indicate that the Chinese real estate market has started and has advanced to the direction of the basic framework of marketization--distinct property rights, specified market agents, formation of the adjustment function of price. By the end of 1995, the integral REM degree has reached 40%, which is a great progress comparing to the former housing welfare system and the non-marketization system of the whole real estate industry. However we cannot be too optimistic, because the marketization degree and the qualities of marketization are relatively low. Now the marketization degree is not only much lower than the real estate market maturity of developed market economy countries (we assume their REM extent is 100% as reference), but also lower than the national economic marketization degree of China, which is about 60%. The manifestations of low marketization qualities are the unsmoothy market operational mechanism, the weak self-circulation ability of funds, and the lag of monitor and control mechanism. The main causes of these flaws are as follows:

1. The actual effective demand is insufficient, but the relative supply is surplus. The disequllibrium of supply and demand influence the marketization course. Now the national overstocked building amount to 60 million square meters, among which 70% is housing. Although the ratio of housing price to household yearly income reaches 60%, the Engel's coefficient (the proportion of food consumption expenditure of resident family) is fairly high, the proportion of citizens' expenditure upon food is high, which affects citizens' expense upon housing. The current housing expenditure stands for less than 20%.
2. The speed of the housing system reform is low, the old housing distribution system still take effect, which refrain the REM course.
3. The development of reform measures are not balanced, for example, the land marketization degree and the real estate finance deepening extent are less than 20%, especially the later concentrated on the real state development credit, and the proportion of housing consumption credit is too low, about 5%, which hold up the integral marketization degree.
4. The lag of law and regulations and the effective intermediary service system hold up the whole REM course, especially the imperfection of laws on housing property rights and housing transfer, and the abnormal service items and fee standard of property management keep the resident from entering the housing market.
5. The faint marketization perception, especially the nonchalant housing marketization idea is one of the main factors that influence China's REM progress.

Table 7.15 The REM Extent of China And Tianjin (%)

	Year	Private Rate of Housing M_1'	Housing Expenditure Proportion M_2'	Housing Price/ Income M_3'	Finance Deepening Degree M_4'	Multiplicity of Investment M_5'	Land Marketization M_6'	Housing Price Marketization M_7'	Degree of REM M'
China	1986	34.48	14.80*	40*	4*	36.81	-	17.72	21.12
	1987	35.47	13.86*	50*	4*	43.16	-	21.69	24.03
	1988	38.82	12.47*	60.6	4*	51.81	-	27	27.80
	1989	41.52	12.47*	60.4	4*	52.44	-	30.84	28.77
	1990	40.40	12.47*	41.8	4*	36.73	-	24.42	22.83
	1991	50.30	12.47*	45.6	4.65	32.59	0.5	22*	24.02
	1992	49.08	14.27	25	8.5	31.03	3.78	21.47	21.86
	1993	51.05	16.73	30	18.5	50*	11.83	26.28	28.94
	1994	54.08	18.47	75	15	55*	16.21*	33.50	38.18
	1995	57*	19.53	60	15	71.4*	19.75*	32.60	39.33
Tianjin	1994	27.48	11.2	45.6	13.75	31.86*	16.21	65*	30.16
	1995	52.83	15.6	40	31.15	31.86	19.75	70.48	37.38

Note: 1. Figures with "*" are estimated values.

2. If the index value has been adjusted, we adopt the adjusted value in this table.

THE COUNTERMEASURES OF EXPEDITING THE CHINA'S REM

How can we push on China's REM according to the former analysis? In summary, we need both the "hard" measures to directly expedite the REM and the "soft" measures to assist, The two supplement each other. If we have only hard measures without the mechanism guarantee of soft environment, the direct expedition can not last long; vice versa, if we only cultivate the soft environment without the hard measures, the marketization will not move forward, and the cultivation of soft environment will fail at last. Obviously the direct push--on by hard measures and the system guarantee of soft environment are rather relative.

The Directly Pushing on by Hard Measures

Hereby the direct push--on by hard measures mean to directly promote the transactions and expedite the marketization course by measures such as adjusting the relationship of supply and demand, and taking advantage of price level. Such measures involve the following:

1. Changing the development guidelines, and transforming the pattern of supply pushing to the pattern of demand pulling. Under the influences and inertia of scarce economy, the development pattern of Chinese real estate industry is supply pushing as the national economy. The housing supply mainly depends on the investment from the government and the enterprises. In fact, the ultimate source of these investments are the deduction of employees' wage (i.e., housing consumption share), because we adopted low wage and housing welfare system under the traditional planned economy. The housing consumption share ought to be component of employees' wages (V), was deducted as public accumulation (M) to invest in housing, that is to say, the effective demand of housing turned into the housing supply, which result in the insufficient demand of housing market and the relative supply surplus. Therefore in order to accelerate the REM and housing commercialization, we should change our development guidelines to transform the housing construction investment only from the government and enterprises to be direct monetary distribution of housing, i.e., making the national housing welfare (housing consumption share) to be part of the wage. This change of relationship of supply and demand will increase the effective demand of housing, not only motivating the residents to enter the housing market, but also do good to rationalize the rate of rent to price and to expand the real estate market.

2. Developing housing consumption credit, and increasing the effective credit-backed demand. This is one of the important measures to increase the effective demand, and to overcome the "Barrel Effect", which restrict the integral advance of China's REM. The "Barrel Effect" indicates that the maximum volume of a barrel is determined by its shortest side. We can see from the former section that the real estate finance depth

degree is the lowest index value, only about 15%, much lower than the average level 40%. Among the small amount of real estate credit, the proportion of housing consumption credit is much lower, less than 5%. So the expansion of the housing consumption credit is very urgent, moreover, it is feasible because we can increase the residents' housing purchasing power by only adjusting the real estate credit structure. In addition, we can increase the ratio of loan to housing price, extend the repay term, carry out the loan repayment guarantee service item, create the new real estate financial tools, gradually realize securitization of mortgage claim, establish the second level mortgage market, so as to increase the real estate finance deepening degree.

3. Deepening the housing reform, cutting out the link with the old real estate system. On the one hand, we should allocate housing through the monetarzation, and dismiss the residents' ideas of depending on the old system to get welfare house, letting the residents select houses from the market by themselves with their "money votes"; on the other hand, we should raise the housing rent, while transforming the housing investment from the government and units to individuals, so as to rationalize the relationship of rent and price, and to realize the marketization of rent. Thus people who thought that buying house was not so worth as renting one before will go to the market to by home, and the housing market volume will be enlarged.

4. Implementing different policies to indirectly increase the effective demand. From the index value of housing price to household income, which is about 60%, we can infer that the housing purchasing power has increased, but there exist significant gap on housing purchasing power among the high, middle and low income earners. Therefore the government should establish the corresponding housing price series according to the residents' income variations: the high--income household buy the commodity housing at market price, the middle--income family buy home at cost price or small--profit price, the low--income household receive the housing subsidy from the government. To the middle or low-income family, these measures indirectly increase their effective demand. It is sure that the proportion of household buying housing at market price will gradually increase along with the progress of REM.

In addition, we should expedite the marketization of land transfer. The low marketization degree of land transfer is one of the main factors resulting in the "Barrel Effect" and restricting the overall level of China's REM. Accelerating the land marketization proceeding can directly expand the real estate market. During the reform course we should adopt various land use policies following the international conventions, i.e., to the ordinary housing land, we should carry preferential policy, making land price no more than 20% of housing construction price. Though the land marketization degree is low at present time, the proportion of land price to the housing price is high, even about 40%of the price in economical and comfortable housing (Anju Project). Therefore, in the course of accelerating land marketization and increasing land price, carrying out different land use policies to lower the residential land price can indirectly increase the effective demand of housing market.

5. Developing the second level real estate market, invigorating circulation and expanding marketization space. Among the whole real estate market system, besides the horizontal structure---land market, building property market, and the reproduction structure---development market, circulation market, consumption and property management market, there exist longitude structure---the first, second level market characterized by the transfer of land property right. At present time, China has only set up the first level market. During the course of real estate system reform, partial property rights and other policies on the transfer of property rights restrict the re-transfer of real estate, thus affecting the normal, public, and reasonable formation of the second level market. On the contrary, these policies result in illegal underground market. We should redesign the arrangement of property rights, for example, admitting the public housing with partial property rights to be transferable, and admitting the original units which had the ownership to share the real estate appreciation, normalizing the transaction of the use rights of the public houses (Fu Shihe, 1997a); cleaning up and rectifying the underground transaction of land use rights that the users got from the government with no pay, to make the transaction public and legal by levying on making--up land price or land revenues (Fu Shihe, 1997b). All these measures can activate and develop the second land market, and promote the orderly market competition, preventing from the disorder in the course of marketization.

The Cultivation of Soft Environment

Hereby the soft environment means that we should guarantee and promote the normal and rapid advance of REM by changing the ideas and mechanism, and establishing laws and ordinances. These measurements include as follows:

1. Changing the residents' perceptions of housing and strengthening the propaganda of housing marketization and commercialization. The residents should depend on the market instead of "mayors" to realize their housing dreams. Perception is one kind of ideology, which is one of the most important institutional arrangements that can reduce the cost of affording other institutional arrangement services. Though housing marketization and commercialization as a successful institution of developed market economy countries has been transplanted into China, whether it will fail or succeed depend on the compatibility of Chinese housing perceptions. Obviously the traditional perceptions of housing welfare and the residents' psychology that unwilling to consume by debt are obstacles in the course of housing market. Not until the residents understand that the house as a commodity, is not only a consumption item, but also an investment instrument, moreover, an effective method to accumulate human capital, and the residents are willing, and brave enough to borrow money from the banks to realize their housing dreams, does the housing market get a qualitative leap.

2. Perfecting the real estate laws and regulations system. As an important institutional arrangement, laws and regulations are the prerequisites of the real estate transfer and the realization of property rights. Currently the Chinese real estate laws and regulations are far from being perfect, some of which are absent, such as the laws on the exchange of use right; some of which are no longer suitable to the requirements of situations development. Therefore it is an urgent task to improve the real estate legal construction.

3. Establishing the monitor system of real estate boom and depression, strengthen the government's macro--adjustment abilities to real estate economy. On one hand, the government should promote the real estate market, and actively push on the development of real estate industry; on the other hand, the government should control the over-speculation of real estate, and avoid the expansion of real estate bubble, which is the continuous increase of real estate price at a rapid speed straying away from the market fundamental value. The crash of the real estate bubble will cause serious loss to the last holders, and the bank loans will not be repaid. The expansion and collapse of Japan's bubble economy produced great loss on national economy, and one of the main causes is that real estate price was out of the control of government. Therefore the government should strengthen the monitor and adjustment of real estate investment, price and credit etc., to ensure the sustainable and stable development of real estate industry during the course of marketization.

4. Developing and improving the intermediary service system of real estate. There are many kinds of intermediary service items: marketing, evaluation, lawyer service, property management and so forth. The facts from developed market economy countries indicate that: in a mature real estate market, undoubtedly there exist great number of real estate brokers collecting information and bringing together transactions; there exist many appraisers affording evaluation service and lawyers with legal service; there exist all kinds of property management companies affording complete or special after--sale service. These professions reduce the transaction cost of real estate market and increase the market operational efficiency. Chinese real estate intermediary service market has only just stared and urgently needs developing and improving, especially the popularization of property management can remove the worries of home buyers on housing maintenance and management and thus can encourage residents to purchasing housing.

5. Strengthening the studies of real estate economic theories. In addition to the theories directly connected with REM, such as real estate property rights, real estate market, real estate price, real estate investment and risk, real estate financial theory etc., the more important problems mow are as follows: what is the position of real estate industry in China's industrial structure? Is it a pillar industry or non-pillar industry? Can housing industry be the new economic growth pole? What is the relationship between the development of real estate and bubble economy? These problems are still in discussion. Only when we clearly understand the industrial position of real estate industry, can we make correct industrial policy and developing plan, thus can we both promote the rapid progress of real estate industry and REM, and avoid the

real estate bubble resulting from feverish investment and over--speculation. So theoretical studies are necessary to the REM, which is one of the main tasks to cultivate soft environment.

REFERENCES

Blanchard, Oliver J. and Mark W.Watson, *"Bubbles, Rational Expectations and Financial Crisis"*, in *"Crisis In the Economic and Financial Structure"*, edited by Paul Watchtel, Lexington Books, New York, 1989

Blanchard Oliver J. and Stanley Fisher, 1989, *Lectures On Macroeconomics"*, The MIT Press

Bi Baode, *Research on China's Land Market*, The Press of People's University of China, 1994

Cai Derong, *The Theory, Practice and Reform of Framework of China's Urban Housing Systems*, Chinese Statistical Press, 1991

Cao Zhenliang, Hao Shouyi, *"An Introduction To Land Economics"*, Nankai University Press, 1989

Cao, Zhenliang, "An Introduction To Housing Economics", Nankai University Press, 1992

Cao Zhenliang, Dong Shoukun, *"Modern Real Estate Development And Management"*, Zhongxing Press 1989

Cao Zhenliang, *"The Reform of State-owned Housing Systems And Property Rights Boundaries"*, Chinese Real Estate, 1996,Vol.6, 1996

Cao Zhenliang, *"The New Economic Growth Pole And Hot Consumption Item, Housing And Real Estate"*, 1998,Vol.1, 1998

Cao Zhenliang, Li Sheng, "The Strategic Position of Real Estate Industry In China's Industrial Structure Adjustment", Nankai Economic Studies, 1995,Vol.6, 1995

Chai Qiang, *"Analysis and opinions on the prices of commercial houses"* Beijing Real Estate Vol 3, 1997

Cheng Guangting, *Studies On Urban Housing Problems of Foreign Countries*, Peking Science & Technology Press, 1991

Construction Ministry, *"The Statistical Report of Real Estate Development in 1994"*, 1995

Construction Ministry, *"The Analysis Report of Real Estate Development in 1995"*, 1996

Fu Shihe, *"The Analysis of China's Current Real Estate Market Situations"*, Modern Real Estate, 1995,Vol.4-5, 1995,

Fu Shihe, *"The Market Entrance Regulations of Land Allocated with No Pay"*, "Modern Real Estate", Vol.1 1997

Gary Eldred, *"Real Estate Analysis and Strategy"*, Harper & Row Publishers, 1987

Greer Gaylon E. and Fawell Michael D., *"Investment Analysis For Real Estate Decisions"*, Dearborn Financial Publishing, Inc. 1993

Lu Xianxiang, *"The Western New Institutional Economics"*, Chinese Development Press, 1996

Ma Kewei, *The Encyclopedia of Chinese Reform: Volume of Land System Reform",* Salian Press, 1992

Meng Xiaosu, *"Real Estate Investment and Transaction"*, Chinese Earthland Press, 1993,

Qiu Zeyuan, *"Renting Housing Or Buying Housing"*, The Press of People's University of China, 1992,

Yang Lu, Wang Yukun, 1994, *Housing Reform: Theoretical Introspection and Realistic Choice,* Tianjin People's Publishing House

Zhang Yuanduan, Zhang Yunqing, 1992, *The Encyclopedia of Chinese Reform; Volume of Real Estate Industry*, Dalian Press

Zhu Tianxun, *"Housing Finance"*, Reform Press, 1990

Chapter 8

CHINESE TECHNOLOGY MARKET AND ITS DEVELOPMENT

Technology market is the important component of Chinese socialist market system. As a component of production element markets, technology market not only has the general characteristics of general market, but also possesses its own peculiarities. Therefore, before investigating Chinese technology market, we shall first define some basic concepts concerning technology market, on the basis of which, we'll research and describe the development of technology market.

TECHNOLOGY AND TECHNOLOGY MARKET

Technology and Technology Commodities

Although almost all people know the word "technology", yet different people hold different views about it. To sum up, there are several chief statements as follows:

1. Technology is the skill the people apply natural science knowledge and experience to perform kinds of production and non-production in the field of production, and the way by which people utilize natural force to transform nature in light of the principle of science. The basic expressions of technology are in designing, producing, installing and utilizing kinds of tools of labor (including mechanical equipment i.e.), designing all kinds of techniques and procedures, utilizing properly and effectively object of labor and protecting resources and natural environment, as well as, processing object of labor to convert it into use-value needed by people.
2. Generally speaking, technology refers to various means of operation and technology abilities that are developed by people according to their practice experience of production and the principals of natural science, including not only the corresponding production tools and other material equipment, but production process or means of operating procedures as well.

3. Technology contains three indivisible portions, they are laborer's skill, labor tools (including mechanical equipment), and labor object. In fact the definition covers the three elements of productive forces. Consequently, the people who hold the view think that technology is basically the same as productive forces.

In our opinion, technology on the technology market includes both that in the field of production and life, but also management approach, decision method, plan method, organization approach, exchange method, method of sales promotion and circulation and so on, that is to say, technology exists in all the fields of market. It may be technology in several stages such as technology in lab, technology after primary test and middle test, yet it can be mature technology or intermediate technology that needs to be developed and perfected. In the technology market, we should comprehend technology in a broad sense.

Technology commodity is the object of transaction on the technology market, but not all technologies can be traded on the market. As the exchangeable commodity on the technology market, technical commodity should possess some qualification, or else technology can not be exchanged because it hasn't characteristic of commodity. Then, in order to be exchanged, what qualification should exchangeable technological commodity possess?

Clear and definite boundary

The exchangeable technical commodity should possess clear and definite boundary, which is defined clearly by characters or technical quota. Only if boundary of technology is clear, technology can be independent, in-adhesive transaction object with background technique and definite space and time. Technology without definite boundary of object will be non-exchangeable.

Definite ownership

As exchangeable technology, it must have a definite governor or owner who may be government, collective or individual. A kind of technology may be owned by one or more owners. In general, technology without definite ownership can not be regarded as being exchangeable.

Reliable guarantee

The exchangeable technology must be monopolistically guaranteed by owner. The guarantee has broad sense. It's either legal guarantee such as patent law and trademark law affirming industrial property right, law against unfair competition ensuring know-how, or non-legal guarantee such as the existence of technological gradient keeping technology from spreading.

Technology Market

Market is the outcome of social economy. The concept of market isn't invariable, but changes along with the development of economy. During different history periods and on different occasions, it possesses different implications. The conventional concept of market refers to people's transaction behavior and places where people trade with each other. As the scale of complicated exchange expand step by step, exchange does not have to take place in fixed places. Therefore, modern market refers to not only specific transaction place, but also the sum total of relations in which all buyers and sellers achieve transaction and it is the totality of complex exchanges. Market includes both supply and demand that connect with and restrict each other, that is, it's the unity of both.

As a part of market system technology market might be defined as the totality of exchange relations to achieve buying and selling of technical commodity (exchangeable technology) and convert it into real productive forces. Technology market has the following forms.

Intermediary agencies for technology transfer

Intermediary agency is an organization that provides service for the trade of technological commodity, whose key responsibility is to link up the buyer and the seller engaged in trade of technological commodity. It has various of forms such as organization engaged in compiling and issuing information concerning technological commodity, or the standing organizational department of technology market, whose aim is to communicate information of trade among the buyers and the sellers

Agencies for technological consultation and development

The organization should take part in deepen-working such as conversion from laboratory technology to technology of elementary test or middle test, besides being the bridge between the buyer and the seller of technological commodity. It also provides the buyer with the corresponding services that the buyer need for technology.

"Scientific shop" and technology market

Scientific shop originates in Holland at the beginning of 1970's, and then it emerged one after another in France and Japan. A fairly famous shop is "Wang Xiang IDEA" in Japan, which is engaged specially in various productions of new inventions and test samples. Many inventors are willing to give their inventions to the scientific shop for placing goods on trial sale, then see its commercial value and social reaction.

The above-mentioned technology market refers to visible market that centers around the buyer and has the fixed venue. Technology market includes not only the comprehensive standing market, but also the market held irregularly. It may be a membership organization made up of many sellers and buyers such as Northern Technology Market in Tianjin, or the individual market that includes only one seller such as professional enterprises for scientific research running according to market system. Invisible market doesn't have fixed place and standing organizations. It exists in the transaction between the buyer and the seller.

GENERATION AND DEVELOPMENT OF
OVERSEAS TECHNOLOGY MARKET

Technology market generates and develops along with the development of economy and the division of labor. Division of labor society leads to separation between the owner and the user of technology, market economy promotes enterprise to obtain new technology. Under such historical conditions, there was non-gratuitous technology transfer, and then technology market came into being. Development of technology market in some capitalistic countries was along with technological progress and development of great industry production. The development of the technology market can be divided into three stages: generation, growth and maturity.

Generation of technology market

Before great machinery industry, market economy wasn't developed, scientific and technological achievement hadn't obvious effect on physical production and didn't become the commodity of value. Generally speaking, transfer of technology depended on relations of master and apprentice, relatives or was granted in the form of bestow from the feudal monarch and royal family to businessman and craftsman who they appreciated. During this period, there wasn't still obvious transaction of technology. In the 1470's patent institution comes into being in Venice Italy, where business is the most developed which initially affirms the commercial characteristic of technology by law. Pumping-up irrigation machine invented by Galileo in 1594 was awarded 20 years' patent right. However, because market economy wasn't still developed and patent institution couldn't have important effect, scientists only provided gratuitously their invention for society. Technology might be copied and imitated. After half a century, along with development in commercial trade, patent institution had been spread from Venice to Britain. At that time British capitalist economy had developed rapidly. To obtain more profits, capitalists incessantly adopted new technology to increase production and pledged strongly to affirm technology as their privately owned property by laws so as to monopoly technology. Under that circumstance, Britain formulated "monopoly law" in 1623, which was the first patent law of world and possessed embryonic form of modern patent institution. The law regulated that people who utilized patented technology owned by others must pay costs. Hence, the generation of patent institution was the beginning of technology transaction.

Growth of technology market

After mid-18th century, industrial revolution had succeeded in Britain. Great machine industry took the place of handicraft production, capitalist economy experienced further development and the world stepped into the period of industrial revolution. In the process of industrial production, technology took the leading status; science and technology had been gradually becoming the crucial factor of production and means by which enterprise sought profit. Development of society and economy led to demand for technology that became the impetus on development of in technology exchange. During the period, development of capitalist market economy impelled most countries to set up their own patent institution. For instance, America set up its patent law in 1770; Sweden in 1819, France in1791; Holland in 1809; Austria in 1810 and Russia in1812. In view of this history, we can figure out the level of production and the level of development in science and technology in different countries.

During this period, although capitalist economy grew rapidly, market competition wasn't very violent. The basic trend of market was that the demand exceeded the supply and the price was very high. As a result, the main task of enterprise wasn't in urgent need of new products and technology, but to increase production. Consequently, although technology transaction had developed universally, to a great extent it still was restricted.

Maturity of technology market

At the beginning of 1930's, the world economic crisis swept through almost all capitalist countries, the problem of capitalist market became even more acute. Especially after World War II, the production developed rapidly as the third revolution of science and technology went deep. At this time, the basic trend of market was that the supply exceeded the demand, because market competition became very violent. The enterprise must open up incessantly new products and new technology in order to increase profit and to contend with competitor, therefore, the demand for technology and requirement for developing market came into being. In the meanwhile, development of technology itself also called for the development of international technology market. High disintegration and integration demonstrated by the development of modern science and technology promoted their worldwide specialized coordination. There was no possibility or necessity that individual country or enterprise did research in every field of technology. All countries realized that they should make good use of the current scientific and technological achievements. Therefore, technological trade was breaking through the border of countries and becoming more and more international. As a kind of specific commodity, its importance began to be recognized and treasured. The volume of international technological trade increased rapidly, which was 2 billion dollars in 1965, 11 billion in 1975 and 40 billion in1985. Within 20 years, it had increased by 20 times. Large amount of scientific and technological achievements have been spread not only from developed countries to developing countries, but among developed countries.

DEVELOPMENT OF TECHNOLOGY MARKET IN CHINA

Implementing commercialization of technological achievements and establishing and opening technology market are significant breakthroughs of China's reform of the management system for science and technology. They are also important steps in deepening coordination reform between scientific and technological system and economy system .In the past two decades, Chinese technology market has developed rapidly and is catching up with the international market which has been developed for hundreds of years. Comparing the status of technology market in China with the process of development of international technology market, we may divide the development process of Chinese technology market into 4 stages.

The stage without technology market (1949-1978)

During this period, planned economy was practiced in China, there were no conditions that enabled technology to become an exchangeable commodity. Thus, technology market didn't exist.

Formation of technology market (1978- April 1985)

It started from national convention on science and technology convened in1978. In the meeting, Deng Xiaoping put forth that science and technology constitute productive force, which provided preparation of pubic opinion for commercializing technology market and open technology market. Hereafter, initial budding appeared in China's technology market; organization of scientific research started to sell their technological achievements. For instance, in 1980, technological service cooperation was set up in Shenyang, which investigated the selling and buying of technological achievements and played the part of "match-maker" between the seller and the buyer. In 1981, technology fair was opened in Wuhan and Shenyang, more than 500 scientific and technological achievements were exhibited and more than 100 invitations for bid were raised by enterprise only in the area of Wuhan. In January 1981 the first technology market newspaper started publication in Tianjin. According to incomplete statistics, there were more than 1100 organizations for developing and inter-exchanging technology above the level of city, and more than 3000 organizations for technological service and consultation which had formed coordinated network. Technology fairs were held in China for more than 240 times in which volume of business was from several millions to 10 millions at every turn.

During this period, technology transfer and technological service were non-gratuitous or partly non-gratuitous, but start point was still only to give suitable compensation to owners of technology. Technology hadn't become real commodity yet. In the mean time, technology market was affected by planned economy. As a result, the main characteristic of China's technology market was the lack of the effective demand of enterprise—the buyer of technologies.

Growth of technology market (April 1985--November 1987)

This stage was symbolized by the issuing of the first patent law in China. As the first law defining technical commodity and standardizing technology market, patent law indicated that technology market was becoming standardized, institutionalized and regularized in China.

On May 15, 1985, the first national trade fair of technological achievements opened in Beijing .The 28 teams for technological transactions, coming from 29 provinces, cities or autonomous regions, 49 ministries, military industries (3000 units in total) provided about 15000 kinds of technologies for transfer. The fair lasted 25 days, and there were about 310 thousand exhibitors coming to the exhibition. During the period, 15182 agreements were signed; the negotiated trade volume reached 8 billions RMB yuan.

Meanwhile, technology trade was developing prosperously everywhere. According to incomplete statistics, the volume of business completed really on the technology market had reached 2.3 billions yuan in China, which was more than three times as much as that in 1984.

Initial maturity of technology market (after November 1987)

The beginning of this stage is symbolized by issue of the first law on technology contracts-"Technology Contracts Law of the People's Republic China". The purpose of the law on technology contracts is to "protect legal rights of parties related to technology contracts and to uphold the order of technology market". This indicates that China's technology market has stepped up on the orbit of legality and is developing into system of socialist technology market facing to both domestic and international market and utilizing both domestic and international resources, in which market system will be strengthened, market organization and market structure will be perfected, market order will be standardized, and which accords with law of development in science and technology and law of market economics operations.

ESTIMATION ON THE EXTENT OF DEVELOPMENT IN TECHNOLOGY MARKET

As a whole, China's technology market develops rapidly. Within 10 years, it has achieved great accomplishment, compared with the same achievement that capitalist countries spent hundreds of years in achieving. However, China's technology market develops from zero under traditional planned system, whose starting point is relatively low. Hence, in order to make a research on the development of technology market, we shall quantify the process of technology market with market open degree. So we make the following device.

First we shall measure the opening degree of China's technology market by the process from planned management to market adjustment. Based on statistics available, we have selected four indices to measure the opening degree. They are: a. increment of transaction volume of nationwide technology market; b. increment of three types of patent application processed; c. increment of non-service patent application and foreigner's patent application processed; d. Increment of self-raised fund in the expense of science and technology research activities.

Index "a" represents the opening degree of science and technology market by the increment of technological commodity transaction. Index "b" and index "b" indirectly reflect the opening degree by measuring the increment of inventors' voluntary application of patent. Index "d" reflects the development pace of technology market by observing the increase of non-state fund in science and technology researches.

To dynamically reflect the opening progress of China's technology market, we selected four key years: 1979, 1985, 1990 and 1995 to observe.

The year 1979 is starting of China's reform when the technology market is still within discussion, so we assume the opening degree technology market is "0".

1985 is the initial development of China's technology market when degree is relatively low, so assume it to be 15%. Based on the ratio of all economic data of 1990 and 1995 with 1985, we calculate the increment of these data during the periods, hence, we can reach the opening degrees of technology market in 1990 and 1995.

Besides, we need to explore into the degree of freedom of the development of China's technology market. Degree of freedom is used to reflect the maturity degree of a market. Owing to lack of information, we select the following two index to measure the degree of freedom of China's technology market: a. amount of applications for patent induced by market (non-service patent application and foreigner's patent application processed). b. proportion of self-raised fund in the expense of science and technology research activities.

Finally, with arithmetical average method, we count out synthetically marketization degree of Chinese technology market in 1985 1990 and 1995. The next we should analyze it concretely

Increment of Transaction Volume on Technology Market

The increment of transaction volume on technology market directly indicates marketization degree of China's technology market. In 1984, the volume of business of technology transaction was 7.6 billions, but ten years later in 1995, it has researched 26.835 billions, 3.53 times as much as that in 1984. Suppose that the volume of business in 1985 remains on the same level as that in 1984, and increases at 15%, the increment of volume of business on technology market by 1995 can be demonstrated in Table 8.1.

Table 8-1 Increment of Transaction Volume on Technology Market

Year	1985	1990	1995
Volume of business on technology market (billion)	7.6	7.510	26.834
Increment rate (%)	10	9.88	35.31

Increment of the Three Types of Patent Application Processed

It's a significant symbol of generation and development of Chinese technology market that patent application is submitted. Three types of patent application which includes 14,372 items were submitted in 1985, in 1995 it has researched 83,045 that is about 6 times as much as that in 1985. Suppose that marketization degree estimated with three types of patent application submitted is 10 percent, we show the open degree of Chinese technology market in Table 8.2.

Table 8-2 Increment of the Three Types of Patent Application Processed

Year	1985	1990	1995
Three types of patent application submitted(item)	14372	41469	83045
Increment rate (%)	10	28.85	57.78

Increment of Non-service and Foreigner's Patent Application in China

Before technology market was opened, invention and creation were accomplished by scientific research units, school and technicians of factory and enterprise during their work. Inventions accomplished that were not reached during work were not acknowledged. Scientific achievements made by foreign people were totally ignored in China's technology market. After patent law was issued, the process of invention is no longer restricted by their identities and nationalities. Therefore, domestic non-service patent application and foreign patent application submitted can indicate the extent of development and maturity of China's technology market. Suppose the increment of the three types of domestic non-service and foreigner's patent application submitted in1985 is 15%, we show measure the increment by 1995 in table 8.3

Table 8.3 Increment of Non-service and Foreigner's Patent Application in China

Year	1985	1990	1995
Non-service and foreigner's patent application submitted (item)	10039	29850	63132
Increment rate (%)	10	29.73	62.89

Increment of Self-raised Funds in Scientific and Technological Activities

Before China's technology market was opened, the funds for scientific and technological activities were directly allocated by government or enterprise. Data in "China statistical Yearbook" indicates that by the end of 1989, there were four resources of funds for scientific and technological activities: higher authorities allocation, self-raised fund, loans of bank and others. That is to say, it comes from various channels, and that self-raised funds is indispensable part of funds for scientific and technological activities. Along with the increase of marketization degree, the proportion of self-raised funds in funds for scientific and technological activity is becoming larger and larger. Therefore, the generation and development of self-raised funds is an important symbol of the development of China's technology market. As there was no data as to the self-raised funds for science and technology market in "China Statistics Yearbook" in 1985, we assume that the increment of it in 1985 also as 15% with reference to the other 3 indexes, hence, by 1995 the increment of self-raised fund is demonstrated in Table 8.4.

Table 8.4 Increment of Self-raised Funds in Scientific and Technological Activities

Year	1985	1990	1995
Raising funds on the own (billion)	0	17.443	37.695
Increment	0	15	32.42

Synthesizing the increment of the four indexes in the four years, the open degree, or marketization progress of China's science and technology market in 1979, 1985 1990 and 1995 are shown in Table 8.5

Table 8.5 Open Degree of Chinese Technological Marketization

Year	1979	1985	1990	1995
Increment rate of volume of business	0	10	9.88	35.31
Increment rate of three types of patent application submitted	0	10	28.85	57.78
Increment rate of non- service and foreigner's patent application submitted	0	10	29.73	62.89
Increment rate of raising funds on the own	0	0	15.00	32.42
Open degree of marketization process of technology market	0	7.5	20.87	47.10

Marketization Progress of China's Technology Market

We first measure the development degree of China's technology market with degree of freedom. This can be demonstrated by the proportion of self-raised funds among all the funds of scientific and technology activities and the proportion of non-service patents and foreigners' patents processed among all the patents processed in Table 8.6 and Table 8.7.

Table 8.6 Freedom Degree of Sources of Funds for Scientific and Technological Activities (in 100 million RMB yuan)

Year	1990	1995
Scientific and technological funds income (total)	403.26	875.56
Self-raised funds	174.43	376.95
others	55.71	153.51
total	230.14	530.46
Freedom of funds sources (%)	57.07	60.59

Table 8.7 Freedom Degree of 3 Patents Processed

Year	1985	1990	1995
Applications processed of 3 patents (in total)	14372	41469	83045
Non-service applications processed	5078	24966	48967
Foreigners applications processed	4961	4884	14165
Total	10039	29850	663123
Freedom of patents processed (%)	69.85	71.98	76.02

By arithmetically averaging the results of Table 8.6 and table 8.7 with that of Table 8.5, we can learn about the marketization progress of China's technology market. See Table 8.8

Table 8.8 Technological Marketization Progress of China (%)

Year	1979	1985	1990	1995
Open degree of technological market	0	15	33.18	75.82
Freedom of the sources of activity funds	0	54	57.07	60.59
Freedom of patent applications processed	0	69.85	71.98	76.02
Marketization progress of technological market	0	46.28	54.08	70.81

Besides measuring development of technology market with opening degree of the market, we shall still consider two other indexes: fairness degree of technology market and connection between domestic technology market and international technology market.

The fairness degree of technology market may be embodied by perfection of law system. We may measure it with the ratio between laws and regulations that perfect technology market needs and laws and regulations already issued in China.

Since 1978, the standing committee of the national people's congress has issued directly more than 10 laws related to technology market, including "Patent Law of the People's Republic of China", (passed in march 12, 1984), "Copyright Law of the People's Republic of China", (passed on September 7, 1990), "Law on Prevention of Unfair Competition of the People's republic of China" (passed on September 2, 1990 and "Law on Technology Contracts of the People's Republic of China", i.e. The issuing of these laws deepens and improves the fairness degree of technology market.

The extent of connection between domestic technology market and international technology market is to indicate internationalization degree of technology market. In this article, we quantify indirectly open degree of technology market by the ratio between scale of technical objects protected clearly in China and scale of technical objects affirmed in the world, as well as the ratio of the amount of international conventions China has joined to the totality of international convention.

After joining WIPO in June 1980, China has joined in many conventions, including "Paris Conventions for Protection of Industrial Property" (March 1985), "Madrid Agreement" (October 1989), "Convention for World Copyrights" (October 1992) and "Patent Cooperation Treaty" (PCT) and so on. Moreover, China also has participated actively "Agreement on Trade-related Aspects of Intellectual Property Rights" of GATT and attributed to the achievement of the agreement.

As for the scale of technical objects, China has done lots of work to draw up and amend law so that scale of technical objects protected gradually is broadening and approaches to international. For instance, China starts implementing October 1991, "Regulations for Protection of computer Software", which makes the scale of technical objects in China step largely toward internationalization that was issued in. In September 1992, China amended patent law, adding new patent property of article such as foods, drinks and relish, as well as medicines and materials obtained by chemical method.

At present, it's difficult to estimate the fairness degree of technology market and the degree of connection between domestic market and foreign market in figures, therefore, in this article, we defined the development degree of China's technology market with the opening degree and freedom degree. only use indicators of the open degree of technology market to estimate the development of Chinese technology market.

From the results of the measurement, we can see that that technology market starts late in China, yet develops slowly. But judging from the other side, the development of technology cannot match the requirement of economic growth for science and technology. In "Outline of the ninth five-year plan for economic and social development and the long-range objective for 2010 of the People's Republic China", it is pointed out clearly that it is further development in technology market that can help us rejuvenate the country by applying science and education, accelerate scientific technological progress, convert pattern of economic growth and achieve strategy on sustainable development.

SUGGESTIONS FOR ACCELERATING DEVELOPMENT
OF CHINESE TECHNOLOGY MARKET

Speeding up the Reform of Scientific and Technological System and Finish Transformation of Organization for Scientific Research Run as Enterprise

At present, the main problem existing in China's scientific and technological system is the lack of incentive mechanism and that scientific research organization have not enter into the circulation of market economy. Therefore, it is essential to reform system of production department of technology commodity in force to strengthen its vigor. Under the principal of "stabilizing one, broadening others", we should make most scientific research organizations, especially technological development and technological service, accomplish management of enterprise or transformed into enterprise. Some organizations might be reorganized into enterprise groups or become the center for development of technology run as enterprise by shareholding enterprise system.

Adjusting Structure of Organization for Scientific Research and Strengthening Concentration of Scientific Research and Lessening the Gap of Lack of Effective Supply for Technical Commodity.

The lack of effective supply of technical commodity is that technical commodity that scientific research organizations or producers can supply doesn't really meet the demand of buyers for technology. In China's technology market, there are a number of technologies that are far away from practice in production and the proportion of technology lacking elementary test and middle test is very large. The main reason is that there are lots of producers who can't satisfy specific and complex requirements of buyers for technical commodities in China. The structure of most scientific research organizations is very simple and scale of organization is small. Moreover, the concentration degree of scientific research is low. As far as computer technology is concerned, there are 90 independent electronics institutes, whose business is scattered and repeated in the low level. Because concentration degree of scientific research is low, computer technology has been lagged behind the advanced world level to the great extent. On the contrary, American IBM corporation has 30000 personnel who are engaged in scientific research, 32 departments of research, the characteristic on production in science and technology of IBM is that the corporation has many personnel, much money and projects, and that concentration degree of scientific and research is very high. In IBM Corporation selection of question for scientific research is decided through negotiation among institutes of scientific research, engineering departments, production sections and marketing departments. There is the regular procedure by which transfer development of research achievements into production, thus IBM's computer technology is among the best of all the candidates throughout the world.

It's proved in practice in several decades that the structure of production of technical commodity under the level of low concentration degree of scientific research has hampered seriously the effective supply for technical commodity and development of technology market in China. Thus, in order to make up for the lack of effective supply of technical commodity, we should do our best to build up "center for development of production", "engineering center", and "the middle test base", which is run as enterprise and high concentration degree of scientific research.

Regulating Structure of Enterprise and Making it be Main Body of Research and Technology Transfer to Make up the Lack of Effective Demand for Technical Commodity.

The lack of effective demand for technical commodity is that the buyer of technical commodity hasn't enough ability to digest and absorb technical commodity on the technology market. Under the present conditions in which the relation of Chinese industrial structure is loose and scientific research is out of line with production, technological progress must be hampered seriously so that allocation efficiency of scientific technological resources is greatly lowed. In order to improve service efficiency and benefit of Chinese scientific technological resources and propel science and technology forward, we must firstly remove the structural hamper on the way of scientific and technological progress. Since policy of reforming and opening to world has been practiced, we have been emphasizing that economic development depends on science and technology, and science and technology is oriented to economic development, but we haven't conscientiously researched the way for combination of science and technology and economy, and ignored the lack of effective demand of enterprise for technical commodity. Specifically speaking, because the structure of industry is not rational, industrial concentration degree and the level of specialization are low, organization for scientific research is dependent of enterprise and concentration degree of scientific research is low in China, enterprises find it hard to look for technology that suits themselves, not to mention that enterprise becomes the market subject of technological transfer and research and development of technical commodity.

In order to make up for the lack of effective demand for technical commodity, we should deepen our reform to make both scientific and technological resources and economic resources be matched and recombined, and also have concentration degree of industry high and strengthen coordination of specialization to get micro-structure of industry rationalized. There are two aspects of the way by which structure is rationalized. One is to develop and improve enterprise's digesting, absorbing and developing strength, also to make scientific and technological structure and economic structure rationalized; the other is to conduct institution invocation of the current independent organization for scientific research and make the organizations run as enterprise or enter into enterprises.

Enhancing the Construction of Intermediate Organizations and Strengthening Intermediate Links of Technology Market.

We should devote great efforts to developing all kinds of intermediate organizations for technological transaction, developing types of services facing to society such as consultation, technology inter-broker, information service, intellectual property and valuation of assessment i.e.. and gradually forming networks and services system for technological transaction covering urban and rural areas. All of that is effective means to make China's technology market prosperous. According to principles of combination between specific duty and concurrent post, we should set up the groups of technological brokers with distinct Chinese characteristic and improve their professional level and professional ethics, and make intermediate organization be auxiliary to promote development of technology market

Strengthening and Perfecting Construction of the Legal System Popularize and Improving Legal Consciousness of Market Subject and Strengthen Enforcement of Law on the Technology Market.

Market economy is legality economy, marketization must be accompanied by institutionalization, only technology market on which law is standardized can be called as technology market indeed. One of the weak sectors of China's marketization of technology is legal system building. In China, market subject lacks consciousness to protect itself with law and standardized behavior of transaction, legal sense is very weak and efficiency of market is low, market administrative interference often happens and enforcement of law is not sufficient .it has had an effect on equity of market.

Hence, to strengthen legal system building is a significant segment to safeguard the order of technology market. First of all, we should devote our efforts to propagate and draw out lawful regulations on intellectual property right such as "Law on Technology" , "Patent Law" , "Trademark Law" , "Copyright Law" , "Law on prevention of unfair competition" and "Regulation for Protection of Computer Software" i.e. and strengthen protection of intellectual property right to protect spiritual and economic rights that party should enjoy on scientific and technological achievements and to prevent patent right, trademark right, copyright, copyright of computer soft and other scientific and technological achievements from plagiarizing and infringing. Moreover, we protect owner's right keeping commercial secrets and keeping secrets of technical information that can bring economic benefits for owner and is not known by the public, and also, prohibit anyone to obtain, reveal and permit others to use owner's commercial secrets and forbid violating agreements or act of tort to right that the owner holds commercial secrets.

Secondly, we should strengthen enforcement of law on technology market, perfect legal binding system and punish severely behaviors violating fair trade and unfair competition. Moreover, we should break up division and blockade among departments, locality and industry and stop local protectionism, and also, in accordance with the law, we should investigate to establish the civil responsibility and the criminal responsibility of the party who infringes legal rights and interests of others, monopolies illegal technology or makes a deal by fraudulent means. Only in this way can we shall set up the operating mechanism of technology market which possesses not only both incentive and constraint, but both equity and competition.

REFERENCES

Chen Zongsheng, Gu Zhe *"Technological Progress and Selection of Labor Intensive Technology"* Nankai Economics Research, No. 6, 1996

McM (translated by Chen Zongsheng and Wang Lihua, et al) *"Unfair Trade Behavior"* China Social Science Press. 1997

Yang Jisheng *"Technological Commodities and Technology Market"* Tianjin Science and Technology Press 1986 *"China Statistics Yearbook"* 1994-1996 China Statistics Press

PART III
MARKETIZATION OF MAJOR INDUSTRIAL SECTIONS: MEASUREMENTS OF MARKETIZATION OF AGRICULTURE, INDUSTRY AND FOREIGN TRADE

Chapter 9

MARKETIZATION PROGRESS OF AGRICULTURE

The economic reform starting in 1978 in China is, in essence, a marketization process whose ultimate target is to transform from traditional central-planned economy to modern market economy. How far the transform has gone and to what extent it can further go on have always been one major concern that many economists and scholars have been discussing. To measure the marketization degree of Chinese agriculture can be tough owing to the extreme complexity of modern market structure, operational mechanism and agents involved.

It is well known that the great economic evolution in China originated in rural areas and agriculture, and then extended to the rest of the Chinese economy. Therefore, marketization in rural areas and agriculture bears special significance. In this chapter, by measuring agricultural marketization, we will analyze the factors leading to agricultural marketization, to measure the achievements in agricultural marketization and to predict the possible upper limits of agricultural marketization.

IMPLICATION OF AGRICULTURAL MARKETIZATION

Implication of Agricultural Marketization

At first, Market is viewed as a place where commodities can be exchanged freely. With the deepening of social division of labor, its implication has completely changed. Market in a modern sense is considered not only as a place to exchange residual commodities but also as an institute to allocate resources and distribute surpluses, which is the base and core of modern economy. Correspondingly, there is another institution, government control. Market and government interventions are two ways of allocating resources and distributing residue in an economy. Marketization, therefore, is a process of transformation of resource allocation and residual distribution from government control to market. Simply speaking, it means that people choose market rather than government to allocate resources and distribute residue, more generally speaking, fulfilled by the law of value (through visible and invisible market transitions among people). In other words, marketization refers to the change of any transaction of a product or factor from government control into market coordination, meaning that more activities of resource allocation and residual distribution are finished in market, not controlled by the regulation of government.

The fulfillment of marketization is the results of marginal transformation of each transactions, which means the transformation from government control to market transaction Direct transactions are not the only way of resource allocation with the highest efficiency. While there is externality in direct transactions, government intervention could be a best choice. It is externality that makes government excessively extended. Moreover, government control has a characteristic of economy of scale. Therefore, in reality, government frequently surpasses its limit to replace market. The exact meaning of marketization is to restore market transactions in sectors where there is no externality.

The collective agricultural production in People's Commune for almost 30 years made the government control not only replace external market transaction in agricultural sector, but directly diminish all market transactions in agricultural production and distribution as well. The distribution from production factors to products was completely controlled by the planning organizations on behalf of the government. Personal exchanges were viewed as illegal and severely prohibited. This over-regulating behavior was one of the reasons that resulted in inefficiency of agricultural production and low income of rural populations. Reform in this area is to resume market transactions in economic sectors where market is the best way to maximize resource allocation. Implications of agricultural marketization in system transformation era are therefore to transform from planned system of resource allocation and residue distribution to market system.

Transformation from planned system of agricultural resource allocation and distribution to market system means:

1. establishment of market system, i.e., to replace government with market in such sectors as agricultural production, operation, distribution, etc.
2. generation and development of market subjects. Since in traditional planned economy market was rejected, there were no market subjects whatsoever. One of the targets of marketization reform is to rebuild and develop market transaction subjects and diminish externality of transaction.
3. establishment and perfection of market organizations (mostly intermediary organizations). Organizations result from transaction cost. If transactions are fulfilled just by one to one exchanges, the transaction cost will surpass the welfare that results from the improvement of resource allocation by market transactions. The establishment of market organizations is to reduce transaction cost and to make good use of market system in resource allocation and residual distribution. It should be noted that this kind of organization is different from governmental organization in that it represents the interests of some part of people instead of all the people, and it is generated to make the market transaction more efficient. The above three points may not be adequate to fully

describe the concept of agricultural marketization, but they are the chief content of agricultural marketization.

Agriculture Marketization and Industrialization, Urbanization

Modern agriculture has developed far away from the small-scale and self-sufficient peasant economy. It must be viewed not only as a source to provide raw materials for a growing non-agriculture but also obtain essential support in production factors and technology. The economic development induced by the emerging and developing of nonagricultural sector is what we call industrialization. Industrialization, therefore, results in population concentration and cities, which is called urbanization. Industrialization and urbanization will increase market transaction; more and more transactions will be between agricultural and non-agricultural sectors, rural households and urban residents.

There are two types of transactions that agriculture can provide raw materials and life necessities for non-agriculture and obtain support from the latter. The first one is government transactions. Under traditional planned economy, the transaction between agriculture and industry was the result of government co-ordination, i.e. the government withdraws agricultural surpluses to support industry and allocate domestic manufactures to subsidize agriculture. The second one is market transaction. Government-dominated intervention in transaction in the early stage of industrialization usually was usually in favor of industry while against agriculture. To realize the target of industrialization, the transaction against of agriculture will finally result in inefficient resource allocation and unequal residual distribution, at the expense of less outputs and lower income in the agricultural sector. On the contrary, market-dominated transaction can make full use of resources and benefit both industry and agriculture. Therefore it is market transaction that balances the transactions between agriculture and industry in the process of industrialization and urbanization. Definitely government intervention can not be excluded in the process.

China now is situated in a stage when industrialization, urbanization and marketization co-exit and co-develop. Industrialization and marketization help agriculture rid of the inefficient traditional self-sufficient commodity production and transaction, and promote the marketization level of agriculture. Therefore, agriculture marketization is a function of economic development, but it is not the focus of our discussion.

RETROSPECT OF THE COURSE OF
AGRICULTURE MARKETIZATION OF CHINA

Chinese rural and agricultural sector before reform was fully regulated by the government, which meant that the government stipulated almost all the profit limits of economic subjects, and gave no permission to free transactions among individuals. Therefore, the elementary marketization reform at this stage is actually a marginal transformation of transaction from state controlling to market regulating. The reform does not result in the welfare loss for most people, and so it is easy to be realized at less cost.

The Stages of the Reform of Agriculture Marketization

The reform in rural area of China consists of the following types.

Replacing reform.
This reform is characterized by the replacement of collective operation with household responsibility system, which leads to the replacement of government transaction with market transaction.

Direct incremental reform:
Increments in excess of the plan-controlled stock were directly managed through market transaction, i.e., country market and fair exchanges were permitted after the state had purchased and distributed the resources and surpluses ordered. With the increase of increments, direct market transacting reform gradually transforms to replacing reform in the whole. For example, the initial market transaction of agricultural outputs will put all the agricultural products on the market which finally diminish the planned allocation.

Complementary reform:
With the marketization reform of agricultural products, the production materials are marketized meanwhile. The government no longer provides subsidiary agricultural production materials

Stock subsidiary reform:
The reform is characterized by providing subsidies to urban residents while freeing control upon prices of agriculture outputs, so as not to damage their welfare.

These four types can basically cover all the marketization reform in rural areas and agriculture, but can outline those in other fields of the economy.

Because of the sequence of marginal transformation, the marketization reform is explicitly phased. During the course of agricultural marketization, the establishment and development of agricultural product markets occupies an important position. Therefore, according to the marketization degree of agricultural products, the marketization can be divided into three stages:

1. Stage I (1978-1984). In this stage, the collective management system was replaced by the household responsibility system. Some market factors were gradually introduced. The scope of the state purchasing and distributing dwindled, the procurement price increased, and especially, the direct increment market transaction occurred. The articles of unified government purchasing and distributing staples reduced from 113 in 1981 to 60 in 1984, the purchasing prices of 18 agricultural products increased by 22.1%.

2. Stage II (1985-1991). The characteristics of this stage are that it speeded the transformation from government control to market-oriented system. The main steps adopted are: replacing the unified government purchase and distribution system with a contract purchase system; reducing the quantity of agriculture staples purchased by order; increasing the scope of negotiated purchase and marketing system and gradually relaxing price control over agricultural products. From 1986 to 1991, the purchasing prices of agricultural products, state pricing ones were reduced from 17 to 9, and in the selling prices, the state-pricing ones were reduced from 14 to 7. The price formation of agricultural products planning-pricing decreased from 94.4% in 1978 to 25.2% in 1990.

3. Stage III (1992 to present). In this stage, the course of marketization was accelerated and the market system of agricultural products was established. In 1992 and 1993, contract purchase was cancelled in a few regions, market-pricing system was realized. The formation of consuming prices of agricultural products was basically decided by market transaction.

With the marketization reform of agricultural products, other sectors such as productive resources reform, marketization reform of agricultural input, country market establishment and the establishment and perfection of rural intermediary organizations, etc. were also experiencing rapid development. These progresses are, as that of agricultural products, characterized by progressive.

Two Types of Market Transactions and Two Marketization Courses

China's rural reform absolutely boomed village markets and there have been 66,585 country fair trade markets in Chinese rural area in 1995 according to statistical data. This trend is still going on. This is surely the achievement of marketization, but it is a problem deserving deep consideration whether it is able to reflect the degree of agriculture marketization.

There were two types of transactions in China's rural and agricultural sector: the country fair transaction and the modern agricultural transaction.

1. Country fair transaction. The transaction subjects are the local agricultural residents of a certain region. There fair transaction is to regulate supplies by adjusting surplus product, exchanging surplus product A for other's surplus product B. It is different from what we call barter though, for its purpose is not for high profits and the market is filled with price haggling, also, the transaction cost is very high. This market transaction aiming to satisfy consuming should be classified as small commodity exchange by Marx's theory, but it contains different implication in current situation.

2. Modern Agricultural Market transaction. Modern market transaction is to make profits with products from specialized production. Also, the consumers are mostly the non-agricultural population in or out of the region. The subjects are diversified, local

agriculture households, non-agricultural population and consumers out of the region. What is most important is that there emerged a group of people who lives on market transaction business. Generally they are well informed and good at transaction, and able to optimize resource allocation.

There are direct and indirect relationships between these two types of transaction. The country fair transaction of the agricultural products can be considered as the basis of modern agricultural market transaction and is developed from village market. According to the classical theoretical analysis of Blundell, country fair transaction is at the bottom of the market economy and the modern agricultural transaction is on the top.

The boom of country market fairs in the early phase of rural reform demonstrates the construction of the basic market system. This simple face-to-face exchange is the base of modern market economy. The marketization reform meanwhile makes modern high-level economic activities occur in rural and agricultural sectors. Accordingly, the co-existence of the two kinds of market transaction makes it essential for us to measure two types of agriculture marketization: the marketization of agriculture household (in micro-economical perspective and the marketization of agriculture reform in macro-economic perspective). Marketization of rural households means the process in which economic activities of rural households--he new subjects of agriculture operating gradually transfer to market transaction. Before the reform, all the transactions were controlled by government and the two parties within one transaction are not equal either in position or in power. As government is more influential and prevalent, the economic game rule therefore is regulated by government.

The macro-agricultural marketization refers to the process in which market allocates resources through open market transactions in place of government controlling. Both the marketizations can reflect the process of market reform to some degree. Comparatively speaking, macro-agriculture marketization is the real symbol of the maturity of marketization reform. Therefore, the boom of country fairs does not necessarily equal to the high level of marketization. Hence, we need to realize the two markets, two types of market transactions and further realize the two levels of agriculture marketization

MEASUREMENT OF AGRICULTURAL MARKETIZATION

The co-existence of two types of agricultural marketization means that to precisely reflect the degree of China's rural and agriculture marketization, it is necessary to analyze from two perspectives. Moreover, the following prerequisite must be assumed: there is no market transaction in the centrally planned system, and the agricultural marketization is completely brought forth by rural area marketization.

Indexes for the Measurement of the Course of Agricultural Household Marketization

Agricultural household is family farm whose chief economic activities are agricultural production, and its objective is to maximize outputs for certain amount of input. Therefore, marketization of agricultural household is composed of input marketization and output marketization. Generally, agricultural household purchases productive materials and sells agricultural products in local country fair. Sometimes they exchange with other local households for machines, labors and capitals, etc. This local country market cannot evolve to modern market system unless modern agriculture is established and developed. So far, agriculture is still dispersed by families, and land tenure was extremely decentralized and uncirculable in China, which determined that the main objective of Chinese agriculture is still self-sufficient. Hence, it is country market transactions that still dominate both the inputs and outputs market exchanges today.

Measurement of the Marketization of Household's Input for Production

Currently, the household's input for production includes crop and planting cultivation, livestock breeding, fishery and forestry. As natural resources in each region are different, emphasis of each region varies from one to another. In addition sideline business based on agricultural products that individual household is engaged in should also be regarded as agricultural production behavior.

Currently, the main input of agricultural household covers the following production materials: land, seeds (or young livestock), fertilizer, machinery, labor, chemicals, fodder, etc. Among them, the marketization level of land is still zero as it is still owned by the nation and allocated to individual household to plant but not be allowed in market transaction. Therefore, the following formula can be adopted to measure the level of marketization of household's input for production:

$$MD_p = \sum_{i=1}^{n} N_i \times M_i \tag{1}$$

where MD_p is the degree of Marketization of household's input, M_i is the cost ratio of market-purchased input into total inputs, including all that purchased and provided from own resources, N_i is the cost ratio of input I to total stock of productive inputs, that is, weight.

Measurement of the Marketization of Household's Output

Similarly, the formula for measuring output marketization can be developed as follows:

$$MD_m = \sum_{i=4}^{n} B_i \times M_i \tag{2}$$

where *Bi* is the value ratio of agricultural products *i* to total agricultural produced by individual household. *Mi* is the ratio of products *i* for sale to the total stock (including all that for sale, own-consumption, planned purchase, ordered purchase and taxation).

Measurement of the Marketization of the Household's operation

Given the degree of the Marketization of household's management as *MF*, then *MF* should be the average weight sum of *MDp* and *MDm*. As the output includes profits, the weight of *MDp* and *MDm* theoretically should be more than the input. So, their weight is respectively $1/(2+i)$ and $(1+i)/(2+i)$, where *i* is the profit rate. The formula is:

$$MF=[1/(2+i)]\times MDp+[(1+i)/(2+i)]\times MDm$$

In a simpler way:

$$MF = MDm +[1/(2+i)]\times(MDp - MDm) \tag{3}$$

For better understanding, we shall further explore into the relationship between the degree of structural transformation of farm operating system and the profit, given the relationship between *MDp* and *MDm* the same.

1. Given *MDp* > *MDm*, *i*>0, if *MDp* and *MDm* are constant, then *MF* shall decrease when *i* increases. Actually, any changes in variable *i* will alter *MDp* and *MDm* when *MDp* > *MDm*.

    MDp> *MDm* indicates that the government still controls much in agricultural output transaction, the agriculture outputs are mostly purchased and distributed, or ordered by the government. Any increase in *i* indicates the government increases the purchasing and ordering price, the farm households therefore prefer planned sales than market transaction. It results in MDm's corresponding decrease; and if *MDp* remains constant, then *MF* decreases. The other possible reason which results in *i*'s increase is that the government subsidizes inputs, so, if *MDp* decreases, and MDm remains constant, then *MF* will decrease.

    Similarly, when *i* decreases, then MF will increase.

2. Suppose *MDP*<*MDm*, *i*>0, if *MDp* and *MDm* are constant, *MF* will increase when *i* increases. In fact, if *MDp*<*MDm*, when *i* increase, *MDm*, and *MDp* will increase, which leads to increase of *MF*.

As agricultural inputs in China have been basically supplied by the market, and the government exerts control over transaction of agricultural outputs, that is to say, *MDp*>*MDm*. Thus, the protective policies and subsidiaries to agriculture undoubtedly increase profits of agricultural household and slows down the pace of marketization of their operation.

Measurement of the Marketization of the Household's Operation at the Present Status

Based on the index system described above, we've obtained three groups of data by sample quantitative survey. As it is difficult to get detailed record of household's expenditure, the data were estimated in average by the interviewees, which can approximately reflect the fact.

Sample questionnaire survey 1.

The survey area is Daizhai Village in Xixian county, Henan Province. The background information of the village is: there is no township enterprise; people basically live on agriculture; about 60% of labor force have left the village and gone into cities to work as peasant workers; only 1.5 *mu* of land per capita; the agriculture is mainly crop and plant cultivation; the most important sideline business is hog raising; and agricultural products are rice, wheat, red linen, oil plant, cereals, etc. According to 30 interviews, the main farm inputs involve chemical fertilizer (25.71%), seeds or young livestock (15.42%), fodder (38.56%), machinery (19.28%), agricultural chemicals (1.03%), the proportion purchased in market are respectively 95%, 70%, 40%, 85%, 100%. According to model (1), the degree of production input marketization is 68.06%. Among the agricultural outputs are rice (60.87%), wheat (14.78%), hogs (17.39%), red linen (4.53%) and cereals (1.30%), and the proportions for the outputs sold through market transaction are, respectively, 50%, 10%, 66%, 98%, and 5%. According to model (2), the degree of output marketization is 47.72%. If the annual market wage for farm labor input is   1500 and the rate of profit is about 30%, then, according to model (3), MF is 53.08%.

Sample questionnaire survey 2:

The survey region is Shudong Village in Huaiyin county, Jiangsu Province. It also is classified as backward region in north of Jiangsu Province. The basic situation is that there are: no township enterprises, 10 percent of labor force work in other regions outside of the village, the main agriculture is crop and plant cultivation, hog raising, and its agricultural staples are rice, wheat, oil plant and cereals. The calculation showed that *MDp* is 49.6%, *MDm* is 49.88% and *i* is 13.95%. According to model (3), *MF* is 49.77%.

Sample questionnaire survey3:

Survey region: Tanggu District, Tianjin. Most of its households are engaged in two or more agriculture undertakings, and the agricultural staples are grain, livestock and vegetables, which comprise of 22.8%, 59.6%, 10.15% respectively of the staples for sale. According to *Tanggu Statistical Year Book, 1995,* the proportion for sale of each is 27.27%, 90.88%, 97.99%. According to model (2), *MDm* is 70.44%. As *MDp* calculated by *Tanggu* rural survey organization is about 90%, *i* is 67%, then MF is 77.78%.

Measurement of the National Agricultural Household's Marketization.

According to a national survey in 1993 conducted by the central policy analysis office and observation office of the Ministry of Agriculture, 89.64 % of farm input was purchased and 35.13 percent of outputs was sold in the market directly or indirectly. Considered that the profit level is 47.62(i) according to *China Statistical Book, 1995*, MF is 57.14%.

The above1data offer evidence that national degree of the marketization of agricultural household operation has reached a higher level, about 60%, and there are regional differences in agricultural household's marketization. The degree of agricultural household's marketization of Tanggu District, the suburb of Tianjin, for example, is rather high, about 70%. The marketization levels of the two backward regions, however, are as low as about 50%. Moreover, the degree of farm input transformation is higher than that of the output transformation, the national-scale spread is 54.51%. The case of sample 2 is somewhat different in that the degree of farm input transformation is a little less than that of input, which is because there is large population compared with limited farmland in this region. Consequently hog raising plays an important role in agricultural production, and its inputs account for 54% of the total farm inputs, while mostly from self-provided fodder. This results in the relatively lower degree of input transformation. Moreover, 90% of the hogs raised are sold in the market which balance the two.

Measurement Index System of Agriculture Marketization

The above measurements index system and statistical data measure the degree of agricultural household's dependence upon market transaction in the present stage. Most of the market transaction of the agricultural households are carried out in country fairs. The marketization of agricultural household just reflects the basic construction of the agriculture market. Its reflection of the marketization degree of the allocation of agricultural resources and residue distribution is not precise. From a wide point of view, agriculture marketization refers to an institutional change in agricultural productive resources allocation from government control to market transaction. The following analysis, therefore, is to measure certain region's macro agricultural marketization from the viewpoint of resource allocation and residual distribution.

Agricultural resources are made up of three categories: labor force, land and capital. As being mentioned above, land is state-owned and uncirculable, we may measure the marketization degree of agricultural resources allocation in the other two respects: labor force and capital. In general, no matter how to allocate resources and distribute residue, pricing is necessary. The marketization degree of the price is an important indicator in agriculture marketization. Also, as the way to realize agricultural resources allocation is mainly by agricultural product circulation, the marketization of agricultural product circulation means the transformation from planned purchases, ordered purchase and planned distribution system to market transaction structure. It is also an important index to reflect the degree of agriculture marketization. Therefore, we may measure the degree of the marketization of the agriculture as a whole through the following formula:

$$M_t = \sum_{i=1}^{n} C_i \times M_i \qquad (4)$$

Where M_t is the degree of agricultural marketization by index i, C_i is the weight of each index.

In the following, it is going to be explained how to measure the four indexes and their results.

Measurement of the Marketization Degree of the Agricultural Labor Forces (M_1)

In the collective economy period, the labor market did not exist, as the labor liquidity is strictly under government control; both employment and wage were fully arranged by the Department of Labor Employment. Laborers had no choices but the amount and efficiency of their contribution.

In the early period of reform, the implementation of the Household Responsibility System intensified the density of labor input in agricultural production. However, with the release of forbidden employment area and labor liquidity, large numbers of non-agricultural industries emerged and exodus of labor force occurred, the density of labor force therefore cut down, labor efficiency improved, and for the first time, agriculture began to grow definitely in China.

The brisk of non-agricultural industries gave agricultural labor force another alternative apart from the agricultural labor: they may choose between agriculture and non-agriculture. The transition of the two alternatives rid of the government control upon agricultural labor force, and labor market appeared. To some extent we can say that it is the boom of non-agricultural sector that resulted in the rise of labor market.

On the other hand, the development of agricultural labor market was indispensable from the change of the agricultural operation system. The transformation from household farming system to operational agriculture system meant the final formation of labor market, for in an operational agriculture system, the labor was seeking maximum profit. The key factor determining the transformation was the shift of surplus labor force. Compared with labors in household agriculture, labors in non-agricultural sectors were completely market-oriented and their choices were realized by free market exchange. It can be said that the quantity of the exodus of labor directly reflects the degree of labor market development.

As there were still differences between towns and countries in the period of reform, the main agricultural labor force shift was within country regions, that is, shifting from agriculture to township enterprises and other non-agricultural industries. Later in 1990's comes out the "rush of farmer job seekers' shifting" from the cropping sector. As they could not become state-owned enterprise workers, most of them entered private business sectors and collective enterprises in cities and rural countries. Accordingly, it is reasonable to represent the amount of labors shifting out of agriculture by measuring that in non-agricultural sectors in the same region.

The above analyses show that today's Chinese agricultural production is still going on in traditional ways and being too intensive in labor force, the best index chosen to measure the degree of agricultural labor marketization in marketizational reform is the proportion of non-agricultural workers to the total agricultural labor force in the region. The index is also one of the accurate ones available.

Measurement of the Marketization of Agricultural Investment (M₂)

Agricultural investment can be broken into two types: liquid production investment and fixed asset investment.

In the period of collective production, the subjects of investment are government and country collectives. The basic peasants' unit or the production unit is only responsible for labor-intensive activities in certain community. The country collective on behalf of the government owns and disposes almost all of capital input, both liquid and fixed. In this stage, the agricultural capital market is not existent.

The transformation of agricultural operation mode from collective to individual household makes the subject of liquid capital investment change from the state and collective to agricultural households. The liquid production investment was completely free of government control. However, since most of Chinese rural areas have vast population and limited farmland, the ratio of return on investment is low, so the capital accumulation resources are also limited. So agricultural cultivation is just a means of survival and the liquid input is just a responsibility, rather than an open market behavior. It can not represent the marketization degree of agricultural investment.

With the transforming of operating system, the subjects of investment involve three layers: the state, collective and individual. The state invests and controls large-scale massive agricultural infrastructure; the collectives are in charge of small-scale fixed asset input on capital construction, and the households are responsible for part of fixed production inputs, such as purchase of farming tools. With the development of non-agricultural sectors in rural areas, the investments of the latter two are no longer confined to agriculture. To the collectives, the purpose is to maximize profits with limited capital based on returns of investment. An excellent example of this is the stagnation of collective fixed input resulted from the diminishing comparative advantage of agriculture. To the household, the limited capital makes his selection depending on agricultural comparative advantage further. Moreover, external capitals absorbed in this stage are still resulted by market transaction. Accordingly, the proportion of individual, collective, external capital of fixed capital investment is affected by market mechanism. Compared with the portion invested by the state, theirs is the product of the marketization. The rate of the marketization level of agricultural capital can be represented by measuring the proportion of investment in fixed agricultural asset from collective, the individual and foreign capital.

Measurement of the Marketization of Agricultural Product Transaction (M₃)

As has pointed in the report, the country market transaction took place between agricultural households could not be interpreted as modern market transaction. The marketization induced by it can not fully reflect the level of agricultural marketization in rural areas. Only the transactions between agricultural and nonagricultural population can be considered as the best way to allocate resource and distribute surplus. There are two types of transactions between agricultural and non-agricultural population: the first one is government transaction, whose characteristic is to plan and order purchase of agricultural residue and then distribute to nonagricultural population. It is the main way adopted in the centrally-planned economy. The second one is the transaction by means of markets between agricultural and non-agricultural population. It is strongly prohibited in central-planned economy. So the increase of this type of transaction can be considered as reflecting the strengthening of the degree of marketization. Therefore, the proportion of direct and indirect transaction to total transaction can realistically measure the agricultural products circulation market.

Measurement of the Marketization of Agricultural Product Price (M_4)

Price is a sign that reflects not only the scarcity of resource and residue, but also the equality of their allocation and distribution. It can be also considered as the outcome of the two types of transactions: the mandatory price set by government and the market price set by market transaction. Before reform, the prices of all the agricultural products are mandatory, the degree of marketization therefore is zero. Accordingly, the proportion of market set price to total agricultural product price can be adopted to measure the price system transformation of agricultural products.

Detailed Exploration into the Weight in Formula 4

Weight is an important index for exactly measurement of the level of the overall agricultural marketization, therefore:

1. In the analysis of agricultural production and exchange procedure, the weight of each is 0.5 respectively.
2. The weight of labor force and capital in the input market can be measured by the elastic weight in the agriculture production function (C-D function). According to some analysts, the elastic weights are 0.34, 0.66 respectively.
3. As it is rather difficult to determine the weights of the contribution of price marketization and products exchange marketization to overall agriculture marketization, we assume they are the same. The formula 4 therefore can be evolved as:

$$Mt = 0.17M_1 + 0.33M_2 + 0.25M_3 + 0.25M_4 \qquad (5)$$

Measurement of the Course of Agricultural Marketization as a Whole

According to the specified index system and Formula 5, we've reached part of the data of agricultural marketization in some provinces and cities.

Table 9.1 The Degree of Agricultural
Marketization and GNP in Some Provinces and Cities

District	M_1	M_2	M_3	M_4	M_t	Per Capita GNP(Yuan)
Beijing	88.17	76.08	31.64	91.5	70.88	8240
Tianjin	72.27	92.97	37.37	91.5	75.18	6075
Shanghai	68.01	57.19	50.00	91.5	65.81	11700
Shandong	52.38	92.76	24.93	91.5	68.62	3222
Zhejiang	47.34	94.04	36.13	91.5	70.99	4431
Jiangsu	41.00	91.59	42.78	91.5	70.76	4308
Guangdong	43.00	76.36	18.26	91.5	59.94	4938
Hebei	43.16	90.30	30.52	91.5	67.64	2682
Jilin	42.00	84.86	9.78	91.5	60.46	2868
Anhui	27.17	93.98	28.27	91.5	65.72	1672
Henan	26.76	94.93	34.12	91.5	67.27	1867
Sichuan	17.90	87.89	17.23	91.5	59.19	1911
Shanxi	29.04	91.96	30.52	91.5	65.63	1041
Xizang	2.16	92.88	11.11	91.5	56.67	1642
Xinjiang	24.28	71.52	51.02	91.5	63.35	2980

Remarks:

1). Data of $M2$ are obtained form relevant data in "China Statistics Yearbook" (1995)

2) The price marketization of agriculture staples in 1994 is 91.5%

3) $M3$ is the proportion of non-state economy in the purchase of agricultural and sideline products in wholes and retail trade, which more accurately reflects the marketization of agricultural products circulation

Figure 9-1 is obtained according to the data in Table 9-1.

Figure 9-1 The Degree of Agricultural Marketization and the Level of Economic Development of Some Provinces in 1994

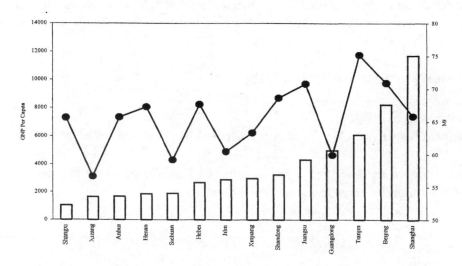

According to the Indexes designed above and Formula 5, it is possible to obtain the sequential data about China's agricultural marketization (1978-1994) (See Table 9-2), and draw the figure of the course of agricultural marketization (See Figure 9-2).

Table 9.2 The Degree of China's Agricultural Marketization (%)

Year	M1	M2	M3	M4	M5
1978	9.23	10.00	5.60	5.61	7.67
1979	9.38	20.00	11.6	6.65	12.75
1980	9.42	30.00	17.7	8.19	17.94
1981	9.09	40.00	20.9	9.36	22.31
1982	9.19	46.78	21.7	10.23	24.98
1983	9.32	63.25	23.9	10.52	31.06
1984	14.48	75.32	32.0	11.81	38.26
1985	18.83	80.14	63.0	17.32	49.68
1986	20.89	72.34	64.7	18.84	48.30
1987	22.58	76.18	70.6	19.46	51.49
1988	23.82	78.33	76.0	19.85	53.86
1989	22.88	73.67	64.7	20.62	49.53
1990	25.87	70.63	74.8	20.84	51.61
1991	26.32	70.40	77.8	21.84	52.61
1992	28.14	58.03	81.8	24.42	50.52
1993	32.86	61.68	90.0	41.34	58.78
1994	33.33	66.19	91.5	57.10	64.66

Remarks:

1). M_1 is cited from *China's Agricultural Statistical Yearbook,* 1995, Chinese Statistical Publishing House.

2). M_2 is cited from *China Statistics YearBook* of relevant years.

3). M_3 is cited from LU Zhongyuan and HU Angang, *The Influence of Marketization Reform upon Chinese Economy Operation*, Economic Research Journal, No. 5 1993; The data in 1992, 1993 and 1994 are calculated according to China's Agricultural Statistical Yearbook (1994 and 1995), Chinese Statistical Publishing House.

4). M_4 is cited from *China Statistics Yearbook* (1994 and 1995) and *China Rural Area Statistics Yearbook* (1995)

Figure 9-2 The Course of Agricultural Marketization in China

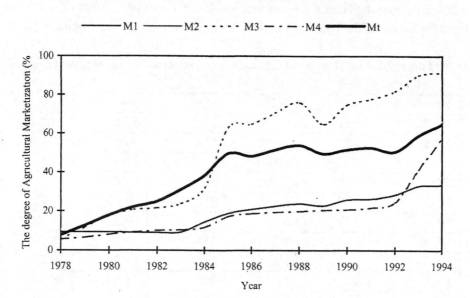

Analysis on the Measurement of Agriculture Marketization

The above index system and data available have measured the progress and the status of China's agriculture marketization. We can learn from the data and chare of 1994 that:

1. There exist objective differences of agriculture marketization level among different regions, especially the level of separate marketization. From table 9.1, we can learn variable coefficient of each index as $Vm1$=53.6%, $Vm2$=12.7%, $Vm3$=0, $Vm4$=43.5%, Vmt-7.8%, Vrg=72.5%, which indicates that similar to GNP, the level of marketization of both labor and agriculture output differentiate among regions. However, the agriculture marketization as a whole over all regions are roughly the similar and Vmt=7.8% a little more equal among regions. The main reason is that the difference in price marketization of all the regions is 0, and the difference in input marketization is also very small, in addition, the both indexes weigh much in weighted sum.

2. The level of agricultural labor force marketization is closely related to the level of economic development. The higher the development, the higher the level of agriculture marketization, for instance, the marketization levels of Beijing, Shanghai and Tianjin are all above 65%, and those of Guangdong, Jiangsu and Zhejiang are above 40% too. However, the level of under-developed area is only 20%, some even less than 10%, such as Tibet, which is only 2.16%. It indicates that the course to a market-oriented agriculture is a process of transformation from agriculture-depending system to nonagricultural sectors-depending system.

3. There is negative relationship between level of agricultural investment marketization and that of economic development. More highly developed areas such as Shanghai, Guangdong and Beijing have less agricultural input-marketed level, that of Shanghai is 57.19%, 30 per cent below average level of 15 provinces. On the contrary, the level of some less developed areas such as Anhui, Henan, Sichuan and Shanxi were all above 90%. Only Tianjin, Zhejiang and Jiangsu are exceptions. This is mainly because the prosperous and developed town enterprise feedback to agriculture and collectives invest more in infrastructure.

4. There is a relative close relationship between the level of overall agriculture marketization and the level of economic development, judged by agriculture marketization and distribution of economic development. The higher the marketization level of agriculture, the higher the economic development, which is clearly demonstrated in the above graphs. This is clearly demonstrated by the relationships of the two tendency lines in chart 9.1. The result is what we expected. Yet they cannot be completely co-related parallel, as marketization is just one of factors that affect economic development.

The above is the status analysis of China's agriculture marketization. Some conclusions can be drawn from the marketization data of 1978-1994and graphs above:

1. The course of marketization is distinctly phased. There are three phases in this course. The first phase is between 1978 and 1984, when each index shows a rapid growth, i.e., M1 increased from 9.23% to 14.48%, M2 increased from 10% to 75.32% in 1984, and the level of agricultural structural transformation increased from 6.67% to 38.26%. The second phase is between 1985 and 1992, when each index experienced slow growth, especially, M3 and M4 were experiencing fluctuation, M1 and M2 went up slowly and the level of agriculture marketization stayed at 50% for a quite long time. The third phase is from 1993 to now, when each index enjoys rapid increase again, i.e., M4 increases quickly from 24.42% in 1992 to 57.10% and the level of agriculture marketization also increases from 50.52% to 64.66%.

2. So far as individual index is concerned, M1 has always been experiencing slowly rise. It reaches only 33.33% in 1994, which means that only one third labor force is employed by market transaction. In developed countries, however, M1 is the highest index and almost reaches 100%. The reason that M1 in China is low is that:

   a. There is a huge population with little land and households were separately operated.
   b. Traditional farm operating system still plays an important role in agriculture production and rural education lagged far behind necessity and most farm labors still satisfies with self-sufficiency.
   c. Traditional ideas and life styles still dominate rural employment.

3. M2 has been high since reform but fluctuates thereafter. The main reason is that the state has decreased infrastructure investment. Meanwhile, the collectives and

individual households also decrease their investment, as the comparative interest of agriculture was low. In 1985 M2 reaches the peak and agriculture production begins to fluctuate. Thereafter, the government re-strengthened investing power and M2 began to decrease year after year, in 1992 it reaches 58.03%. After 1992, as agricultural staples circulation market is opened and its prices are raised considerably, so the comparative interest of agriculture increases, M2 begins to increase again.

4. The price marketization and circulation marketization of agricultural staples are even more characteristics of phases. For example, in 1984 the level of price-marketed transformation is just 32%; in 1985 it has reached 63%. The reason is that the main channel of Chinese agriculture marketization is price and circulation system transformation.

AN ANALYSIS ON THE FACTORS CONTRIBUTING TO AGRICULTURE MARKETIZATION

Based on the theoretical analysis, we have measured the marketization course of Chinese agriculture in two levels. In this section, we are going to explore into the key factors which induce the rise of agriculture marketization institutional change factors, market subject growth factors, and organizational change factors.

Agriculture marketization consists of three aspects: formation of market institution system, development of market subjects and establishment/perfection of market organizations. Therefore, the inducing factors of marketization can also be accordingly divided into three groups: institutional change factors, subject growth factors and organization change factors.

Institutional Charge Factors

Agricultural institutional change in China is mainly interpreted as the course from traditional centrally planned economy to market economy, that is, market replaces government in agricultural production allocation and exchange

Given *MAD* be a measure of agricultural transition, a function can be developed as follows:

$$MAD = fa \ (IC, AM, LF, AIr, ID, FE, GF...) \tag{1}$$

IC represents the institutional change of agricultural producing and operating system. There are three types of agricultural producing and operating system: household farm, managerial farm and collective farm. Moreover, household farm includes modern household farm and traditional family farm; collective farm includes *Kolk Hoz* (represented by former Soviet) and people's Communes (represented by China). Modern household farm and managerial both can be viewed as a produce of market economy. Family farm in some way is also dominated by country market transaction. Collective farms, whereas, still managed by government. The promoting agriculture producing and operating transition in China is to replace people's communes by household responsibility system as the unit of production and accounting, which is similar to family farm in that they are both village market directed and have less government intervention.

AM represents level of agricultural specialization, modernization and large-scale, which are interrelated. There are two ways to realize specialization, modernization and large-scale: first, by government intervention and investment to form fare large-scale productive unit to specialize in single region, which, however, is low efficient and will result in wastage of resources. Second, under the functions of market, the inner demand of economy development causes agricultural production more and more to depend on capital input, and agricultural specialization, modernization and large-scale can be achieved through competition in market. Comparatively, the latter is a better way to allocate resources efficiently, and to promote agriculture to develop fast and smoothly. So, the level of agricultural specialization, modernization and large-scale should be viewed as not only a product of marketizaton, but also a way to serve all links of agriculture production, exchange and distribution and promote marketization.

LF represents a measure of liquidity of ownership and tenure of agricultural fixed capitals (including land), which also is a basic condition of agriculture market. Currently in China almost all fixed capitals can be exchanged freely except ownership of land. The reform of agriculture must require tenure of land can be exchanged freely.

AF represents development of rural financial market. Financial instrument as the intermediary of transaction is one of the most significant characteristics of modern market transaction. Rural financial market is an indispensable part of agricultural market system. With the scope of market transaction deepening and broadening, the demand for financial instrument has become more and more great. To a certain extent, the development of financial market imposes a restriction on agricultural marketization. In the period of people's commune, the business of the rural financial agencies is state-directed. After the reform, the nature of the financial business has been changing, and some new financial instruments are arising, but the development of rural financial market is not satisfied the demand of market operation. Therefore, rising the developmental level of rural financial market will promote the reform of marketization more deep and perfect.

AIr represents the price ratio of industrial and agricultural products. In the period of the planned-economy, for accelerating industrialization, the government extracted the agricultural surplus through the distortion of pricing. The exchange of products between industry and agriculture was carried out under state monopoly for purchase and marketing. The reform makes the product exchange between industry and agriculture to increasingly depend on market, which requires a reasonable price ratio. The marketization of agricultural product price is a course of the price ratio of industrial and agricultural products becoming more equitable, which reflects the degree of agricultural marketization, and at the same time, adjustment to more equity will promote agricultural marketization.

ID represents the level of industrialization and urbanization, which embody the level of the economic development of a country or a region. Industrialization and urbanization mean that labor is drawn from agriculture, then demand pressure on agriculture increases, and this pressure acquires agriculture to be oriented to urban market. On the other hand, marketization is a function of the level of economic development. Therefore, industrialization and urbanization can promote agricultural marketization.

FE is rural living level. Rural living level has a close relation to agricultural marketization. Below self-sufficient level, the lower the living level is, the higher the degree of agricultural marketization is. At self-sufficient level, the degree of agricultural marketization reaches the lowest point. After the living level exceeds self-sufficiency, the higher the living level is, the higher the degree of agricultural marketization is, because the agricultural surplus can be used to exchanged for other productive and living goods. At present, rural living level has exceeded self-sufficiency in China, so raising the rural living level will promote the agricultural marketization.

GF represents the function of government in agricultural development, which means how much service the government provides for smooth operation of agriculture market. These kinds of service mainly include four aspects: (1) providing information service; (2) input and extension on agricultural technology and research; (3) input on education, hygiene in rural area; (4) input on agricultural fundamental construction. The increase of each service above will definitely accelerate the process of agricultural marketization.

The eight factors mentioned above are the main factors that contribute to agriculture marketization in the three aspects of production, exchange and allocation. According to the way they influence transformation of market system, these factors can be divided into compulsory factors, such as IC, GF, etc. which push forward the transformation through government intervention, and inductive factors such as AM, LF, ID, FE which accelerate agriculture marketization by market direct.

Market Subject Growth Factors

Agriculture market subject mainly refers to the subjects of market transactions, including both individual agricultural household and rural organizations involved in market transaction. Subject of market transaction is the result of marketization reform, but the core of market operation as well. The development and growth of market subject is an important sign of marketization reform. Given MGd be a measure of the development of market subject, then

$$MGd = fg(FF, AE, AG...) \tag{2}$$

FF is a measure of self-dependency of single household, while self-dependency means the subject of production gradually gets free from government control and is influenced by market. The improvement of self-dependency depends on diminishing of government intervention.

AE is the market subject's level of cultural quality and market transaction consciousness, where market subject means market participant and agent. Rational economic person is essential to efficient market operation and avoiding market failure. Moreover, market economy is an information one, so the improvement of market subject's cognitive ability is necessary for market mature. To improve the market subject's level of cultural quality and consciousness of market transaction needs human capital input.

AG is a measure of the cooperation among market subjects. Nowadays it is dispersed individual household who dominates Chinese agricultural market. Uncertain risks of the market may severely affect the operation of them, which in the long run prevent marketization going further. Therefore, the cooperation and unification of households are beneficial to the deepening of market reform.

Organization Change Factors

Organization here refers to market intermediary agents instead of organization of market subjects. It includes all intermediaries serving for market transaction. Such as, circulation organization for rural cooperation economy, financial intermediary, technological intermediary, information intermediary, etc, all of which are included in certain market and serve it. A fully operating market must include all of these intermediaries and an objectively existent market is a component of them. Each market must have its own transaction place, circulation organization, financial intermediary and so on. Therefore, transition of market intermediary can be demonstrated in the growth of market as a component. Given Mod be the measurement of market intermediary change, then,

$$Mod = fo\ (OQ,\ OM,\ OT,\ OG...) \tag{3}$$

Where *OQ* is the amount of market intermediaries; *OM* is the scale of market intermediaries; *OT* is the specialization and modernization degree of the intermediaries; *OG* represents the cooperation among intermediaries. The improvement of specialization and modernization of intermediary means the junior market evolves to a future market and finally future contract market, each evolvement indicates the progress of market-oriented marketization.

Chinese agricultural intermediary is completely the result of agriculture marketization reform, part of which is evolved from the original intermediary organizations, connecting government and farm household, i.e., current agriculture financial organizations, agricultural material and staple circulation organizations, technology popularization organizations. These organizations have, to some extent, been market intermediaries, but still not in pace with development of the market and their organization structure and function needs further improvement. The other intermediaries are developed by government or farm household in the process of market transformation.

These mainly are: 1) specialized market, which is composed of all kinds of intermediaries specializing in certain transactions. The characteristic of it is that it has specialized transaction venue and transaction organization, such as all kinds of wholesale market of agriculture staples. They are mostly established by government and collective. 2) circulation entity of rural economy, mostly they are production companies combing the function of production and sales, such as household unity revolving around core agriculture household, or specialized production/cooperative organization revolving state-owned business. The participants of this levels of intermediary from the state, the collective to farm household. 3) technology associations in rural area, whose services cover each step of agriculture production and circulation. 4) financial intermediary such as rural save association, which has experienced long slowly developing and still is in junior stage. All these newly established intermediaries have been important part of rural and agricultural market and the development of them will further promote operation of agricultural market.

Inducing Model of Agriculture Marketization

As mentioned before, agriculture marketization is induced mutually by system transition factors, market subject growth factors and organization transition factors and is the function of all three:

$$Mt=ft\ (MAd,\ MGd,\ Mod) \tag{4}$$

Therefore we can arrive at the inducing model of agriculture marketization:

$$Mad=fa(IC,\ AM,\ LF,\ AF,\ Alr,\ ID,\ FE,\ GE...) \tag{1}$$

$$MGd=fg(FF,\ AE,\ AG...) \tag{2}$$

$$Mod=fo(OG,\ OM,\ OT,\ OG...) \tag{3}$$

$$MT=ft(Mad,\ MGd,\ Mod...) \tag{4}$$

It is possible to get the actual model by hypothesis of certain function, however, the focus of this section is to qualitatively describe the progress of agriculture marketization. Its improving and deepening depends on the variables listed above. In Table 9.3 are listed the changes of some indexes in the reform of agricultural marketization. The correlation of them to agricultural marketization is clearly demonstrated in the table.

Table 9-3 Changes of Factors Restricting Agriculture Marketization and its Relationship to Agriculture Marketization

Year	Growth of financial market of agriculture (%)	Consuming index of peasants	Non-agriculture level	Number of high school graduate in rural area (in 10000)	Number of country fairs	Level of agriculture marketization
1978	0.032	104.4	79.59	--	33302	7.67
1979	0.028	106.9	77.78	--	36767	12.75
1980	0.042	109.3	77.47	7.9	37890	17.94
1981	0.044	107.9	75.97	9.4	39715	22.31
1982	0.049	107.6	75.09	13.1	41184	24.98
1983	0.059	109.1	75.29	21.6	43515	31.06
1984	0.107	112.4	75.60	27.8	50365	38.26
1985	0.111	113.9	78.18	41.3	53324	49.68
1986	0.142	102.4	78.93	57.9	57909	48.30
1987	0.165	104.2	78.70	75.0	58775	51.49
1988	0.155	106.1	80.32	81.0	59178	53.86
1989	0.167	99.10	81.07	86.3	59019	49.53
1990	0.185	99.50	79.86	89.3	59473	51.61
1991	0.222	106.8	81.52	94.5	60784	52.61
1992	0.270	109.3	83.73	96.7	64678	50.52
1993	0.286	106.1	80.01	102.5	66551	58.78
1994	0.265	106.5	79.00	107.6	66585	64.66

Source: *China's Statistical Yearbook* (of each relevant year)

ACHIEVEMENTS OF AGRICULTURE MARKETIZATION

The premise that marketization brings about the change of world economic system is that it results in the growth of social wealth. It is widely accepted among economic study that a perfect market can realize Paulette ultimization. The Chinese agriculture marketization from traditional planned purchase and distribution circulation system to household responsibility market system confirms this. At least the following social wealth has been increased ever since agriculture reform: The reform of agriculture marketization in China has increased social wealth at least in the following aspects:

1. The implementation of Household Responsibility system freed many potential agriculture labor forces to nonagricultural sectors, which developed tertiary and town enterprises and changed the ever-existing rural unitary economic structure.

2. The boom of nonagricultural sectors in rural area, which resulted in market transformation, increased not only material wealth but also population in rural towns and cities, which also resulted in urbanization by means of developing small towns.

3. There is clear agriculture increase in this period of reform with less labor input and without any more evident capital and technology input. The increase owes much to the agriculture marketization. We can see clearly the relationship between increase of GNP, GAP and the market-oriented transformation degree of agriculture in the following table.

Table 9-4 Relationship between GNP, GAP and Agriculture Marketization

Year	GG	GL	GK	FG	FL	FK	Mi
1981	4773	43725	961.06	2180	29836	29.21	22.31
1982	5193	45295	1230.4	2483	30917	34.12	24.98
1983	5809	46436	1430.6	2750	31209	35.45	31.06
1984	6962	48197	1832.8	3214	30927	37.12	38.26
1985	8557	49873	2543.2	3619	31187	36.94	49.68
1986	9696	51282	3019.6	4013	31311	35.06	48.30
1987	11301	52783	3640.9	4675	31720	42.11	51.49
1988	14068	54334	4496.5	5865	32308	46.17	53.86
1989	15993	55329	4137.7	6534	33284	50.65	49.53
1990	17695	56740	4449.3	7662	34177	67.22	51.61
1991	20236	58360	5508.8	8157	35016	85.00	52.61
1992	24036	59432	7854.9	9084	34855	112.7	50.52
1993	27232	60220	12457.9	10995	33258	131.2	58.78
1994	30390	61470	16370.3	15750	32690	160.0	64.66

Sources: *Chinese Statistics Yearbook*

Given GG be Gross National Production, GL be gross labor input, GK be gross capital input and Mi be a measure of agriculture marketization, then GG is function of GL, GK and Mi. Also, given FG be Gross Agricultural Production, FL be agricultural labor input, FK be agricultural capital input, then FG should be function of FL, FK and Mi, which are:

$$GG=f(GK, GL, Mi) \text{ and } FG=g(FK, FL, Mi)$$

respectively. Moreover, hypothesize the two functions are simple Line function, i.e.,

$$GG=a_0+a_1GK+a_2GL+a_3Mi; \quad FG=b_0+b_1FK+b_2FL+b_3Mi$$

With data provided in the table and recursive analysis, the two functions are:

(1) FG = −2355.12 + 72.74FK + 0.0073FL + 78.71Mi   AR − sq = 0.956
    (−0.4073) (9.297)   (0.0371)   (2.918)   F − st = 94.268

(2) GG = − 46155.52 + 1.2627GL + 0.8606GK − 230.9038Mi   AR−sq=0.995
    (−14.651) (14.956)   (12.917)   (−7.761)   F−st=975.415

as T-test of independent variable FL in (1) is not distinct, we can say that increase in labor is no more a basically push to increase in agriculture production. Without FL in (1), we get:

(3) FG = − 2143.38 + 72.83FK + 79.10Mi   AS − q = 0.960
    (−2.45) (10.33) (3.34)   F − st = 155.52

Also, from (3) we can get:

(4) d(FG)=72.83d(FK)+79.10d(Mi)

This formula demonstrates that each 1% increase in transformation degree of agriculture will result in increase of 79.10 billion yuan in GAP. In 1994 about 18% 0f GAP increase is the result of better resource allocation by agriculture marketization.

Function (2) is somehow out of our expectation. The coefficient of GK which is 0.86 shows that each increase of 100 million in infrastructure will result in 0.86 billion increase in GNP. Also, the coefficient of GL which is 1.26 demonstrates that each increase of 100 million labor in labor input will result in 1.26 million increase in GNP. However, the agriculture marketization is reverse to increase in GNP, i.e., each increase of 1% in Mi will result in decrease of 23 billion in GNP. This is contrary to our hypothesis. Since Chinese economic development has outgrown labor-push forward period, GL can be omitted. Therefore we find Mi contributes much to GNP.

TREND OF AGRICULTURE MARKETIZATION

There are two aspects of Chinese agriculture marketization:

1. Freedom from traditional self-efficiency agriculture in economic development, namely, market-oriented transformation of household.
2. Transformation from planned system to marketed allocation system in resources allocation, in other word, overall marketization of agriculture.

As a matter of fact, household marketization is shared by all types of economy in advancement, while overall marketization is typical of Chinese agriculture. The developed countries have experienced an anti-marketization agricultural process, where government strengthens its power on agriculture control and protection, which finally results in protected agriculture, such as the US, Canada, German which characteristic of large plantation, even as small plantation typical of France and Japan.

Thus, Chinese agriculture marketization can not be viewed as a unidirectional process of proceeding. From view of theory, the higher the economy is developed, the more agriculture depends on market transaction, with the theoretical maximum is 100%. That is to say, all the agriculture inputs, outputs and circulation depend on market transaction. However, it is impossible in the real world, especially in agriculture. So the maximum is still open to debate.

First, the marketization of agricultural labor force will go on to about 80-100%: agricultural labor force has complete choice of employment. Secondly, the agricultural input transformation which is measured by infrastructure will slow down. Government will play a more and more important role in agriculture fundamental construction for there will be less capital input substituted by labor input and government will burden the risk of agriculture. According to some developed country, the limit should be 30-50%. Third, price of agriculture staples will experience an anti-market process which means more and more items of agriculture staples will be priced by government to protect agriculture, its limit should be 40-60%. Fourth, the marketization of agriculture circulation system will speed. Most of the national-scale transaction will be under no control and international trade will be protected by government, the limit will be 80%. Accordingly, we get the reasonable up-limit, which should be between 60% and 80%.

In general, the current Chinese agriculture should be no more pursuing the improvement of overall marketization level, but the adjustment and deepening of the steps of the marketization progress. Some marketization should go on, some others may have reached up-limit. Protective model agriculture will be our future choice.

REFERENCES

Chen Zongsheng *"Allocation of income in economic development"* Sanlian Bookstore, Shanghai People's publishing house 1994

Chen Zongsheng *"Surpassing Dilemma"* Chinese Economy Publishing House

Lu Zhongyuan, HU Angang. *"The influence of marketization reform upon Chinese economy operation"* "Economics Research" vol. 5, 1993

National Statistics Bureau *"Chinese Statistics Year Book"* 1980-1996 Chinese Statistics publishing house

Wang Yuesheng *"Re-exploration into the Cost and Harvest of Reform in Different Reform Modes"* "Economics Research" vol. 3, 1996

Wang Jiguang *"Chinese Grain Problems"* "economy research" vol. 3,1996

Ye Xingqing *"On the Reform of the Supply System of Public Product in Rural Area"* "Economics Research" vol. 6, 1996

Chapter 10

MEASUREMENT AND ANALYSIS OF THE COURSE OF INDUSTRIAL MARKETIZATION

The transformation from traditional centrally planned economic system to market economic system is one of the two critical transformations which have great significance to the realization of the future economic development targets in China. Industry plays an important role in national economy. Therefore, the degree of industrial marketization is undoubtedly a focus of attention of first concern of the economic theory circle and strategic departments.

INDEX DESIGN

The marketization of an economic activity can be measured from many aspects. In this chapter, it is scheduled to be measured from the following aspects:

In an economic system whose economic activities center on market, the economic subjects inevitably regards economic interest (both short-term and long-term ones) as their major, if not sole, objective. Each economic subject does not pursue either social interest, nor assume any social function or adjustment function. This is an important sign of the marketization of economic activities. From this point of view, studying the degree that economic subjects pursue economic interest can serve as one of the measurements of the marketization degree of the economic system. When economic subjects pursue economic interest, the first sign is the system's full use of production factors (capital, labor force, resources and facilities). The second one is that the economic system organizes its production according to the market rules so as to ensure the sales of product and the realization of profit. The last one is that the economic system attaches importance to the formation of future productive capacity and efficiency, which are the important condition to guarantee the continuous profits.

Index 1: Utilizing rate of labor forces (F_1)

F_1 = the amount of industrial efficient employment/total amount of industrial employment

The amount of effective industrial employment refers to that of employment that matches a given capital and is decided by the needs of production. When industry is run under the rule of market efficiency, it will not hire unnecessary labor forces. Therefore, the ratio of required labor force in production to the total labor force is one of the indexes in measuring the marketization degree of industry.

Index 2: Utilizing rate of capital (F_2)

F_2 = output value created by per hundred yuan capital in industry / output value created by per hundred yuan capital in foreign-funded enterprises

In market economy, as one of the productive factors, the capital must be fully utilized by economic entities in market economy.

Index 3: Ratio of sales to output (F_3)

F_3=sales value of industry product / gross industry output

The index reflects the degree of realization in industry output value. Under market economic system, the economic subject can only obtain profit on condition that the product is sold out. Therefore, the economic subject must adjust its production according to the requirement of the market instead of its own production capacity.

Index 4: Investment-profit elasticity (F_4)

$$F_4 = F\,[(k_1-k_0)/k_0]/[(e_1-e_0)/e_0]$$

In F_4, k_1 and k_0 is the amount of auto-investment of report period and base period in industry enterprise respectively. E_1 and E_0 are economic effectiveness index of report period and base period respectively in industry. $F(x)$ is self-defined in function. It equals 1 when x>0, or 0 when x 0.

Investment is expected to obtain high return when economic efficiency increases. That enterprise increase investment at that time is the normal response to the market and we can regard its marketization degree as one. On the contrary, its marketization degree is zero.

In a system centering on market economy, the government should participate and interfere with enterprises' economic activity to the minimum under market economic system. The intervention with micro-enterprise operation does not conform to the principles of market economy. Therefore, the lessening in the degree of government involving economy is important sign of economic system marketization. Accordingly, The lessening index of government participation and intervention is also an important one in measuring marketization degree of economic activities.

Index 5: Ratio of non-state-capital to gross capital in industry (F5)

F_5 = non-state-capital in industry / gross capital in industry

In economic system activities, market is the basic means of resources allocation. People who have the right to dispose production factors can decide the investment of the production factors into the production of goods to realize his target. In this process, it is the market rather than the government who guides the allocation of production factors. In non-state owned enterprise, the capital is not invested by the state; thus, the ratio of non-state-capital to gross capital in industry is an important indicator of industrial marketization process.

Index 6: The degree of enterprise's independence (F6)

F_6 = 1 − (planned sales value of industrial output + planned raw materials supply value of industrial output + state-priced industrial output value Z multiple counting) / gross industrial output value.

In market economy, enterprises decide the production of products and sell them in the market to cash the investment. The state guides the strategy by macro-control instead of direct intervention.

In the economic system where market is the core of the economic activities, economic subject can form various preferential economic behaviors according to its institutional characteristics such as preferences for free and fair competition and contractization of economic relationship, etc. Therefore, inclination of some economic behaviors is also an important index in measuring the marketization degree of economic system.

Index 7: The bid ratio in construction industry (F_7)

F_7 = the project number of bid in construction industry/ total project number of construction industry in the same period

Transaction through bidding proves to be the most efficient way of transaction. The bid ratio reflects whether the economic subjects attach great importance to efficiency, and the bid is also the degree of equality in market competition. Since the bid ratio of other industry is not easy to obtain, the one in construction project can present the degree of bid ratio in general.

Index 8: Rate of Contracts being executed (F_8)

F_8= the amount of contract executed / (the amount of contract ought to be executed + the transaction amount having not been contracted)

Normalized economy order is essential to the smooth operation of market mechanism. When economic subjects transact with one another, the signing and execution of contract is one of the reflections of orderly running in economy. Only by signing contract can economic subject effectively protect his interests. The contract execution rate represents the level of contractization within an economic system.

Index 9: Industrial enterprise bankruptcy rate (F_9)

F_9 = the number of enterprise bankrupted / the number of enterprise whose asset is short of debt in the same period

"Survival of the fittest" also applies to market economy. That some enterprises go bankrupt is a natural product of market competition. That an enterprise who does not go bankrupt although its asset is short of debt is not economic subject's preferential behavior, especially that of the creditor under market economic conditions. The rate of enterprise's bankruptcy reflects marketization degree of economic system from the point.

Index 10: Degree of service socialization of enterprise (F_{10})

F_{10} = welfare amount paid by enterprises / total welfare amount

In the market economy, as a production unit, enterprise assumes no other social obligations than salary and insurance for employees. The benefit of the employees should be issued by the state organizations instead of the enterprise. In other word, the society should provide service for enterprise production. Therefore, the socialization level in enterprise's service is one of the indicators that reflect marketization degree of economic system.

Lastly, the way of measuring overall marketization degree in industry is to arithmetically average all indicators in each group, then geometrically average all the group value calculated. Its result reflects marketization degree in industry.

INDEX CALCULATION[3]

Table10.1 Indexes of the Industrial Marketization Degree (%)

Year	1983	1985	1988	1991	1993	1994	9595
F1	54.38%	54.38%	48.1%	42.46%	54.85%	55.62%	54.26%
F2	49.46%	64.71%	70.30%	72.32%	82.93%	98.78%	82.29%
F3	96.5%	95.54%	95.97%	94.27%	95.95%	82.56%	96.34%
F4	100%	100%	100%	100%	100%	100%	0
F5	15.53%	19.12%	22.83%	25.19%	34.15%	38.52%	40.09%
F6	10%	-	-	64%	86.2%	85.3%	84.4%
F7	0	-	-	-	-	52.16%	57.51%
F10	1.51%	1.11%	0.64%	0.69%	0.72%	0.9%	0.82%

Remarks: - = unavailable
  the ratio of net value of industry in 1980 to fixed net asset
  proportion of sales of independent enterprises
  cited from statistics report of State Statistics Bureau.
  replaced by the market price with of production materials.
  bidding rate of state-owned construction enterprises and that of other construction

For a long time China has carried out high employment rate policy, which results in surplus personnel in enterprise. The situation has not been improved significantly after reform. According to our estimate, the utilization rate of labor force in 1983 and 1995 remains approximately the same (in 1983 it is 54.38%, in 1995 it is 54.26%). The chief causes for the problem are 1). There is no major laws or regulations governing employment system, and there is not unemployment insurance, which results in surplus personnel in enterprises. 2) Although foreign-funded enterprises and private enterprises with higher utilization rate have increased remarkably, the advanced technology and equipment leads to higher rate of surplus personnel in the enterprise. The surplus enterprise personnel can not be resolved and the utilization rate of labor force can't be improved.

Judged by the result of calculation, capital utilization rate in industry has increased remarkably after reform. In one aspect, this is because the government has conducted some changes as to the utilization means of capital, which promoted state-owned

---

[3] The data involved in this book is calculated according to *China Statistics Yearbook*, if not specified.

enterprise consciousness of utilization rate. In the other aspect, it is because the comparative utilization rate of our contrast—foreign-funded enterprises is also cutting down. In 1994, the abnormal situation of capital utilization rate is due to policy of the government which affects other enterprises more than state-owned one, thus the difference in utilization rate of capital between state-owned enterprises with the foreign funded enterprises become small.

The sales rate of industrial product has always remained high apart from that in 1994. Yet the sales rate in 1983 is not comparable to that in 1995. In 1983, the high sales rate is realized via state planning while in 1995, over 95% of products are sold by enterprises' own effort. The rate of 1995 is much high compared with that in 1994. There are several factors contributing to it, partly because enterprises have developed adaptability to the market. Indicator 3 shows that marketization level of industry has increased.

The marketization progress reflected in indicator 4 does not match our impression. It indicates non-marketization tendency of enterprise's investment. From 1983 to 1995, enterprises begin investing independently, irrespective of the actual economic situation. It is reflection of enterprise's investment desire when no hard budget constrains is imposed. After the economic reform, the ratio of non-state-owned capital increased year by year, from 15.53% in 1983 to 40.09% in 1995. Included in the non-state-owned enterprise are both collective enterprises and the township enterprises, foreign-funded enterprises and other types of enterprises. The prosperity of them greatly stimulates the development of the Chinese economy.

By 1992, Chinese reform in industry has been always progressing around the decentralization of power, which can be perceived from the gradual rising of value on indicator 6. This further indicates the improvement of marketization degree of industry. It is worthwhile to mention that in 1994 the government controls the price and sales of products a bit more than ever for the sake of administering inflation, which indicates that the rights of enterprise haven't been safeguarded and the government can take back the rights granted at any time.

As a means of transaction appropriate to market economy, invitation for bid and bidding do not grow fast enough in our country. The invitation for bid started in construction industry in 1984. By 1995, the bidding rate reached 57.71%. It reflects the unbalance and inadequate growth of the market.

Chinese enterprises always inherit the tradition that enterprise function as society, which hasn't changed after reform. All the benefit of employees and the salary and benefit of the retired employees are covered by enterprises. After the reform, the situation has not been changed, and even the proportion of welfare expenses paid by society (the civil administrative departments) has decreased (1.51% in 1983; 0.82% in 1995). Today, the change of such situation is becoming increasingly urgent in today's reform.

Because the rate of contract execution and that of enterprise bankruptcy are not easy to calculate, we can only provide some descriptive statements afterwards.

According to the previous method of calculating marketization degree of industry, the marketization degrees of industry from 1983 to 1995 lists are as follows:

Table 10.2 Degree of Industrial Marketization.

Year	1983	85	88	91	93	94	95
Marketization degree of Industry (%)	7.86	23.47	32.08	31.34	46.52	48.42	49.86

Remarks: as regards to the unavailable data, the speed of average development estimator takes their place.

Chronologically speaking, industrial marketization has developed considerably after the reform. Next, we are going to briefly analyze its situations.

JUDGEMENT ON THE PRESENT MARKETIZATION PROGRESS OF INDUSTRY

Genuine Marketization Economic Subject of Industry has not been Developed Yet in Micro Layer of the Economy

In market economy, profit is ultimate goal of all enterprise behaviors. Enterprises are self-independent, self-responsible, self-developing and self-restraining economic subject. After more than ten years' of reform, the '4-self' enterprises is gradually shaping. This can be clearly demonstrated in the non-state-owned enterprises, while in state-owned-enterprises, the situation does not improve substantially.

1. Enterprises have not fully utilized the production factors. Their behaviors are not or cannot be market-oriented. This is mainly reflected in the surplus labor forces. Before the reform, enterprises' requirement for labor force is completely under government arrangement and allocation. The incoming and outgoing of staff were controlled by superior authorities. After the reform, especially after the issue of the regulation governing the employment of labor in 1992, enterprises began to be granted the right of employment in name. Yet the application of the right was restricted in many aspects (According to a questionnaire survey conducted by "Chinese Entrepreneur", in 1995, only 74.8% employment rights was actually granted to enterprises). Out of the consideration for social stability, government authorities forbade enterprise from dismissing surplus labor to the society. Such phenomena exist both in state-owned enterprises, collective enterprises and non-state-owned enterprises. We estimate that the proportion of surplus labor force in industry is about 45%.

Another reflection of enterprises' ineffective of production elements is the low rate of capital utilization in enterprises. Capital of an enterprises is to develop production and make more profit. Only when enterprises maximally utilize the capital can they make profit. But in China, the enterprise as an economic subject plays the role of the society. It is not only responsible for the living of employees but for their direct relatives. A large amount of fund is invested in non-productive field like hospital, kindergarten, and can not create further profit. Although the utilization rate of industrial capital that we have measured is relatively high, part of the reason is that the rate of foreign-funded enterprises is also cutting down (in 1988 the ratio of product value to fund is 1.216, but in 1995, it drops to 1.096). Definitely, enterprises have their complaints (the underdeveloped social security system and the unmatched development of market system). But the objective result is that enterprises can not freely allocate the production factors as the market economy subject should do.

2. State-owned enterprises have not formed the efficient stimulating and restraining mechanism. In traditional planned economy, the state directly operates enterprises: the state invests in enterprises; the products are allocated by the state; prices are determined by the state, therefore, realization of value of the product does not depend on the market. After the reform in 1978, Chinese government has takes many steps to accelerate enterprise to develop in the self-operating and self-responsible direction. Yet these steps did not resolve the motivation of enterprise development. Enterprise is not independent utilization subject of the property, and can not dispose the property; hence, it is not responsible for the consequence of economic activities. This inevitably resulted in that enterprises put the state's property at stake. In 1993, Chinese Central party issued decision on setting up socialist market economic system and to finally free the state from limitless responsibility for enterprises. Yet the decision has not been satisfactorily carried out in practice. The first reason is the issue of representative of the state capital. Government financial department, management department of the state property, as well as administrative authority of industry all think that they are the representatives and continue interfere with the operation of enterprises. Secondly, the soft restraint upon enterprises has not been relieved yet. According to related investigation, when the fatal fault of investment strategy in state-owned enterprises arises, 31% of enterprises don't know who is responsible and 38% of enterprises state that it is the leading group who is responsible.(i.e., no one is responsible).

Although non-state industry enterprises has achieved much better in marketization, state owned enterprises still dominate half of the whole industry, therefore, the current enterprise does not deserve the tile of economic subject.

Government's Direct Interference with and Participation in Economy have Decreased to Some Extent

One of the indicators of government's direct intervention with economy is its control over enterprises. Before the reform, enterprise is just a subsidiary to the government. The government exerts direct control over all steps of state-owned enterprise: what, how and for whom to produce are all decided by the government. From 1979 and on, the state council has issued several documents decreasing the scale and degree of government control over enterprise. In the course, enterprises have gained much self-independence in operation. As far as the government's administration on goods and materials are concerned, among the sales income of productive materials, assigned price by the government is only 13.89%. The government's planned distribution of goods and materials decreased from 256 types before the reform to 20 types in 1993. The goods administered and planned by the government decreased from 188 types to 23. In 1995, the value of goods and materials planned and distributed by government is only 25% of gross output value of industry (Jiang Xiaowei and Song Hongxu, 1995). These indicate that the degree of direct interfering with economy by government decreases. But failure in separating the functions of government from those of enterprises still exists, which is mainly reflected in administrative intervening in the appointment of managers and middle-level cadres and in enterprises' routine operating activities. All of these showed that government's management function have not shifted from micro control of macro management and control yet.

For over two decades since reform, the degree of government's participating as economic subject in economy has decreased vertically: the proportion of state-owned enterprises' assets in industry to total industry assets is 84.47% in 1983, it deceased to 59.91% in 1995. Yet the original problem of dispersed investment of state capital still exist, as a result, the big state enterprises are not big enough while the small ones are underdeveloped. None of the major state-owned enterprises can be listed among the 500 gigantic enterprises of the world. On the contrary, many of the small enterprises are in heavy losses. The number of enterprises in loss accounts for 1/3 of all the state-owned enterprises. Since mid 90's, Chinese government put forth the strategy to focus on the major enterprises while putting the small ones to market. This is a major step taken by the government to accelerate the progress of economic system market. What deserves noting is, even in western countries with mature market economy, state-owned enterprises still exist, and the government intervenes with economic activities to some extent. It is our target to prioritize the distribution of state capital, and to adjust the structure of industry, so that state capital can be made the most use and improve the development of overall production capacity.

Behavioral Preferences of Various Economic Subjects Indicate that There Is a Long Way in the Construction of Marketization

Marketization is not only a process of system construction but also a process of the transformation of ideological concepts and fosterage of market awareness.

Preferential behavior demonstrated by economic subjects not only shows the degree of marketization of the society but promotes or depresses the function of marketization. We are going to explore into the degree of industrial marketization via the situation of invitation for bid/bidding, that of the contracts execution, that of enterprise bankruptcy and the socialization level of enterprise service.

Invitation for bid/bidding is one of efficient competitive methods and form of transaction. The rate Invitation for bid in state-owned building enterprises' contract project was only 34.5% in 1995. The local protection and administrative intervention are one major reason of it. Many departments ignore the efficiency and superiority rule for the sake of their own interests, which is owe to the following reasons. One is the failure in separating the functions of government from those of enterprises; the other is our country hasn't established a set of market rules that can maintain fair competition and so has not restrained economic entities efficiently.

In market economy, economic entities adopt universally contracts to contact with each other. At present there are problems in the disorder of contract and low execution. According to the estimation in1992, the number of unexecuted contracts is one billion, about one third of contracts signed the year. The capital involved is between 300 billion to 400 billion yuan. This reflects that our market rules are imperfect and economic entities have no self-regulation needed in market economy condition.

Chinese "*Law of Bankruptcy*" came into effect in November 1988. By the end of 1994, there are 3010 bankruptcy cases settled by law procedures. In 1994, the enterprise bankruptcy rate is 1.9 per ten thousand. But at present the number of enterprises, which should to be bankrupted, is about 15 percent of all the state-owned enterprises. The sharp contrast indicates that a large number of insolvent enterprises struggle to exist under the support of several of non-market factors. These factors are 1. local governments; 2. specialized banks; 3. the requirement for social stability.

The local government officials regard bankruptcy a shameful thing to their performance, so they are against local enterprises going bankruptcy. The specialized banks are against bankruptcy firstly because of consideration for their own performance, secondly, if enterprises go bankruptcy, the bank shall never be able to collect the loan into the enterprises. The third factor is because currently China has not set up complete system of unemployment protection. It is difficult for unemployed people to be re-employed.

There is another obstacle to the development of our market economy, that is, the social services do not agree with the demand of market economic system. Up to now, China has owned the characteristic that enterprise plays the function of society. Once people are employed by enterprises, the enterprises shall be responsible for everything of the employed people. As a result, such system imposes a heavy burden upon entrepreneur, distracting them from attention upon business. Although after the reform, some steps as to social protection and service have been taken yet the essential situation is not improved. The severe competition of market economy needs socialization of enterprise service, but too many social functions that enterprises undertake have hindered the progress of marketization in our country.

Above all, the behaviors of economic subjects in China have not fully been adopted to the requirement of market economy for various reasons, which brings about much difficulty to the development of industrial marketization.

From above three aspects of industrial economic subjects' behavior, the state of the administration on industry by the government and matched social system, the progress of marketization in our country does not seem optimistic. Industry is just one department of national economy. The industrial marketization demands the efforts of industry itself, but it requires the cooperation of the whole society.

REFERENCES

Chen Zongsheng, *"Outgrow Economic Dilemma"* , Chinese Economy Publishing House, 1995

Chen Zongsheng, *"Perfecting unemployment protection"*, Guide To Opening Up, No. 3, 1995.

Jiang Xiaowei and Song Hongxu, *"Study of market-economy's degree in China"* , Administration World, No. 6, 1995.

"Observation of behavior of various investment subjects", Business Administrator's Study Information, No. 14-15, 1995.

Wang Zhenzhong *"Wage income and manpower resources allocation in China foreign funded enterprises"*, Economic Research Journal, No. 9, 1995.

Chapter 11

STUDIES ON THE COURSE OF
MARKETIZATION OF CHINA'S FOREIGN TRADE

World economy has become integrity ever after human being evolves to industrial society. The economic development of one country is indispensable to the overall development of the world. The market of one country becomes an important composition of world market. Foreign trade, as a major part of national economy, is a key link to the world market. Hence, the marketization situation of one country's foreign trade embodies the marketization level of its national economy as well as the level of integration with the world economy or that of mixture with the world market. Therefore, the researches of the marketization of China's foreign trade constitute an indispensable component of the studies on the marketization process of China's economy. The foreign trade system of our country started from the founding of new China, and developed after the "Open Policy" to the outside world, especially following the 14th Congress of the Party that has determined to form a system of socialist market economy, which has further accelerated the marketization process of China's foreign trade.

The marketization degree of one country's foreign trade should be judged by both quality and quantity. The quality refers to the investigations on the evolution of one country's foreign trade system and how the system facilitates the process of the marketization; the quantity refers to the establishment of an index system measuring foreign trade marketization so as to indicate the level of marketization. We will begin our investigations with the two aspects mentioned on the marketization process of China's foreign trade.

MARKETIZATION COURSE OF CHINA'S FOREIGN TRADE SYSTEM

During the course of the marketization, China's foreign trade system has experienced changes in three stages, namely, stage of centralized planned system from 1949 to 1978; stage of planned economic system reforms from 1979 to 1991; stage of transition to market economy from 1992 to the present.

Stage 1 (1949-1978): China's foreign trade system in the beginning of its founding, affected by the situations both at home and abroad, coincided with the highly centralized planned economy system, was a centralized one. Foreign trade was just to regulate surplus and deficiency on the premise of self-sufficiency under the guidance of the planned economic theory as well as the ideology of self-reliance. Therefore, it is a foreign trade system that both the management and the operation were conducted by the government. The government was responsible for the profit or loss of the foreign trade, and the function of the government was mixed with that of the enterprise. As a result, this system made trades of imports and exports reach equilibrium as a whole, which ensured the balance of China's international payment and maintained a lower domestic price level. Yet on the other hand, it severed the organic relations between China and world economy, extremely fettered the development and expansion of the foreign trade as well as the whole national economy.

Stage 2 (1979-1991): In December, 1978,the 3rd Plenary Session of the 11th Central Committee determined a line of ideological emancipation and seeking truth from facts, and shifted the focus point of the party and the state to the socialist economic construction; made a strategic decision of reform and opened door to the outside world; while carrying out the reform of the economic system, gradually implementing the reform of the foreign trade system.

This stage can also be divided into three sub-stages:

During the period from 1979 to 1987, according to the following principles formulated by the state council as government bureaucrats being separated from enterprises; agency system in foreign trade; integrating industries, technology with trade; and combining imports with exports, etc, part of the management authorities in foreign trade were transferred to a lower level; the experiments of integrating industries with trade were made; the planned parts of the foreign trade were simplified; the contracting management system of imports was instituted. Through the reforms mentioned above, the system of our foreign trade began to initially extricate itself from the past irrational conditions, and developed in the direction adaptable to openness to the outside world and building up a planning commodity economy. The reforms implemented in this period laid a foundation of a rational and scientific system of foreign trade. But, in general, some essential problems in the former system of foreign trade were still not resolved, for instance, the fiscal system of internal unified revenues and expenditures were still not fundamentally changed; the foreign trade enterprises did not have a general adoption of enterprise principles; the distinction between governmental duties and enterprise obligations was not drawn clear; the macro-managerial measures and the economic regulation system of the state were still very weak.

During the period of 1988 to 1991, based on the contract experiences of specialized foreign trade enterprises in the previous stage, the State Council issued "Regulations on Issues Related to Speeding and Deepening Reforms of Foreign Trade System", which mainly referred to a comprehensive implementation of the contract responsibility system in foreign trade, requiring local governments, all specialized foreign trade companies and all industrial & trade corporations to separately make a contract with the central government for target of producing foreign exchanges by exports, amounts of the earned foreign exchange turned over to the state and target of economic benefits; the target of a contract generally remained unchanged for three years. The local branches of specialized foreign trade companies and a part of the industrial & trade corporations separated themselves from their headquarters, and simultaneously linked to local finance. The targets of contract were dispersed to foreign trade management enterprises and production enterprises for exports; the contract units were responsible for its profits and losses; the proportion of foreign exchange earnings was retained by disparity. The experimental reforms of sole responsibility for its profits and losses were carried out in light industries, arts & crafts and clothing industry. In order to implement the contract responsibility system of management in foreign trade, the state took a series of necessary reforming measures such as relaxing control of foreign exchanges, implementing a policy of export refund, shifting part of powers to the lower level by the Ministry of Foreign Economic Trade, so on and so forth, which strengthened the capacity to regulate macroeconomy by economic levers, and created an external environment for foreign trade enterprises to take advantage of market mechanism and set an autonomous management.

Judging by three years' practice, the comprehensive implementation of contract responsibility system of management in foreign trade basically changed the former situation of complete responsibility for profits and losses by the central government, aroused the zeal of governments both central and local for expansion of exports, strengthened the self-controlled mechanism, promoted integration of industry with trade and a close contact between production and sales, and ensured the state foreign exchange earnings. But, there still existed some defects in this reform of the system such as the foreign trade enterprises were still not entirely responsible for their profit and loss, which fostered interregional and interdepartmental blockades and barriers, created unbalanced competitions among different regions as well as different enterprises, led to enterprises' short-term behaviors, led to operation under severe loss because of neglection of the changes in domestic and international business environments. After three years of contract operation, on Dec.9, 1990, the State Council gave out "Resolutions on Issues Related to Further Deepening and Perfecting Foreign Trade system", determined that foreign trade enterprises should be responsible for their own profits and losses without fiscally export subsidy. But no more success was achieved than ever. Generally speaking, the reforms of foreign trade system in this stage were implemented under the condition that the socialist planned economic system was being gradually shifted to market economy, and based on product economy. Although the contract responsibility system of management in foreign trade has had some features of market economy, it still retains some essential characteristics of former system as a transitional system. Much more efforts are still needed to develop foreign trade in accordance with the economic law of international economy and the standard of international trade.

Stage3 (1992 to now): In October, 1992, General Secretary Jiang Zemin made a speech in the 14th Congress of the Party, defining a new reforming objective of foreign trade system, that is, "deepening the reform of foreign trade system, establishing a newly-typed foreign trade system as soon as possible which is suitable for the development of socialist market economy as well as in conformity with the standard of international trade." Conforming to the standard of international trade means to be up to the standard of GATT. The objective of GATT is to foster global economic growth by promoting world trade, free and impartial. It is realized by an implementation of unconditioned multilateral MFN treatment, reduction of tariffs and other trade barriers, promotion of trade liberalization, making full use of world resources and expansion of commodity production and exchanges. Its basic principles are the following, namely: free trade, no-discrimination, tariff reduction, no amount or number limits, impartial trade, self-protection, transparency, and negotiation & mediation.

According to the basic principles and the relevant clauses of GATT, there still exist a lot of aspects that are not in conformity with GATT in our correct foreign trade system. For instance, although export fiscal subsidy was cancelled, it artificially constituted an export subsidy that the state supported loss-making enterprises and foreign exchange market supplied foreign exchanges at the rate higher than official rate; and some practices such as goods of import & export administered by different levels and managed by classification, could not make enterprises get into market with equal opportunity, and were harmful to the principle of impartial trade; the kinds of goods managed by import & export licenses and by quotas were too many ,which conflicted with the principle of general cancellation of quantity limits; besides, there was lack of enough transparency in foreign trade administration; the tariff rate was still on the high side though reduced, so on and so forth.

In 1994, the state implemented a new round of comprehensive reforms in foreign trade system, centered on the reform of foreign exchange management system. The direction of this reform was an unified policy, equal competition, responsibility for one's own profit and loss, integration of industry with trade, implementation of agency system, etc. in order to establish a foreign trade operation system meeting the current international standard.

The main measures taken in this round were:

Integrating exchange rates;

Establishing a sole, manageable floating exchange rate system based on market supply and demand, Renminbi exchanged for foreign money with qualifications under current accounts;

Abolishing the retained system of foreign exchange earnings and the target of turning them over to the state;

Establishing foreign exchange business market between designated banks;

Canceling mandatory plans of imports & exports;

Promulgating the first *Law of Foreign Trade* of our country;

Further giving impetus to more liberal management of foreign trade enterprises;

More quickly vesting with management rights in foreign trade the state-owned production enterprises, scientific research institutions and commercial goods & materials enterprises;

Quickening the reform and construction of chamber of commerce of import & export,

Improving its institutional framework, strengthening its coordinating service functions;

Perfecting the coordinating service mechanism of foreign trade management;

implementing modern enterprise system;

Quickening the shift of management mechanism of foreign trade enterprises.

The implementation of the reform of the foreign trade system in this round has strengthened the coordinating functions of market economic mechanism, improved the terms of foreign trade, significantly accelerated the process of marketization of the foreign trade, which has attained initial results.

MEASUREMENT OF THE MARKETIZATION COURSE OF CHINESE FOREIGN TRADE

Before 1978, Chinese economy was a closed one; foreign trade was just a supplement to national economy. In the eyes of enterprises, foreign trade was just to adjust the surplus or shortage of products rather than a means to develop market. After the reform, Chinese economy transformed from centrally planned to market-oriented; the reform of foreign trade system gradually ties Chinese economy to the world. The independence and initiation of enterprise in foreign trade activities became intensified. The segregation of domestic market with world market was diminished. Meanwhile, the mechanism of government control over foreign trade also transformed from administrative demand to indirect control by means of market. The marketization course of Chinese foreign trade can be reflected in the following aspects.

Operation Subjects in Foreign Trade Constantly Expanded, and the Monopolistic Pattern of Foreign Trade Gradually Changed

In the initial stage of opening to the outside world, the enterprises engaged in foreign trade were only about 20 state-owned foreign trade corporations and their affiliated branches, which operated under a typical planned economic model. After the reform, the operation subjects in the foreign trade definitely increased and government intervention with foreign trade gradually decreased. The traditional monopolistic pattern was broken. Now there are over 10,000 foreign trade enterprises in our country, including central government foreign trade corporations, central industrial trade corporations; local foreign trade companies, industrial trade companies, agricultural trade companies, technological trade companies, production enterprises (group), scientific research institutions, commercial goods & materials enterprises. More than 200,000 foreign-funded enterprises are registered in 1994, among which 90,000 have started business. These have initially formed a multilevel and pluralized operational pattern of market economy.

What deserves our note is, from 1990's and on, with the increase of the amount of foreign-funded enterprises and the enlargement of their scales, their role in Chinese foreign trade is significantly improved. The effect of foreign-funded enterprises upon the increase of Chinese foreign trade can be clearly demonstrated in Table 11.1. In 1995, the export and import of foreign-funded enterprises amounted to 109.82 billion dollars, representing 39.1% of total imports and exports of China. By 1996, the imports and exports of foreign-funded enterprises increased to 137.1 billion dollars, its proportion in the whole state increased to 47%.

Table 11.1 Position of Foreign-Funded Ventures in Total of China's Imports and Exports (1980-1993) (100 Million US Dollars)

Year	Import & Export (Total)	Foreign-Funded Ventures (total)	Sino-Foreign Joint Ventures	Sino-Foreign Cooperative Ventures	Solely Foreign-Funded Ventures	Proportion of Total Imports & Exports
1980	381.4	0.43	0.42		0.01	0.11
1981	440.2	1.43	1.31		0.12	0.32
1982	416.0	3.29	2.79		0.61	0.79
1983	436.1	6.18	0.99		5.19	1.42
1984	535.5	4.68	1.77		2.91	0.87
1985	696.0	23.61	21.04		2.57	3.39
1986	738.4	30.12	27.14		2.98	4.08
1987	826.5	43.30	39.36		3.94	5.24
1988	1028.0	82.03	74.99		7.04	7.98
1989	1116.8	137.09	99.68	22.19	15.22	12.28
1990	1154.4	201.21	141.68	30.95	29.08	17.43
1991	1356.3	289.54	190.99	43.37	55.17	21.35
1992	1655.3	437.27	276.70	64.29	96.28	26.42
1993	1957.1	671.60	400.21	109.16	161.34	34.32

Sources: "YearBook of China's Foreign Economic Trade 1994/1995" and "YearBook of China's Foreign Economic Statistics", Chinese Social Science Press.

Dependence Level on Foreign Trade has Greatly Risen

The dependence level on foreign trade is a very important index measuring the level of a country's openness to the outside world as well as the marketization process of a transitional country. The greater the dependence level on foreign trade, the higher the level of openness as well as of marketization process of the country is. Before the open policy to the outside world, China's dependence level on foreign trade is very low (4.9% in 1978), so most enterprises does not care about the changes of supply and demand in international markets. So far, the dependence level on foreign trade has amounted to 20%. In other words, 20% of domestic products must be sold in world markets, and 20%

products and intermediate inputs demanded in the domestic market have come from world markets. In this situation, nearly all the enterprises have felt the competitive pressure coming from world markets. It has become an indispensable part of an enterprise's managing activities to take advantage of every opportunity existed in the two kinds of resources and the two markets both in abroad and home.

Table 11-2 Changes in China's Dependent
Level on Foreign Trade (million US dollar)

Year	Export	Import	GNP	Dependent level (%)
1978	9750	10890	210703	4.90
1980	18100	19900	201696	9.42
1986	31148	43172	271880	13.67
1988	47520	55270	401514	12.8
1990	62433	53819	376102	15.45
1991	71892	63843	386516	17.56
1992	84858	80597	458692	18.04
1993	91737	103881	549323	17.81
1994	121047	115681	522172	22.67
1995	148770	132080	690017	20.35

Sources: "*YearBook of China's Foreign Economic Trade 1996*", Chinese Social Science Press, 1996;

"*From Planning to Market: Report on World Development 1996*" Chinese Finance Press, 1996;

"*Abstracts on Chinese Statistics, 1996*" Chinese Statistics Press, 1996.

Protection Level of Non-Tariff Barriers has Obviously Declined and Domestic Market Further Opened

It is the main obstacle to trade development that restricting imports of foreign products by non-tariff barriers. In the past several decades, China has made distinguished progress in clearing those barriers. Great changes have taken place in the traditional centralized planning management; the managing field of charters and quota are gradually lessened; the development of transparency in trade policy is well known.

The centralized planning management in foreign trade is a typical feature in China's traditional system. Before 1978, all imports and exports were implemented according to annual plans. The targets of the plans were dispersed to 12 main foreign trade corporations. The corporations owned monopoly powers in their own business fields of centralized planning management have still been kept entirely. The plans of foreign trade made by the state mainly referred in order to seclude domestic markets from foreign markets. Up to 1984, the situation of central planned management still remained unchanged. The main foreign trade plans made by the state were the following such as purchasing plans, export plans, appropriation plans for export goods, plans for export goods turning to domestic markets, import plans, foreign exchange plans, and including finance, transportation, package, wages, so on and so forth. After 1985, fields of centralized planning management were largely lessened, no longer making and giving plans for foreign trade purchases and appropriations, canceling domestic sales plans as well. Furthermore, the mandatory plans were lessened and the guidance plans were enlarged in the export plans as well as in the import plans.

Up to 1991,in the export plans, the merchandises in the mandatory plans covered 30% of China's total exports; and those in the guidance plans covered only 15%; and those in no plan-listed amounted 55%. In the import plans, the goods in the mandatory plans covered 20% of China's total imports; other 20% of the total only stipulated their special uses and amount of money; and those out of the plan adjustment covered about 60% of the total imports.

China has resumed license management in foreign trade since 1980. In 1988,the goods in the import license covered 53 items, among which the production materials and raw materials amounted to 23 items, including steel and steel bloom. The goods in the import license amounted to 50% of the total imports. In 1992,the goods under the control of import quotas and license amounted to 1247 items, covering about 20% of the total import items. In the recent years, China has cut down the items of quotas and license respectively on January 1,1993, on January 1,1994, on June30, 1994, on January 1 1996, on May 8, 1996. Now the goods in the quotas and license management only covered 384 items, amounting to 5%of the total items. The percentage of the goods in the quotas, license and import control has dropped to 25% or so.

In the export license, management was implemented by classification. License management was taken in the first and second class goods. The goods of first class are 21 items, relative to the national economy and the people's livelihood, large and some special merchandises; the goods of second class cover 72 items, related to those high competition and quota restriction in the international market, there are about 17 items in the goods of third class under the control of the export license.

Quickening Reform of Tariff System and Integrating with GATT

As the market economic system was gradually established, China's ties with world market were getting closer and closer, which required China to break with the former tariff system in the planned economic system and build up a new tariff system step by step meeting international trade practices. On January 22,1978,the National Congress passed "*The Customs Law of People's Republic of China*", chapter 5 of which referred to legislation of tariff imposition and management. On May 15,1978, the Customs General Office issued "*A Notice on Imposition of Export Duties*", decided to impose export duties on 34 items of goods, rates from 10% to 60%, an average of 33.4% on March 7,1985, the State Council issued "*Regulations on Import & Export Duties of People's Republic of China*", later revised on September 12, 1987 and on March 18,1992.Since 1991, China has implemented significantly tariff reforms five times in order to reduce the general level tariffs step by step and meet the requirements of GATT on the developing countries.

- The first time, in 1991, the import regulating duties on 16 items of goods were totally cancelled;
- The second time, in the early of 1992,the import duties on 225 items of goods were reduced, a decline of average rate to 43.1%;
- The third time, in 1993, the import duties on 3371 items of goods dropped to 39.9%, a decline of 7.3% in the general level of tariffs;
- The fourth time, in 1994, the import duties on 2898 items of goods dropped to 35.9%,a decline of 10% in the general level of tariffs;
- The fifth time, in 1995, the import duties on 4997 items of goods dropped to 23%, a counting for 76% of the total items of import duties, a decline of 12.9% in the general level of tariff; the main characteristics of this regulation in import duties are: reduction of duties by a big margin; regulation of duty rates by a large scope; encouragement of imports in advanced technological equipment; cancellation of duty items in complete sets of bulk parts; simultaneous implementation of duty reduction and cancellation of preferential policies in imports.
- The sixth time, in 1997, the import duties were again greatly reduced to 17%.

Through these tariff reforms, the duty items set and tariff rates of Chins are much closer to the international trade preferential policies in imports.

The Reform of Management System of Foreign Exchange are Pressing on towards Free Exchange in RMB

Exchange rate is one of the main measures which are taken by the state to adjust the external equilibrium of macro-economy. Before 1994, China's management system of foreign exchange was highly centralized, which took a policy of "Centralizing Administration and Unified Management". Although, since openness to the outside world, the retained system of foreign exchange earnings has been established, and regulation centers for foreign exchange have been built up, which have brought initiatives of enterprises, but, as a lever to regulate the economy, the exchange rate has not played its due role basically.

In 1994, China reformed its exchange control system. The reforms included canceling the system of retaining a certain percentage of foreign earnings by the exporting enterprises; canceling the system of turning over the foreign currency to the central government; taking into effect the system for buying foreign earnings and selling foreign currency by the banks. These reforms realized the target of official rate of exchange (for RMB) being made uniform with the market rate; the single and managerial floating exchange rate system being made based on demand and supply in the market;

foreign exchange transactions being dealt among banks. All these resulted in improving the exchange rate forming mechanism. The state cancelled mandatory plans for receipt and law as the macro control tool to control foreign currency and international receipt and payment. The 1994 exchange control reform made RMB freely convertible in some circumstances under the current account, laying a solid foundation for RMS being finally freely convertible. Meanwhile, the canceling of the system of turning over the foreign currency created a relatively fair environment for all enterprises.

At present China still adopts centralized control over the transactions and flow of foreign currency under capital account. Restrictions are imposed upon the enterprises issuing or accepting foreign commercial loans or borrowings from abroad, etc.   ·

The Marketization Degree of Overall Foreign Trade.

For a transforming country, its marketization degree can be measured by degree of market openness, scope and means of government's control over trade, the initiative of enterprises' participation in trade etc. From the above analysis, we can see that the process of the adoption of the market principle in the foreign trade is progressing in many respects. If we use the above context, meanwhile taking as main indices the foreign trade independence, non-tariff, tariff-rate and the changes in the exchange rate system to roughly measure the adoption of the market principle in the foreign trade, we can arrive at Table 11.3.

Table 11.3 The Extent of the Marketization in China's Foreign Trade (1978-1997)

		1978	1980	1985	1988	1991	1995	1997
The Extent of Marketization (%)	A	0	0	0	0	0	48.9	62.2
	B	0	0	n.a	50	60	n.a	80
	C	0	0	10	10	10	50	50
	D	6.1	11.8	17.1	16	19.3	25.4	25.4*
	Average	1-5	30	9.0	19	22.3	41.4	54.4

Notes "*" is predicted figure

In the table, A is the marketization process induced by the changes in tariff-rate, using the 45% tariff-rate in 1991 as the basis. A=(45%-T)/45%, where T is the average import tariff-rate.

B describes the marketization process induced by the lowering of the non-tariff. It represents the proportion of commodities imported that are not included in mandatory plans, licensing system, to the total imports.

C is the changes in the exchange rate, including its forming system and the process regarding RMB being made freely convertible (Between 1985-1991, there existed the system of retaining of foreign earnings, let's just estimate the adoption of the market principle is 10%)

D is the coinage between domestic and foreign markets. We use the foreign trade independence (import plus export/2/GDP) to express it. Because a cot of merchandise can not be traded, realty business for example. We need to amend the independence index (the independence is 0.8, 0.8 is parameter). D is the amended foreign trade independence. The last in the fable is the average.

Although the above result is only a rough estimation, we can still see clearly the marketization progress in China's foreign trade. Up to 1997 the degree has risen from 2% to 54%. That is a remarkable progress.

ACHIEVEMENTS IN FOREIGN TRADE MARKETIZATION OF CHINA

A Sustained and Accelerated Growth in Imports and Exports

In 1978, China's imports and exports showed a total value of 20.64 billion dollars, among which, the exports accounted for 9.75 billion dollars and imports for 10.89 billion dollars. In 1988, the total value of China's imports and exports reached 102.79 billion dollars, among which the exports showed 47.52 billion dollars, and the imports showed 55.28 billion dollars. In 1996, China's imports and exports amounted to 289.9 billion dollars, among which the exports showed 151.07 billion dollars, and the imports showed 138.83 billion dollars (Table 11.4). The growth speed of the foreign trade in the seventh 5-year plan period has changed the situations that the growth of imports exceeded the growth of exports in the past 40 years or so. The growth of exports has been speeded up (Table 11.5 and Table 11.6).

Rise of the Proportion of Export Amount National Production

In 1980, China's GNP amounted to 447 billion dollars, the exports were 18.119 billion dollars, accounting for 6% of GNP. From then on, the growth of exports has been faster than that of GNP. In 1994, compared with 1980, when the GNP showed an increase of 365%, the total of exports showed a rise of 668%. The proportion of the value of export trade in GNP rises from 4.7% in 1978, 6% in 1980,9.7% in 1985, 10.8% in 1988, and 14.3% in 1990 up to 27.6% in 1994. Its proportions in Gross income at the same time are 5.6% in 1978, 7.4% in 1980, 11.8% in 1985, 13.1% in 1988 and 17.4% in 1990; the proportion in gross output values of industry & agriculture are 3.0% in 1978, 3.8% in 1980, 6.2% in 1985, 6.4% in 1988 and 7.9% in 1990 (Table 11. 7 and 11.8).

Table 11.4 China's Foreign Trade (1950-1996) (100 million US dollars)

Year	Imports & Exports	Exports	Imports	Balance	Year	Imports & Exports	Exports	Imports	Balance
1950	11.3	5.5	5.8	-0.3	1974	145.7	69.5	76.2	-6.7
1951	19.6	7.6	12.0	-4.4	1975	147.5	72.6	74.9	-2 3
1952	19.1	8.2	11.2	-3.0	1976	134.3	68.5	65.8	2.7
1953	23.7	10.2	13.5	-3.3	1977	148.0	75.9	72.1	3.8
1954	24.4	11.5	12.9	-1.4	1978	206.4	97.5	108.9	-11.4
1955	31.4	14.1	17.3	-3.2	1979	293.3	136.6	156.7	-20.1
1956	32.1	16.5	15.6	0.9	1980	381.4	181.2	200 2	-19 0
1957	31.0	16.0	15.0	1 0	1981	440.2	220.1	220.1	0.0
1958	38.7	19.8	18.9	0.9	1982	416.0	223.2	192.8	30.0
1959	43.8	22.6	21.2	1.4	1983	436.1	222.2	213.9	8.3
1960	38.1	18.6	19.5	-0.9	1984	535.5	261.4	274.1	-12.7
1961	29.4	14.9	14 5	0.4	1985	696.0	273.5	422.5	-149.0
1962	26.6	14.9	11.7	3 2	1986	738.4	309.4	429.0	-119.6
1963	29.2	16.5	12.7	3.8	1987	826.5	394 4	432.2	-37.8
1964	34.7	19.2	15 5	3.7	1988	1028.0	475.2	552.8	-77.6
1965	42.5	22.3	20.2	2.1	1989	1116 8	525.4	591.4	-66.0
1966	46.2	23.7	22.5	1.3	1990	1154.4	620.9	533.5	87.5
1967	41.6	21.4	20.2	1.2	1991	1356.3	718.4	637.9	80.5
1968	40 5	21.0	19.5	1.5	1992	1655.3	849.4	805.9	43.5
1969	40.3	22.0	18.3	3.7	1993	1957.1	917.6	1039.5	-121.9
1970	45.9	22.6	23.3	-0.7	1994	2367.3	1210.4	1156.9	53.5
1971	48.4	26.4	22.0	4.4	1995	2808.5	1487.7	1320.8	166.9
1972	63.0	34.4	28.6	5.8	1996	2899.0	1510.7	1388.3	122.4
1973	109.8	58.2	51.6	6.6					

Sources: *YearBook of China's Foreign Economic Trade 1984,* 1994/1995, Social Science Press of China and other materials.

Rise of Proportion and Status of Total Chinese Export Amount in Total World Export Amount

In 1978, China's export trade amounted to 9.745 billion dollars, accounting for only 0.75% of world exports with a total value of 1298.8 billion dollars, standing in the 32nd place. Since opening of China's economy to the world, the exports grow rapidly, and the growth of China's exports is faster than the growth of the total world exports; and the order of importance of China's exports in the world is steadily raised. China's shares in the world exports have been raised from 0.75%, the 32nd place in 1978 to 2.3%, and the 11th place in the world in 1992. In 1994, China's exports surmounted one hundred billion dollars, amounting to 1210.40 dollars, accounting for 2.9% of total world exports with the 11th place (Table 11.9).

Table 11-5 Growth Rate of China's Foreign Trade (by percentage over last year)

Year	Import & Export	Export	Import	Year	Import & Export	Export	Import
1950	100.00	100.00	100.00	1974	32.7	17.4	47.7
1951	72.2	37.1	105.5	1975	1.2	4.5	1.7
1952	0 7	8.7	6.7	1976	8.9	5 6	12.1
1953	22.0	24 2	20.4	1977	10.2	10.7	9.7
1954	2.7	12.1	-4.4	1978	39.4	28.4	51.0
1955	29.3	23.2	34.7	1979	42.1	40.2	43.9
1956	2.0	16.5	-9.8	1980	28.9	33.8	24.7
1957	-3.3	-2.9	-3.6	1981	6.8	14.3	-0.3
1958	24.8	24.0	25.5	1982	-2.7	4.4	-10 3
1959	13.2	14.1	12.2	1983	3.6	1.7	6.0
1960	-13.1	-17.9	-7.9	1984	22.2	10.0	36.8
1961	22.9	-19 7	-26.0	1985	21.0	6.1	35.4
1962	-9.3	-0 1	-18.8	1986	-0.2	4.2	-3.6
1963	9.5	10.7	7.9	1987	13.3	28.5	1.0
1964	18.8	16.2	22.2	1988	18.2	17.1	19.3
1965	22.6	16.3	30.4	1989	2.6	6.9	-1.8
1966	8.7	6.2	11.5	1990	3.1	19.9	-15.6
1967	-9.9	-9.8	-10.1	1991	17.5	15.8	19.5
1968	-2.6	-1.5	-3.7	1992	22.1	18.3	26.3
1969	-0.5	4.8	-6.2	1993	18.2	8.0	28.9
1970	13.8	2.5	27.5	1994	21.0	31.9	11.3
1971	5.6	16 6	-5.2	1995	18.6	22.9	14.2
1972	30.2	30.6	29.6	1996	3.2	1.5	5.1
1973	74.2	69.0	80.4				

Source: *Yearbook of China's Foreign Economic Trade, 1984,1994/1995*

Table 11.6 Growth of China's Foreign Trade
(1950-1990) (by period and by percent)

Period	Import & Export	Export	Import	Period	Import & Export	Export	Import
Reconstruction (1950-1952)	30.8	22.1	38.5	Fifth Five-Year Plan (1976-1980)	20.7	20.3	21.2
First Five-Year Plan (1953-1957)	9.8	14.2	6.1	Sixth Five-Year Plan (1981-1985)	9.8	7.2	11.9
Second Five-Year Plan (1958-1962)	-3.0	-1.4	-4.9	Seven Five-Year Plan (1986-1990)	0.2 13.3 18.2	4.2 28.5 17.1	-3.6 1.0 19.3
Adjustment (1963-1965)	16.8	14.4	19.8	1986	2.6	6.9	-1.8
Third Five-Year Plan (1966-1970)	1.6	0.3	2.9	1987	3.1	19.9	-15.6
Fourth Five-Year Plan (1971-1975)	26.3	26.3	26.3	1988	11 4	12.0	10.6
				1989			
				1990			
				1950-1990			

Source: *YearBook of China's Foreign Economic Trade, 1991*, Chinese Social Sciences Press.

Table 11-7 Proportion of China's Export in GNP (1980-1993)

Year	GNP (value in 100 million RMB yuan)	Export	% in GNP	Year	GNP (value in 100 million RMB yuan)	Export	% in GNP
1980	4,470	181.19	6.0	1988	13,984	475.16	12.6
1981	4,773	220.07	7.7	1989	15,916	525.38	12.4
1982	5,193	223.23	8.0	1990	17,686	620.63	17.0
1983	5,809	222.26	7.5	1991	19,580	718.42	19.5
1984	6,962	261.39	8.3	1992	23,938	849.40	19.5
1985	8,562	273.50	9.5	1993	31,380	917.63	16 8
1986	9,696	309.42	11.2	1994	43,799	1210.40	27.6
1987	11,301	394.37	13.0				

Source. YearBook of China's Foreign Economic Trade, 1994/1995, *Beijing· Social Science Press of China.*

Table 11-8 Proportion and Position of Total China's Export Amount in Key National Economic Indices (1978-1990)

Item	Unit	1978	1980	1985	1988	1990
Total Export	100 million US dollars	97.45	182.72	259.15	406.40	520.67
GNP	100 million RMB yuan	3,588	4,470	8,562	14,015	17,400
Proportion to GNP	%	4.7	6.1	9.7	10.8	14.3
National Income (NI)	100 million RMB yuan	3,010	3,688	7,041	11,533	14,300
Proportion to NI	%	5.6	7.4	11.8	13.1	17.4
Total Output of Society (TOS)	100 million RMB yuan	6,846	8,535	16,603	29,259	37,969
Proportion to TOS	%	2.4	3.2	5.0	5.2	6.5
Gross Output Value of Industry And Agriculture (GOVIA)	100 million RMB yuan	5,634	7,078	13,337	23,723	31,233
Proportion to GOVIA	%	3.0	3.8	6.2	6.4	7.9

Source: *Yearbook of China's Foreign Economic Trade, 1991*, Chinese Social Sciences Press.

Rapid Development in Processing Trade

In early 1980's, China's foreign trade pattern was simple and the processing trade held a very small proportion. Since 1990's, as China's economy further opens to the world, patterns of trade have been increasingly diversified. The foreign trade, including processing imported materials, processing with customers' materials and compensation trade, have achieved a considerable growth. In 1992, the total value of imports and exports in processing trade amounted to 71.12 billion dollars which accounted for 43% of China's imports and exports, among which the export was valued at 39.61billion dollars and the import at 31.51 billion dollars. By 1996, the processing trade has become the largest-scale trade pattern: its total value reached 146.6 billion dollars, for the first time it surpassed half of the total imports and exports, accounting for 51%, an increase of 11% over the previous year; among which the export amounted to 84.3 billion dollars, an increase of 14%; the import amounted to 62.3 billion dollars, a rise of 7%. At the same time, the traditional trade pattern dwindled, a decline of 11% over last year (Table 11.10).

Table 11.9 Position of China's Exports in World Exports by Proportion and Order of Importance(1953-1994) (100 million US dollars)

Year	World Exports (Total)	China's Exports (Total)	Percentage in World Total Exports	Order of Importance
1953	829	10.22	1.23	17
1954	863	11.46	1.33	16
1955	940	14.12	1.50	15
1956	1,042	16.45	1.58	14
1957	1,123	15.97	1.42	15
1958	1,086	19.81	1.82	13
1959	1,159	22.61	1.95	12
1960	1,283	18.56	1.44	17
1961	1,344	14.91	1.11	19
1962	1,419	14.90	1.05	19
1963	1,545	16.49	1.07	19
1964	1,736	19.16	1.10	19
1965	1,872	22 28	1.19	18
1966	2,052	23.66	1.15	18
1967	2,155	21.35	0.99	19
1968	2,401	21.03	0.88	19
1969	2,744	22.04	0.80	21
1970	3,153	22.60	0.72	29
1971	3,513	26.36	0.75	25
1972	4,158	34.43	0.83	25
1973	5,764	58.19	1.01	21
1974	8,415	69.49	0.83	28
1975	8,769	72.64	0.83	28
1976	9,933	68.55	0.69	34
1977	11,269	75.90	0.67	30
1978	12,988	97.45	0.75	32
1979	16,430	136.58	0.83	32
1980	19,906	181.20	0.92	26
1981	19,724	220.10	1.10	19
1982	18,308	223.20	1.18	17
1983	18,078	222.20	1.23	17
1984	19,019	261.40	1.40	18
1985	19,277	273.50	1.40	17
1986	21,157	309.50	1.50	16
1987	24,969	394.40	1.60	16
1988	28,382	475.20	1.70	16
1989	30,361	525.40	1.70	14
1990	34,700	620.90	1.80	15
1991	35,300	719.10	2.00	13
1992	37,000	850.00	2.30	11
1993	36,870	917.70	2.50	11
1994	41,738	1210.40	2.90	11

Source: *Yearbook of China's Foreign Economic Trade*, 1984,1994/1995.

Table 11.10 Changes of Proportion of Processing Trade in Total Import & Export Trade (1992-1996) (100 million US dollars)

Year	Import & Export Trade			Processing Trade			% of Total Import & Export
	Total	Import	Export	Total	Import	Export	
1992	1655.3	849.4	805.9	711.2	396.1	315.1	43
1993	1957.1	917.6	1039.5	786.0	422.4	363.6	40
1994	2367.3	1210.4	1156.9	973.4	521.3	452.1	41
1995	2808.5	1487.7	1320.8	1320.7	737.0	583.7	47
1996	2899.0	1510.7	1388.3	1466.0	843.0	623.0	51

Source: *Yearbook of China's Foreign Economic Trade* and other relevant materials.

Expansion and Distribution Improvement of Foreign Trade Market

China's foreign trade markets covered the socialist countries of former-Soviet Union and Eastern Europe after the founding of new China. From the 1960s, they started to be shifted to the advanced western countries and developing countries and regions. In the 1970's, an important breakthrough was made in China's foreign relations. In 1980, countries having economic and trade relations with China amounted to 174. Since 1980, a pluralistic strategy of development has been taken. Up to 1996, the trade partners of China were distributed in 227 countries and regions. The traditional foreign trade still dominated the market, nevertheless, its growth and position was declining. The proportion of China's trade with advanced industrialized countries was rising (see Table 11.11).

Increasing Improvement of the Structure of Import & Export Commodity

The Structure of import and export commodity reflects the present situation of industrial composition. As China's economic and industrial composition is adjusted and the marketization process of national economy is quickened, a great change has taken place in the composition of import and export commodity.

First, judged by the composition of export commodity, in 1980, the exports of manufactured products amounted to 9.01 billion dollars, accounting for 50.3% of the total exports. In 1995, the exports of manufactured products reached 127.28 billion dollars, accounting for 85.6% of the total exports; among which the mechanical and electrical products became the largest export item of China with the value of 43.86 billion dollars, surpassing the export of textile; the export of primary products was valued at 21.49 billion dollars, dropping to 14.4% of the total export.

Table 11.11 China's Foreign Trade by Country and Region(1978,1988-1990) (100 million US dollars)

Country or region	1978			1988			1989			1990		
	Total	Export	Import	Total	Export	Import	Total	Export	Import	Total	Export	Import
Total	206.38	97.45	108.93	804.90	406.40	398.50	825.83	434.40	391.4	851.18	520.67	330.51
Developing countries and regions	34.09	19.08	15.01	116.11	67.77	48.34	113.37	64.32	49.05	114.41	75.48	38.93
% of total	16.52	19.58	13.78	14.43	16.68	12.13	13.73	14.81	12.53	13.44	14.50	11.78
Advanced industrialized countries	115.45	36.44	79.01	328.78	161.64	221.14	395.81	175.93	219.88	377.68	202.07	175.61
% of total	55.94	37.39	72.53	47.56	39.77	55.49	47.93	40.50	56.17	44.37	38.81	53.13
Former-Soviet Union and Eastern Europe	29.05	14.98	14.16	63.98	31.06	32.92	69.18	33.64	35.54	58.20	30.59	27.61
% in total	14.10	15.28	13.00	7.95	7.64	8.26	8.38	7.74	9.08	6.80	5.88	8.35
Hong Kong and Macao	27.42	26.67	0.75	226.09	132.10	93.99	227.48	146.10	81.38	269.72	189.41	80.31
% in total	13.29	27.37	0.69	28.09	32.50	23.58	27.55	33.63	20.79	31.68	36.38	14.60
Among which: Hong Kong		25.32		220.72	128.57	92.15	222.32	142.67	79.55	264.41	185.83	78.54
Macao		1.35		5.37	3.52	1.85	5.16	3.43	1.73	5.30	54	1.76

Source: *Yearbook of China's Foreign Economic Trade*, 1991.

Secondly, judging by the structure of import commodity, in 1980,the imports of manufactured products amounted to 13.05 billion dollars, accounting for 65.2% of the total imports; the import of primary products was valued at 6.96 billion dollars, holding 34.8% of the total import. In 1995,the imports of manufactured products reached 107.67 billion dollars, accounting for 81.5% of the total imports, lower than the proportion of manufactured products export in the total exports; the import of primary products was valued at 24.41 billion dollars, dropping to18.5% of the total import.

Table 11.12 Structure of China's Export
Commodity in 1953-1993 (100 million US dollars)
(In line with *Classification by International Trade Standard*)

Year	Total Export	Primary Products		Manufactured Products	
		Value	% in Total Export	Value	% in Total Export
1953	10.22	8.11	79.4	2.11	20.6
1957	15.79	10.15	63.6	5.82	36.4
1965	22.28	11.41	51.2	10.87	48.8
1966	23.66	14.27	60.3	9.39	39.7
1970	22.60	12.10	53.5	10.50	46.5
1975	72.64	40.98	56.4	31.66	43.6
1976	68.55	37.44	54.6	31.11	45.4
1977	75.90	40.65	53.6	35.25	46.4
1978	97.45	52.16	53.5	45.29	46.5
1979	136.58	73.15	53.6	63.43	46.4
1980	181.2	91.1	50.3	90.1	49.7
1981	220.1	102.5	46.7	117.6	53.3
1982	223.2	100.5	45.0	122.6	55.0
1983	222.2	96.1	43.3	126.1	56.7
1984	261.4	119.2	45.6	142.2	54.4
1985	273.5	138.1	50.5	135.4	49.5
1986	309.4	112.7	36.4	196.7	63.6
1987	394.4	132.2	33.5	262.2	66.5
1988	475.2	143.9	30.3	331.2	69.7
1989	525.4	150.7	28.7	374.6	71.3
1990	620.9	158.9	25.6	461.8	74.4
1991	718.4	161.5	22.5	556.9	77.5
1992	849.4	170.0	20.0	679.4	80.0
1993	917.6	166.7	18.2	750.9	81.8

Source: *Yearbook of China's Foreign Economic Trade*, 1991, 1994/1995, Chinese Social Sciences Press.

**Table 11.13 Structure of China's Import Commodity
by 1980-1993 (value in 100 million US dollars)**
(In line with *Classification by International Trade Standard*)

Year	Total Import	Primary Products		Manufactured Products	
		Value	% in Total Import	Value	% in Total Import
1980	200.2	69.6	34.8	130.5	65.2
1981	220.1	80.3	36.6	139.9	63.4
1982	192.8	76.2	39.6	116.6	60.4
1983	213.9	58.1	27.2	155.8	72.8
1984	274.1	52.1	18.7	222.1	81.3
1985	422.5	52.9	12.5	369.2	87.5
1986	429.0	56.3	13.0	372.5	87.0
1987	432.1	69.1	16.0	363.1	84.0
1988	552.8	100.8	18.2	452.1	81.8
1989	591.4	117.5	19.9	474.0	80.1
1990	533.5	98.6	18.5	434.9	81.5
1991	637.9	108.3	17.0	529.6	83.0
1992	805.9	132.6	16.4	673.3	83.6
1993	1039.5	142.2	13.7	897.3	86.3

Resources: *YearBook of China's Foreign Economic Trade*, 1994/1995

PROPOSALS ON DEVELOPMENT STRATEGY
FOR CHINA'S FOREIGN TRADE MARKETIZATION

Judging by the analyses above, it can be seen that the marketization process of China's foreign trade has been speeded up step by step, and considerable progress has been made since 1980s, especially since 1990s. The dependent level of the foreign trade has been raised; the terms of trade has been increasingly improved; international economic contacts have been continuously expanded; the ties with international markets have been strengthened day by day. But, undeniably, there existed some problems in the process, for instance, the ideology and conventional practices of pursuing scales and quantities one-sidedly formed under the planned market system for a long time are affecting the healthy development of foreign trade undertakings to some extent; the economic benefits of foreign trade enterprises are declining; the shift of state-owned foreign trade enterprises is behind the times, which get them into dilemma in management; the laws and regulations of foreign trade management are not amplified which disorders its management; the foreign trade markets are over-centralized; the composition of export commodity is not equitable, and the proportion of export goods with deep-processed and highly-added value is on the lower side, etc., which reflects the process of foreign trade marketization still remains an arduous task.

Based on the analyses above in the process and existing problems in foreign trade marketization, the authors have put forward the following strategic proposals on China's foreign trade marketization in late 1990's.

1. Accelerating the implementation of a general economic trade strategy. Further opening domestic market to the world; better integrating of macro-management of foreign economic trade with macro-control in national economy; strengthening the tie of foreign economic trades with the domestic industries concerned, making the most of the leading role of foreign economic trade in adjustment of domestic industrial compositions and product compositions, technological progress and effective deployment in resources, etc., and fostering the shift of economic growth patterns from extensiveness to intensity, and effective growth of national economy; increasingly opening up the range and quality of international markets, promoting the integration of China's economy with world economy, and improving the capacity of taking advantage of foreign markets and resources.

2. Opening all the channels of trade, developing direct trade and various kinds of international economic and technological cooperation; actively participating and upholding regional economic cooperation and the world multi-lateral trade system; realizing the plurialization of markets by the interaction of mutual and multi-lateral trades.

3. Quickening opening process of trade in services; setting up professional directive and regulatory departments, and carrying forward reforms of management system in services, greatly promoting exports in services.

4. Reforms of import system, including the establishment of a new system helpful to improving import compositions, and to promoting introduction and digestion of technology.

5. Strengthening the competitive capacity by an increase of added values of export commodity and by forming a mechanism of export growth mainly relied on qualities and benefits.

6. Speeding up the reforming process of necessary policies in the foreign trade marketization, accelerating the reform of free exchanges in RMB; further reducing the level of tariff rates, regulating the tariff composition, putting duty-free and duty-reduced items into order; standardizing and reducing the non-tariff barriers in the practice of import-export commodity; perfecting a unified, scientific and open system and measures of foreign trade management.

7. Based on the *Law of Foreign Trade*, the special and necessary laws concerned should be made and issued as soon as possible so as to speed up the process of legal system in the foreign trade.

8. Accelerating the development of information industry in foreign trade so as to bring about paperless trade at an early date.

REFERENCES

Chen Zongsheng, et al., *Unfair Trade Practices* (translated), Beijing: Chinese Social Sciences Press, 1997.

Chinese Ministry of Foreign Trade, *A Handbook of Admission to Asian and Pacific Markets*, Beijing: China's Foreign Economic Trade Press, 1997.

Wang Lihua, et al., *On China's Foreign Trade*, Beijing: Foreign Trade Educational Press, 1992.

Yearbook of China's Foreign Economic Trade, Beijing: Chinese Social Sciences Press, 1980, 1984, 1991, 1994/1995.

PART IV
CHINA'S MARKETIZATION OF DIFFERENT REGIONS: MEASUREMENT OF THE MARKETIZATION IN EACH EAST-MIDDLE-WEST AND SOUTH-MIDDLE-NORTH LARGE REGION

MEASUREMENT AND ANALYSIS ON THE REGIONAL DIVERSITY OF MARKETIZATION DEGREE IN CHINA

Since the process of marketization of economic system in late 1970's, there are distinct performances among different regions because of their geographical locations, historical conditions and other factors. However, it is difficult to measure and analyze the difference of marketization degree among them. This is mainly because of the scarcity of statistical data that can reflect the degrees of marketization of different regions.

In this chapter, by exploring into the causes of the regional difference, we attempt to make use of a group of relevant statistical data to set up the index system, to describe the regional marketization degree objectively.

THE CAUSE OF REGIONAL DIFFERENCES OF MARKETIZATION IN CHINA

In China, the process of marketization since late 1970's can be observed in two aspects. The first one which has been discussed extensively is the transition process of the production materials and other commodities which used to be allocated by the government and now are decided by the market. The second one, which has always been overlooked, is the transition from natural economy to market economy along with the development of national economy. It predicates that many self-sufficient production elements and products have been changed as negotiable productive essentials and products. The differences of the marketization degree in each region of China, in general, are related to the two main indications in the process of marketization. Generally speaking, the deeper a region conducts its economic system reform, or the faster a region develops its economy, the higher its marketization degree is. Therefore, in order to explore into the cause of difference of marketization degree, we must begin with economic system reform and economic growth.

Economic System Reform and Regional Differences of Marketization Degree

Reform of economic system is the exterior cause promoting marketization in China. As it only changes the pricing and allocation means of economic resources and commodities, it does not bring about the expansion of the market scale. The reform of economic system driving on marketization, therefore, centralizes in the industries strictly controlled by the central planned economy. These industries mainly include manufacturing, building industry, transportation and communication. They are mostly state-owned. However, in the fields controlled weakly by central planning economy, the driving function of the economic system reform upon marketization is limited. Xiaogang Village, Fengyang County, Anhui Province, for example, was the first one in China who distributed its cultivated field to every rural resident in 1977 and was considered as the pioneer of the rural transformation. Nevertheless, until 1990's, the marketization level of economy in Xiaogang is still very insufficient and the self-sufficiency agriculture is the most important department in its economy. There is a close relation between reform of economic system and the regional differences of the marketization. But the relation does not mean that a region with deeper economic reform definitely enjoy a higher marketization. The latter is also determined by the economic foundation, especially the development of state-owned economy.

In general, the regions with higher marketization degree resulting from economic system reform are mainly the historically developed regions or those weightily invested in the period of the centrally planned economy. These regions include a large of part of the coastal China and some urban areas of the inner China. Before the reform, the manufacturing, as the most important industry in these areas and mainly state-owned, had been controlled by the central government. With the transformation of economic systems, the progress of marketization began in these areas. The systems of central planned economy were replaced by the systems of marketing economy. The power of distributing economic resources and commodities and deciding price of goods and services has been transferred from the central government to the both sides of suppliers and demanders. In those under-developing areas before, especial the areas with a few non-agricultural industries, it has been limited that the transformation of economic systems driving on the progress of the marketization.

Economic Growth and Regional Differences of Marketization

Economic growth is the internal cause leading to marketization in China. Whatever the economic foundation is, the economy capacity shall expand with the expanding of total economic amount, which eventually promotes the increase of marketization degree. It is not only in the field formerly founded and mightily controlled by the central government, but also in the field nearly founded or lightly controlled by the central government that the economic growth drives on marketization. Especially the fields which are developed have a quicker progress of marketization. For example, electronics industry has always been the fastest developed one of all manufacturing industries in China, and the market of electronic products is the most opened one of markets of all manufacturing products in China. The vegetable cropping, a formerly small and mainly self-sufficiency field, has been quickly developing since early 1980s in China. It is mainly because of the fast developing and the founding of a marketizing and efficient distributing system of the vegetable cropping. Therefore, there is a close relationship between the regional differences of marketization and the economic growth. Especially in the formerly under-developed area, the promotion of economic growth upon marketization course may appear even more evident.

Recently, however, it is the rural area whose economy used to depend heavily on agriculture rather than urban areas with the developed manufacturing such as Shanghai, Tianjin, and Shenyang that enjoys a faster economic growth and marketization degree. The reason that these rural areas can attain their fast economic growth lies in that they have a good opportunity of marketing. They can transform their limited production resources to productivity. Accompanied with high-speed economic growth, is the increase of marketization degree.

INDEXES FOR MEASURING THE REGIONAL DIFFERENCES OF MARKETIZATION DEGREE OF CHINA

When we measure the regional differences of marketization of economic systems in China, the statistical data from state and local statistical departments are the sole resources. Because these statistical figures are collected according to administrative divisions, we must regard administrative divisions as regional unit. According to our experiences, the prefecture is the most proper administrative division with measuring the regional economic development level among four levels administrative divisions consisting of province, prefecture, county and township in China. Owing to the limit of time and fund, we cannot collect all statistical figures in prefecture level and only regard province as regional units measuring the regional diversity of marketization of economy systems in China. After analyzing the original statistical materials of "China Statistics Year Book", "China Rural Area Statistics Year Book", "China Urban Statistics Year Book", "China Market Statistics Year Book" and all provinces, we have selected 19 indexes in the five fields that premise of marketization (B_1), Market system building (B_2), Degree of the marketization of goods (B_3), Degree of the marketization of productive essentials (B_4) and Social security marketization (B_5). An indexes system has been established for assessing the level of marketization of region with the 19 indexes. The weight of every index in the indexes system is from the specialists assessing.

Prerequisite of marketization (B_1)

The prerequisite of marketization is a group of statistical figures used as measuring the industrial structure and ownership structure in an area. It includes four figures: C_1 (Ratio of value added of tertiary industry to gross domestic value), C_2 (Ratio of number of employed persons in tertiary industry to total number of employed persons), C_3 (Ratio of value added of non state-own manufacturing to total value added of manufacturing) and C_4 (Ratio of non-agricultural output value to gross output value in rural community). Their detailed means are below:

C_1 (ratio of added value of tertiary industry to GDP)

$$= \frac{\text{Regional added value of tertiary industry}}{\text{Regional GDP}}$$

C_2 (ratio of labor forces in tertiary industry to the total labor forces)

$$= \frac{\text{regional total labor forces in tertiary industry}}{\text{regional total labor forces}}$$

C_3 (ratio of added value of non - state - owned industrial sector to the total added value

of industry) $= \dfrac{\text{regional added value of non - state - owned industrial sector}}{\text{regional total added value of industry}}$

C_4 (ratio of non - agricultural output value to gross output value in rural community)

$$= \frac{\text{regional gross non - agricultural output value}}{\text{regional gross rural output value}}$$

Our purpose in designing this group of statistical index is to measure the economic basis of marketization in the fields of all society (C_1, C_2), whole manufacturing (C_3) and whole rural community (C_4) in every area

Market System Building (B_2)

The market system building is a group of statistical indexes used to measure the development of the goods and productive essentials market systems in an area. It includes four figures below: C_5 (Number of enterprises in wholesale and retail sales trade per a thousand persons), C_6 (Number of employed persons in wholesale and retail sales trade per a thousand persons), C_7 (Number of free markets per a thousand persons) and C_8

(Number of institutions in finance and insurance system per a thousand persons). Their detailed means are below:

C_5 (number of institutions in wholesale and retail sales per ten thousand persons)
$$= \frac{\text{regional number of institutions in wholesale and retail sales}}{\text{regional total population (in 10,000 persons)}}$$

C_6 (number of employed persons in wholesale and retail sales per ten thousand persons)
$$= \frac{\text{regional number of institutions in wholesale and retail sales}}{\text{regional total population (in 10,000 persons)}}$$

C_7 (number of town and rural fairs per ten thousand persons)
$$= \frac{\text{regional number of town and rural fairs}}{\text{regional total population (in 10,000 persons)}}$$

C_8 (number of financial institutions per ten thousand persons)
$$= \frac{\text{regional number of financial institutions}}{\text{regional total population (in 10,000 persons)}}$$

Our purpose in designing this group of statistical indexes is to measure the organization and personnel conditions of marketization in the fields of goods market (C_5 C_6, C_7) and finance and insurance market (C_8) in every area.

Degree of the Marketization of Commodities (B_3)

The degree of marketization of commodities is a group of statistical figures used as measuring developing situation of goods market in an area. It includes four figures below: C_9 (Ratio of total purchases of manufactures in wholesale and retail sale trades to gross manufacturing output value), C_{10} (Ratio of total purchases of farm products in wholesales and retail sale trades to gross agricultural output value), C_{11} (Ratio of total imports value to total purchases in wholesales and retail sale trades) and C_{12} (Ratio of total exports value to total manufacturing and agricultural output value). Their detailed means are below:

C_9 (Ratio of total purchases of industrial products in wholesale and retail sale to gross industrial output value)
$$= \frac{\text{regional total purchases of industrial products in wholesale and retail sale}}{\text{regional gross industrial output value}}$$

C_{10} (Ratio of total purchases of farm products in wholesale and retail sale to gross industrial output value)

= $\dfrac{\text{regional total purchases of farm products in wholesale and retail sale}}{\text{regional gross industrial output value}}$

C_{11} (Ratio of total imports to total purchases in wholesale and retail sale business)

= $\dfrac{\text{regional total imports}}{\text{regional total purchases in wholesale and retail sale business}}$

C_{12} (Ratio of total exports to total industrial and agricultural output value)

= $\dfrac{\text{regional total exports}}{\text{regional total industrial and agricultural output value}}$

Our purpose in designing this group of statistical indexes is to measure the degree of marketization in the fields of manufacturing products market (C_9), agricultural products market (C_{10}) and import and export market (C_{11}, C_{12}) in every area.

Degree of the Marketization of Production Factors (B_4)

The degree of the marketization of production elements is a group of statistical indexes measuring the development of the production factor market in a region. It includes five figures below: C_{13} (Ratio of number of contract employees to total number of employees), C_{14} (Ratio of number of registered unemployment population in labor departments to total number of unemployment population), C_{15} (Ratio of total revenue of advertising to gross social output value) C_{16} (Ratio of transaction value in technological market to gross manufacturing output value) and C_{17} (Ratio of floor space of commercial houses actually sold to that of buildings completed). Their implications are as follows:

C_{13} (Ratio of number of contracted employees to the total number of employees)

= $\dfrac{\text{regional number of contracted employees}}{\text{regional total number of employees}}$

C_{14} (Ratio of number of registered unemployment population in labor departments to the total number of unemployment population)

= $\dfrac{\text{regional number of registered unemployment population in labor departments}}{\text{regional total number of unemployment population}}$

C_{15} (Ratio of total volume of advertising business to gross social output value)

= $\dfrac{\text{regional total volume of advertising business}}{\text{regional gross social output value}}$

C_{16} (Ratio of transaction value in technological market to gross industrial output value)

= <u>regional transaction value in technological market</u>
    regional gross industrial output value

C_{17} (Ratio of floor space of commercial houses actually sold to that of buildings completed)

= <u>regional floor space of commercial houses actually sold</u>
       regional of buildings completed

Our purpose in designing this group of statistical indexes is to measure the degree of marketization in the fields of labors market (C_{13}, C_{14}), advertisement market (C_{15}), technical market (C_{16}) and real estates market (C_{17}) in every area.

Social Security Marketization (B_5)

The social security marketization is a group of statistical indexes measuring the situation of social security in a region. It includes two figures below: C_{18} (Ratio of total welfare funds to total wages of staff and workers) and C_{19} (Ratio of number of towns with the rural social security network established to total number of towns). Their implications are as follows:

C_{18} (Ration of total welfare expense for insurance of on-the-job staff and workers to total wages of staff and workers)

= <u>regional total welfare expense for insurance of on-the-job staff and workers</u>
          regional total wages of staff and workers

C19 (Ratio of number of towns with the social security network established to total number of towns)

= <u>regional number of towns with the social security network established</u>
            regional total number of towns

Our purpose in designing this group of statistical figures is to measure the degree of marketization of in the fields of social security of staff and workers (C_{18}) and rural social security (C_{19}) in every region.

After the investigation and scoring by experts and professionals of Economics Research Office of Nankai University, we obtain here in Table 12.1 the weights of every index in the evaluation system of China's Regional marketization degree.

Table 12.1 Weights of Every Index in Index System of Measuring the Regional Diversity of Marketization of Economy Systems in China

Index (B)	Index (C)	Weight
Pre-determinative condition of marketization (B_1)	Ratio of value added of tertiary industry to gross domestic value (C_1)	0.0539
	Ratio of number of employed persons in tertiary industry to total number of employed persons (C_2)	0.0538
	Ratio of value added of non state-own manufacturing to total value added of manufacturing (C_3)	0.0698
	Ratio of non-agricultural output value to gross output value in rural community (C_4)	0.0624
Formations of market systems (B_2)	Number of enterprises in wholesale and retail sales trade per a thousand persons (C_5)	0.0563
	Number of employed persons in wholesale and retail sales trade per a thousand persons (C_6)	0.0554
	Number of free markets per a thousand persons (C_7)	0.0462
	Number of institutions in finance and insurance system per a thousand persons (C_8)	0.0552
Degree of the marketization of goods (B_3)	Ratio of total purchases of manufactures in wholesales and retail sale trades to gross manufacturing output value (C_9)	0.0560
	Ratio of total purchases of farm products in wholesales and retail sale trades to gross agricultural output value (C_{10})	0.0542
	Ratio of total imports value to total purchases in wholesales and retail sale trades (C_{11})	0.0457
	Ratio of total exports value to total manufacturing and agricultural output value (C_{12})	0.0431
Degree of the marketization of productive essentials (B_4)	Ratio of number of contract staff and workers to total number of staff and workers (C_{13})	0.0623
	Ratio of number of registered unemployment persons in labor departments to total number of unemployment persons (C_{14})	0.0477
	Ratio of t total revenue of advertising to gross social output value (C_{15})	0.0440
	Ratio of transaction value in technical market to gross manufacturing output value (C_{16})	0.0452
	Ratio of floor space of commercial houses actually sold to buildings completed (C_{17})	0.0465
Social security of marketization (B_5)	Ratio of total welfare relief funds to total wages of staff and workers (C_{18})	0.0456
	Ratio of number of towns with the rural social security network established to total number of towns (C_{19})	0.0416

Source: designed by the authors

SITUATION ANALYSIS ON THE REGIONAL DIFFERENCE OF MARKETIZATION DEGREE

Based on the statistical indexes and the weight calculated by experts, we've sorted 19 relevant indexes of the 30 provinces and other provincial units (except Chongqing Municipality City) and applied them in the marketization degree evaluation index system. In this way, we have the general indexes and individual indexes in the five fields of marketization of economy systems of 30 provinces and other provincial administrative units in mainland of China, as demonstrated in Table 12.2.

Table 12.2 General Indexes and Individual Indexes in the Five Fields of Marketization of Economy Systems in Every Province and Other Provincial Administrative Units

Region	B_1	B_2	B_3	B_4	B_5	Total
Beijing	0.789	0.714	0.689	0.699	0.907	0.851
Tianjin	0.648	0.515	0.273	0.376	0.287	0.485
Hebei	0.390	0.377	0.126	0.270	0.126	0.299
Shanxi	0.422	0.296	0.120	0.296	0.149	0.295
Inner Mongolia	0.236	0.301	0.153	0.102	0.080	0.210
Liaoning	0.471	0.525	0.230	0.314	0.522	0.434
Jilin	0.299	0.490	0.230	0.283	0.562	0.381
Heilongjiang	0.222	0.408	0.230	0.159	0.493	0.309
Shanghai	0.743	0.515	0.465	0.518	0.287	0.615
Jiangsu	0.508	0.260	0.153	0.398	0.499	0.376
Zhejiang	0.567	0.525	0.148	0.310	0.207	0.398
Anhui	0.344	0.173	0.093	0.186	0.109	0.210
Fujian	0.530	0.270	0.251	0.270	0.149	0.358
Jiangxi	0.344	0.209	0.093	0.181	0.230	0.227
Shandong	0.399	0.372	0.109	0.350	0.207	0.320
Henan	0.322	0.102	0.082	0.403	0.476	0.270
Hubei	0.385	0.326	0.120	0.265	0.499	0.316
Hunan	0.349	0.357	0.164	0.190	0.207	0.286
Guangdong	0.630	0.464	0.421	0.283	0.247	0.499
Guangxi	0.344	0.255	0.115	0.168	0.465	0.262
Hainan	0.485	0.556	0.208	0.354	0.120	0.411
Sichuan	0.322	0.173	0.115	0.288	0.006	0.229
Guizhou	0.118	0.015	0.115	0.128	0.316	0.134
Yunnan	0.131	0.117	0.322	0.239	0.143	0.249
Xizang	0.177	0.204	0.142	0.000	0.419	0.176
Shanxi	0.304	0.219	0.219	0.270	0.092	0.276
Gansu	0.272	0.179	0.098	0.181	0.132	0.196
Qinghai	0.168	0.184	0.224	0.088	0.166	0.200
Ningxia	0.249	0.250	0.131	0.212	0.178	0.230
Xinjiang	0.181	0.291	0.284	0.106	0.080	0.245

Note: Data in the table only reflected the differences in marketization degree, instead of the actual level, of every province or other unit.

The Sorting and Group Analysis of Marketization Degrees of Economy Systems of 30 Provinces and other Provincial Units

In general, the differences in degree of marketization among every province and other provincial administrative unit approximately parallel those in level of economic development. For example, in the three Municipalities under the Central Administration, Beijing, Shanghai and Tianjin, and some developed provinces such as Guangdong, Liaoning and Jiangsu, the degrees of marketization are high. And in some underdeveloped provinces and autonomous regions, the degrees of marketization are low. (see Table 12.3)

Table 12.3 Sorting of Index in Degree of Marketization of Economy Systems in Every Province and other Provincial Unit

Region	index in degree of marketization	Per capita GDP	Region	index in degree of marketization	Per capita GDP
Beijing	0.851	10265	Hunan	0.286	2701
Shanghai	0.615	15204	Shaanxi	0.276	2344
Guangdong	0.499	6380	Henan	0.270	2475
Tianjin	0.485	8164	Guangxi	0.262	2772
Liaoning	0.434	6103	Yunnan	0.249	2490
Hainan	0.411	4820	Xinjiang	0.245	3953
Zhejiang	0.398	6149	Ningxia	0.230	2685
Jilin	0.381	3703	Sichuan	0.229	2516
Jiangsu	0.376	5785	Jiangxi	0.227	2376
Fujian	0.358	5386	Inner Mongolia	0.210	3013
Shandong	0.320	4473	Anhui	0.210	2521
Hubei	0.316	3341	Qinghai	0.200	2910
Heilongjiang	0.309	4427	Gansu	0.196	1925
Hebei	0.299	3376	Xizang	0.176	1984
Shanxi	0.295	2819	Guizhou	0.134	1553

Resources: YearBook of provinces and table 12-2

If we divide the 30 provinces and other provincial units into the east region, the middle region and the west region, we can also find differences of degree of marketization among them even more sharply. The marketization levels of the east region is much higher than both the middle and west regions. (See Figure 12.1)

Figure 12.1 Degree of Marketization in Main Regions of China

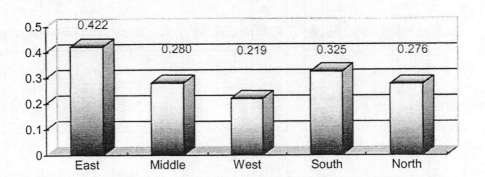

In the east area, 12 provinces and other provincial units included, there are 9 provinces or other provincial units with the index in degree of marketization of economy systems over national average. Only in Hebei Province and Guangxi Zhuangzu Autonomous Region the degree of marketization of economy systems is low. And in the West area, there are 6 provinces or other provincial units among the 10 provinces or other provincial units with the lowest degree of marketization of economy systems. But the difference between South area and North area is not as evident as that among the East, the Middle and the West. In the North area, the average index of degree of marketization of economy systems is a little lower than in the South area. In Beijing Municipality, the degree of marketization is even higher than in Shanghai Municipality. And in Liaoning Province, the degree of marketization is almost the same as that in Guangdong Province.

An Analysis on the Arrangement in Order of Every Field's Index in the System of Evaluation of Regional Marketization Degree

In comparison with the total index of measuring of marketization of economy systems, there are more errors in every individual index in the five fields of measuring of marketization, but they can show more problems.

Table 12.4 Sort and Analysis in Five Field of Indices of Measuring of Marketization in all Provinces or other Provincial Units

Region	B_1	Region	B_2	Region	B_3	Region	B_4	Region	B_5
Beijing	0.789	Beijing	0.714	Beijing	0.689	Beijing	0.699	Beijing	0.907
Shanghai	0.743	Hainan	0.556	Shanghai	0.465	Shanghai	0.518	Jilin	0.562
Tianjin	0.648	Liaoning	0.525	Guangdong	0.421	Henan	0.403	Liaoning	0.522
Guangdong	0.630	Zhejiang	0.525	Yunnan	0.322	Jiangsu	0.398	Jiangsu	0.499
Zhejiang	0.567	Tianjin	0.515	Xinjiang	0.284	Tianjin	0.376	Hubei	0.499
Fujian	0.530	Shanghai	0.515	Tianjin	0.273	Hainan	0.354	Heilongjiang	0.493
Jiangsu	0.508	Jilin	0.490	Fujian	0.251	Shandong	0.350	Henan	0.476
Hainan	0.485	Guangdong	0.464	Liaoning	0.230	Liaoning	0.314	Guangxi	0.465
Liaoning	0.471	Heilongjiang	0.408	Jilin	0.230	Zhejiang	0.310	Xizang	0.419
Shanxi	0.422	Hebei	0.377	Heilongjiang	0.230	Shanxi	0.296	Guizhou	0.316
Shandong	0.399	Shandong	0.372	Qinghai	0.224	Sichuan	0.288	Tianjin	0.287
Hebei	0.390	Hunan	0.357	Shaanxi	0.219	Jilin	0.283	Shanghai	0.287
Hubei	0.385	Hubei	0.326	Hainan	0.208	Guangdong	0.283	Guangdong	0.247
Hunan	0.349	Inner Mongolia	0.301	Hunan	0.164	Hebei	0.270	Jiangxi	0.230
Anhui	0.344	Shanxi	0.296	Inner Mongolia	0.153	Fujian	0.270	Zhejiang	0.207
Jiangxi	0.344	Xinjiang	0.291	Jiangsu	0.153	Shaanxi	0.270	Shandong	0.207
Guangxi	0.344	Fujian	0.270	Zhejiang	0.148	Hubei	0.265	Hunan	0.207
Henan	0.322	Jiangsu	0.260	Xizang	0.142	Yunnan	0.239	Ningxia	0.178
Sichuan	0.322	Guangxi	0.255	Ningxia	0.131	Ningxia	0.212	Qinghai	0.166
Shaanxi	0.304	Ningxia	0.250	Hebei	0.126	Hunan	0.190	Shanxi	0.149
Jilin	0.299	Shaanxi	0.219	Shanxi	0.120	Anhui	0.186	Fujian	0.149
Gansu	0.272	Jiangxi	0.209	Hubei	0.120	Jiangxi	0.181	Yunnan	0.143
Ningxia	0.249	Xizang	0.204	Guangxi	0.115	Gansu	0.181	Gansu	0.132
Inner Mongolia	0.236	Qinghai	0.184	Sichuan	0.115	Guangxi	0.168	Hebei	0.126

Heilongjiang	0.222	Gansu	0.179	Guizhou	0.115	Heilongjiang	0.159	Hainan	0.120
Xinjiang	0.181	Anhui	0.173	Shandong	0.109	Guizhou	0.128	Anhui	0.109
Xizang	0.177	Sichuan	0.173	Gansu	0.098	Xinjiang	0.106	Shaanxi	0.092
Qinghai	0.168	Yunnan	0.117	Anhui	0.093	Inner Mongolia	0.102	Inner Mongolia	0.080
Yunnan	0.131	Henan	0.102	Jiangxi	0.093	Qinghai	0.088	Xinjiang	0.080
Guizhou	0.118	Guizhou	0.015	Henan	0.082	Xizang	0.000	Sichuan	0.006

First of all, we are sure that the marketization degree in Beijing is the highest among 30 provinces and other provincial units. In the sort of five fields of Indexes of measuring of marketization, the first ones are in Beijing. Especially the four among the five indexes, Formations of market systems (B_2), Degree of the commodity marketization (B_3), Degree of the marketization of production factors (B_4) and Social security marketization (B_5), are obviously higher than the second provincial unit.

Secondly, the sequence of the premise of marketization (B_1) is essentially the same as the sequence of the level of economic development. And in the sort of other four among five fields of Indexes of measuring of marketization, there are some contents beyond all expectations.

1. Jiangsu Province is the 7th developed province in China and Guangdong Province is more developed than Jiangsu Province. But the index of building of market systems (B_2) of Jiangsu is the 18th among the 30 provinces and other provincial unit, and in Guangdong is the 8th. The index of building of market systems (B_2) of Jiangsu and Guangdong thus, is far behind their development level.
2. In Yunnan Province and Xinjiang Uigur Autonomous Regions, the index of degree of the marketization of goods (B_3) is the 5th and 8th among the 30 provinces and other provincial unit. But their development levels are after 20th among the 30 provinces and other provincial unit.
3. In Henan province, the index of degree of the marketization of production factors (B_4) is the 3rd among the 30 provinces and other provincial unit. And in Guangdong Province, the same index is the 13th. In Guangdong Province, therefore, the level of economic development is obviously higher in Henan Province.
4. In Shanghai Municipality and Tianjin Municipality, the 1st and 3rd largest City, the index of social security of marketization (B_5) is under the average level of entire country and lowers than in very poor Xizang Autonomous Region and Guizhou Province.

All these phenomena reflect two problems. The first one is that it is not very reasonable of selecting indexes or that there are some errors in original data. In two Metropolis Shanghai Municipality and Tianjin Municipality, for example, social security of marketization (B_5) is under national average. On other way, it shows that the distinct governments and residents are not same of comprehension for the marketization of economic system and do not make same motion in achieving the marketization of economic system.

Estimation of Actual Level of Marketization in Every Province and other Provincial Administrative Unit

According to the estimate of general report in this item, actual level of marketization is 55.0%-68.0% in whole China now. With the number as a cardinal number, we complete the illation of actual level of marketization in every province and other provincial administrative unit according with three level from 55.0% (low), 61.5% (middle) to 68.0% (high).

We can find that there are 12 provinces, municipality in central authorities or autonomous regions with the actual level of marketization over national average among 30 provinces or other provincial administrative units. They are Beijing Municipality, Tianjin Municipality, Liaoning Province, Jilin Province, Heilongjiang Province, Shanghai Municipality, Fujian Province, Guangdong Province, Yunnan Province, Shaanxi Province and Xinjiang Uigur Autonomous Region.

Table 12.5 Level of Marketization in all Provinces

Region	Low	Middle	High	Region	Low	Middle	High
Beijing	72.66%	81.25%	89.84%	Henan	50.68%	56.67%	62.65%
Tianjin	60.62%	67.78%	74.95%	Hubei	51.85%	57.97%	64.10%
Hebei	51.81%	57.94%	64.06%	Hunan	52.28%	58.46%	64.64%
Shanxi	53.29%	59.59%	65.89%	Guangdong	61.32%	68.56%	75.81%
Inner Mongolia	50.96%	56.98%	63.01%	Guangxi	49.64%	55.51%	61.37%
Liaoning	56.77%	63.47%	70.18%	Hainan	53.55%	59.87%	66.20%
Jilin	55.20%	61.72%	68.24%	Sichuan	51.75%	57.87%	63.98%
Heilongjiang	55.60%	62.18%	68.75%	Guizhou	49.65%	55.52%	61.39%
Shanghai	62.78%	70.20%	77.62%	Yunnan	57.97%	64.82%	71.67%
Jiangsu	53.52%	59.84%	66.17%	Xizang	49.09%	54.89%	60.70%
Zhejiang	51.93%	58.07%	64.20%	Shaanxi	55.18%	61.70%	68.22%
Anhui	48.94%	54.72%	60.50%	Gansu	48.97%	54.76%	60.55%
Fujian	55.96%	62.58%	69.19%	Qinghai	53.65%	59.99%	66.33%
Jiangxi	49.91%	55.81%	61.71%	Ningxia	50.04%	55.96%	61.87%
Shandong	51.42%	57.50%	63.57%	Xinjiang	55.91%	62.52%	69.13%

Note: Designed and calculated by the authors, according to each table in this chapter and Table 1-1 in Chapter 1.

However, on an average, the differences in marketization level among the three parts of east, middle and west, and between the parts of north and south are clear (See Figure 12-2). The level of marketization of the west part is a little bit higher than of the middle part, which maybe results from the higher lever of opening up to the outside world along the border of west part.

Figure 12.2 Degree of Marketization in Different Areas if China

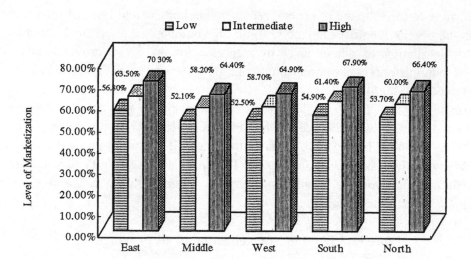

SUGGESTIONS ON IMPROVING THE DEGREE OF MARKETIZATION IN UNDERDEVELOPED AREAS AND REALIZING BALANCED ECONOMIC DEVELOPMENT AMONG DIFFERENT AREAS

In general, there is a close relation between the level of economic development and the degree of marketization of the every area of China. Where the marketization degree is high, the economic development is more advanced. In condition of accelerating progress of marketization, therefore, it is important that heightening degree of marketization in underdevelopment areas for achieving balanced economic development among different areas. According to the sequence of indexes in degree of marketization of economy systems in every province and other provincial administrative unit, we divide 19 provinces or autonomous regions with per capita GDP under national average into three categories and point out several suggestions for each category:

The first category of province (autonomous region), such as Jiangsu Province, Zhejiang Province, Shandong Province, they are low in marketization degree, but high in economic development level. Exploration into the problem reveals that the above provinces are short of central cities which match their economy strength, which restrain their market system development. The provincial capital of Jiangsu-Nanjing, for example, is a city with 2 million urban populations. Yet, its economy strength is far weaker than Suzhou's and Wuxi's which are in the same province and with fewer than 1 million populations. The same case also happens in Zhejiang Province and Shandong Province. The capital Hangzhou in Zhejiang is a city with even weaker economy strength than Nanjing's. The two biggest central cities in Shandong Province, Qingdao and Ji'nan, than Nanjing's. The two biggest central cities in Shandong Province, Qingdao and Ji'nan, both with more than 1 million urban populations are comparatively small in a province with about 90 million populations. We think that it is the first step to accelerate central development in a province or autonomous region with low degree of marketization and high level of economic development.

The second category of provinces (autonomous region), such as Hainan Province, Hubei Province and Hebei Province, they are low in marketization degree and intermediate in economic development level. These provinces and autonomous regions are in the critical stage of the progress of marketization now. Their progress of marketization is mainly restrained by some objective elements, e.g. Hainan Province is in an economic regulation period after a high tide of real estate investing, and its progress of marketization was ceased. In Hubei Province, Capital Wuhan's role as the center of Middle China is still to be demonstrated. It slackens the progress of marketization in the province. In Hebei around Beijing Municipality and Tianjin Municipality, because there aren't close relations between Hebei Province and Beijing Municipality and Tianjin Municipality, its progress of marketization has been restricted. Therefore, to accelerate the progress of marketization in these provinces or autonomous urban, some local policies must be adopted according to local situations.

In the third category of province and autonomous region, poor provinces and autonomous regions are nearly all in middle and west China, they are low in progress of marketization and their economic development level is behind mostly province and autonomous region. The reason that their marketization degree is low is simply because of their economic development level. Meanwhile, the very low degree of marketization restricts the economy development in these provinces and autonomous regions. The central government and the involved local governments must adopt some interrelated policies in accelerating economy development and foundation of market in these provinces and autonomous regions.

REFERENCES

Chen Dongsheng and others. *"Regional Economics"*, Henan People's Press, 1991.

Chen Zongsheng. *"Income Distribution in economic Development"*. Shanghai: Shanghai Sanlian Bookstore and Shanghai People's Press, 1991, 1994.

Hu Angang et al. *"Regional Disparity in China"*, Liaoning People's Press, 1995.

Ma Hong, Tang Jie et al. *"Regional Development and Industrial Policies in China"* China Social Science Press, 1991.

INDEX